Strike a Prose

Books by Cat Ellington

REVIEWS BY CAT ELLINGTON: THE COMPLETE
ANTHOLOGY, VOL. 1

REVIEWS BY CAT ELLINGTON: THE COMPLETE
ANTHOLOGY, VOL. 2

THE MAKING OF DUAL MANIA: FILMMAKING
CHICAGO STYLE

REVIEWS BY CAT ELLINGTON – THE COMPLETE
ANTHOLOGY LIMITED EDITION HOLIDAY GIFT
SET (BOOKS 1 & 2)

REVIEWS BY CAT ELLINGTON: THE COMPLETE
ANTHOLOGY, VOL. 3

MORE IMAGINATIVE THAN ORDINARY SPEECH:
THE POETRY OF CAT ELLINGTON

REVIEWS BY CAT ELLINGTON: A TRILOGY OF
UNIQUE CRITIQUES #1

MEMOIRS IN GOGYOHKA: A BOOK OF SHORT
POEMS AND MEMOIRS

YOU CAN QUOTE ME ON THAT: A COLLECTION
OF QUOTES BY CAT ELLINGTON

REVIEWS BY CAT ELLINGTON: THE COMPLETE
ANTHOLOGY, VOL. 4

REVIEWS BY CAT ELLINGTON: THE COMPLETE
ANTHOLOGY, VOL. 5

REVIEWS BY CAT ELLINGTON: THE COMPLETE
ANTHOLOGY, VOL. 6

I DO: SHEET MUSIC

THE BOOK OF US: SHEET MUSIC

I'M STILL IN LOVE: SHEET MUSIC

SOMETHING IN YOUR EYES: SHEET MUSIC

GETT OUT: SHEET MUSIC

THE FIVE-STAR REVIEW: A COLLECTION OF CAT
ELLINGTON'S TOP-RATED BOOK REVIEWS FROM
1981-2021

STRIKE A PROSE: A FRAMEWORK OF MEMORIES
AND COMMENTARIES IN POETRY

Strike a Prose

A Framework of Memories and
Commentaries in Poetry

Cat Ellington

Quill Pen Ink Publishing

THE BEAUTY OF EXPRESSION™

CHICAGO

Strike a Prose: A Framework of Memories and
Commentaries in Poetry
Copyright ©2022 Cat Ellington

PAPERBACK ISBN-13: 978-1-7370971-1-2

Library of Congress Control Number: 2022362739

Published by Quill Pen Ink Publishing
Chicago, Illinois, USA

Quill Pen Ink Publishing, 2022
The Cat Ellington Poetry Collection
The Cat Ellington Literary Collection
The Cat Ellington Diaries

Cover design: Tommie Mondell for Quill Pen Ink Publishing
Flower art: Watercolors by Ateli
Cover tint: Rosé

Watercolors by Ateli appear courtesy of Quill Pen Ink
Publishing

QPIP | Books: The Boutique Domain

Printed in the U.S.A.

Dedication

To my great-grandmother, Sylvia, and my grandmother,
Bessie—
Who are always with me in spirit

Introduction

Dear reader,

Welcome to my sanctuary of words and freestyle prose: this is *Strike a Prose: A Framework of Memories and Commentaries in Poetry*. The following pages include both *More Imaginative Than Ordinary Speech* and *Memoirs in Gogyohka* in their entirety, as well as seven new works of poetry that were previously unpublished in my books.

I have more to say - about love, life, faith, hope, society, family, friends, etc. And if you enjoyed reading my commentary and my dialogue in *More Imaginative Than Ordinary Speech* and *Memoirs in Gogyohka*, then you will be interested in hearing the rest. Yes, I have more narration through the written word. I even have paintings by Ateli: flowers of various types splashed in vivid hues of watercolor.

So follow along, why don't you. Wisdom, knowledge, and understanding will guide us.

All my love,

Cat

Acknowledgments

Thank you, Lord God, for all of your blessings. Only YOU
have the power to bestow honor, and I love you. Thank you
for guiding my hand through the work I do here on Earth
concerning the written word. It is my passion. And I thank
you for blessing me with the gift in its presentation.

Joe, Nathaniel, Nairobi, Naras, Freddie, and Maurice, I love
y'all. Thank you for your unconditional love and your
never-ending support.

And a very special thank you to those readers who find
enjoyment in my creative writing. I appreciate all of you.

Strike a Prose

A FRAMEWORK OF MEMORIES AND COMMENTARIES IN POETRY

Table of Contents

More Imaginative Than Ordinary Speech:

The Poetry of Cat Ellington

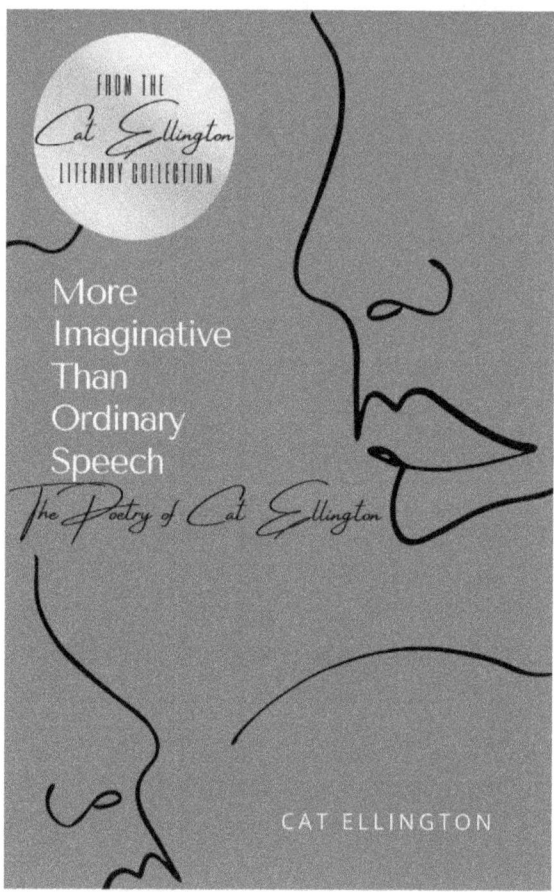

FROM THE
Cat Ellington
LITERARY COLLECTION

More
Imaginative
Than
Ordinary
Speech
The Poetry of Cat Ellington

CAT ELLINGTON

More Imaginative Than Ordinary Speech

Books by Cat Ellington

REVIEWS BY CAT ELLINGTON: THE COMPLETE
ANTHOLOGY, VOL. 1

REVIEWS BY CAT ELLINGTON: THE COMPLETE
ANTHOLOGY, VOL. 2

THE MAKING OF DUAL MANIA: FILMMAKING
CHICAGO STYLE

REVIEWS BY CAT ELLINGTON - THE COMPLETE
ANTHOLOGY LIMITED EDITION HOLIDAY GIFT
SET (BOOKS 1 & 2)

REVIEWS BY CAT ELLINGTON: THE COMPLETE
ANTHOLOGY, VOL. 3

MORE IMAGINATIVE THAN ORDINARY SPEECH:
THE POETRY OF CAT ELLINGTON

More Imaginative Than Ordinary Speech
Speech
The Poetry of Cat Ellington

Cat Ellington

Quill Pen Ink Publishing

THE BEAUTY OF EXPRESSION™

CHICAGO

PAPERBACK ISBN-10: 1733442111
PAPERBACK ISBN-13: 978-1-7334421-1-4
HARDCOVER ISBN: 978-1-7370971-8-1

Library of Congress Control Number: 2022362736

Cover design: Tommie Mondell for Quill Pen Ink Publishing
Cover tint: Purple Pleasure
Flower art: Watercolors by Ateli

Published by Quill Pen Ink Publishing
Chicago, Illinois, USA
https://quill-pen-ink-publishing.business.site/

Quill Pen Ink Publishing, 2019
The Original Poetry Synopsis
The Cat Ellington Poetry Collection
The Cat Ellington Literary Collection

Watercolors by Ateli appear courtesy of Quill Pen Ink
Publishing

"The Black Girl" appears courtesy of The Black Jaguar
Music Company

Hardcover Edition: November 2021

Printed in the U.S.A.

Dedication

To Frank "Tony" McBride—
For assisting in the saving of my life all those years
ago

I will love you always

Preface

Dearest reader,

I cannot begin to tell you how thrilled I am for the release of *More Imaginative Than Ordinary Speech: The Poetry of Cat Ellington*. After receiving the first vision to write this work in 2004, I knew that I would end up having to pull it all together bit by bit over time. And although completing this work had been a challenge—due to my other professional obligations—it is finally finished. It's here now. And I couldn't be more relieved. It wasn't long after the initial vision to create this work was shown that I immediately prepared my research to study poetry book concepts. And while brainstorming ideas for titles—which, if you know me, had to be something uniquely creative—I looked up the word, *Poetry*, in my Webster's Dictionary, and voilá! There it was in the second definition: More imaginative than ordinary speech. Right away, I selected that interesting definition/description to use for the title of the work that would soon come into being: for it had been the unique title that I needed. Added, it was not in use anywhere else. And that made it all the more appealing. Indeed, it was wholly original. And it was me.

With that, I quickly jotted the words down in my notebook and allowed them to settle for a minute. And after a few more days of research, it was decided that "More Imaginative Than Ordinary Speech" would be the title of my book of poetry. And to this day, it still fascinates me.

More Imaginative Than Ordinary Speech. It was perfect. And I loved it. As far as subtitles went, that was relatively easy to decide. I favored The Poetry of Cat Ellington. It would serve as the perfect complement to the distinctive main title. Also, being a writer of songs (primarily), I could appreciate the melodic flow of all the words mingling together in perfect harmony: More Imaginative Than Ordinary Speech: The Poetry of Cat Ellington.
Yes. It was me. And it felt just right.

That was back in 2004. And today—exactly 15 years later—the beautiful vision has come to pass.

More Imaginative Than Ordinary Speech, created to feature many of my selected poems, including *The Long-suffering*, *The Black Diamond*, *The Golden Goose*, *Hot and Humid*, *The Proverbial Diva*, and *The Black Girl* (a bonus from my song catalog), was a joy to write. For is a compilation of which I am very proud. And I do hope that you, my dearest reader, will enjoy viewing this book of poetry as much as I did collecting it over the years.

Happy reading.

Acknowledgments

As always, I honor my Father God, my Lord Jesus—even Christ and Him crucified—and the gloriously awesome Holy Spirit with the first fruits of my praise: for without them, I could do nothing—creative or otherwise. And I do mean that. Thank you, my precious and omnipotent Lord, for everything that you do for me on this beautiful Earth of your making.

To my husband, Joseph, and our three cherished children Nathaniel, Nairobi, and Naras, I extend my sincerest gratitude. I love all four of you with all I have. And it pleases me to say that you're all mine.

Thank you to my beloved brothers, Freddie and Maurice, for all of your love, support, good times, good drinks, and good eats. I love you both.

Thank you to my Humanmade family. I love and appreciate all of you. Thank you for being there.

Thank you to my family of fellows at the Academy of American Poets. I love and appreciate all of you. And I thank you for your kind words.

Joanne at WorldCat, thank you, my dearest lady. I truly admire all of the hard work you do for the World's Largest Library Catalog.

Thank you, team HometownReads, for everything you all do on behalf of local authors across the country. Speaking for all of us, I can say that we appreciate every one of you.

Thank you, Gary Martin. I have loved you since we were kids in junior high, and God knows that I still love you dearly today. Thank you for your genuine friendship.

To my beloved Chad, MWAH! You still look like Rick Astley, baby, even after all these years. Haha. Thank you for just being. I love you, boo.

My dear Derek, thank you, baby. Thank you for all those times you looked out for me. I have never forgotten them, nor will I ever. I love you so much. I always have - and I always will.

For you, my dear Joyce Jackson, I have nothing but unconditional love. Thank you for always keepin' it real with me.

And to all of you, my beloved readers, I extend much love and gratitude. Thank you for absorbing my written witness with understanding.

Table of Contents

26

Coming November 2019: Memoirs in Gogyohka: A Collection of Short Poems and Memoirs

About the Author

The Introduction

WHO AM I?

A Seeker of Truth.
A Finder of Truth.
A Vessel for Truth: for I am whole.

My name is Cat Ellington. And I am a woman who:

Seeks the Truth and Finds the Truth.
Gets to Know the Truth.
Falls in Love with the Truth.
Moves In with the Truth and Strives to Make Love to the
Truth.
Commits Herself to the Truth and Reproduces with the
Truth.
Builds A Solid Unit with the Truth and Contends with the
Truth.
Sometimes Gets Frustrated with the Truth and Cries with the
Truth.
Makes Amends with the Truth and Listens to the Truth.
Passes Time with the Truth.
Grows Older - and Wiser - with the Truth.
Will Die with the Truth: for the truth is what I represent. It is
what I love. And it is what I choose to infuse into my
creative contribution concerning the written word.

But some utterly despise the Spirit of Truth. And they hate those individuals who speak the truth boldly and who prefer to live by it. I have had run-ins with people of this sort in the past. And it is for a surety that I will continue to have run-ins with these types—whether directly or indirectly—in the present and future times. Those about whom I speak will be the ones scoffing the loudest: for they will be the proudest and the angriest. These are the people who will despise me, not so much for spotlighting the truth through the written word, but for being an African-American woman—particularly an African-American woman from the South Side of Chicago—doing it.

Know for a certainty that such hostility will stem from worldly-minded people who are full of hatred, pride, and bigotry - not to mention racism and malice. For these will be tempted to hate my being a visible public figure in the creative arts. Because my style of creativity, where it pertains to my contributions, is not overseen—much less controlled—by them or by people like them. Indeed, this is the truth.

I do me and not anyone else. And I don't - and won't - allow myself to conform to the wishes of anyone else. I write whatever the Spirit moves me, or rather, commands me to write. And if there are people out there who may be offended by my existence and my contribution to the creative arts, particularly in its branches of music, motion pictures, and literature, that's just fine; they have a right to dislike my brand. But I will not "water down" my concentrated efforts to appease anyone, nor will I sugarcoat the truth to make it more digestible to the one willing to shy away from it. That is just not going to happen. I am going to tell it like it is, and that's that. And should there be a few folks who prefer to stand in opposition to my effort(s), then so be it. But I will not don the kid gloves of conformity to appease people. It is just not in my nature. I have to be who I am. It's just that simple. Take it or leave it.

This work features poetry that took its inspiration from many of my experiences in my life. These include racism, lust, homosexuality, interracial love, rage, anger, fear, hatred, depression, manic depression, living life on the streets of the South Side of Chicago, Pentecostal Christianity, etc. Whenever there arose in my life a unique situation worthy of a written testimonial, I took the opportunity to record my witness, pen to paper. And while some of you may find my testimony inspirational, others may label the same as being quite offensive. And that's just as well with me as everything is not for everybody. But trust that my testimony is diverse and prone to mutability.

This portion of my witness I felt compelled to share through poetry. But the remainder of my witness will be reserved for my autobiography. That's right, my autobiography. Hey, if you thought the life story of Tina Turner was something, wait until you get a load of mine! Hee hee, haha. Yes, my dearest men and women, one of these groovy ol' days, my life story will be made public via a memoir. But until then, let's start here.

I love the craft of writing because it's therapeutic, you know? There is simply no other physical gift in existence better than it. Writing is a magnificent gift that should be cherished and nurtured but never trifled with or taken for granted.

For without the written word, nothing that has ever come into being could be or would be: for without the scribbler, what is to be of life?

The written word:
It is the beating heart of my cognitive creativity;
Its life source

It is my power.

The written word emboldens my introvert

It is my power.

The written word:
It salves the wounds of my tribulation,
It covers the scars of my despair

It is my power.

The written word:
It rebukes my persecutor - in swift defense of my honor

It is my power.

The gift of writing is one of the most special. And I am honored to be numbered among the millions of people to whom the Lord has given it.

My dearest men and women? It pleases me to present to you *More Imaginative Than Ordinary Speech: The Poetry of Cat Ellington.*

"Ignorance is not bliss, and neither is the sorrow of the heart."

—Cat Ellington

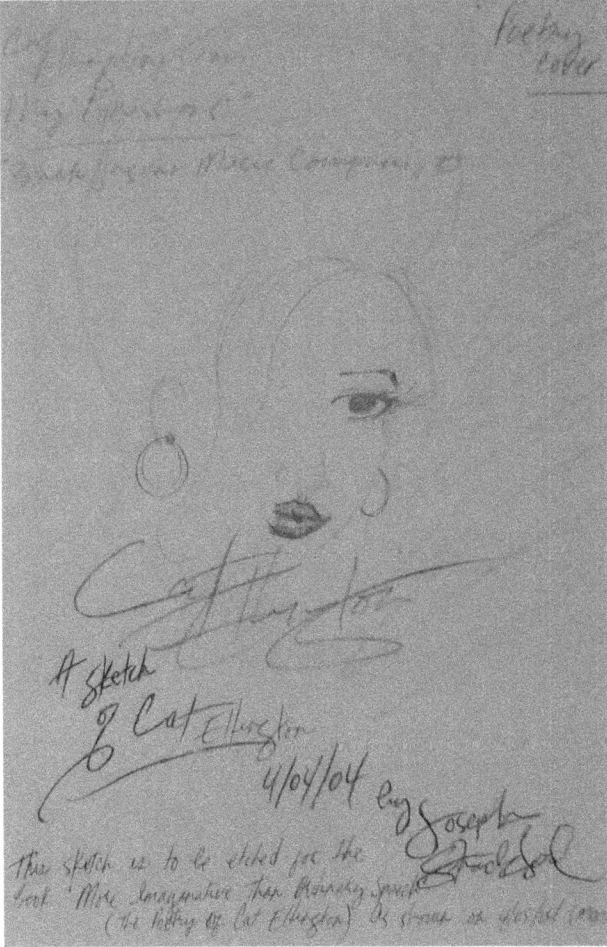

Sketch of Cat Ellington by Joseph Strickland
April 4, 2004
The beautiful vision has come to pass.

Part One

"The Beauty of Being"
Genre: Narrative

The Synopsis

This production of the written word, in poetic form, intends to praise the hated truth while rebuking the beloved lies of this present generation, which breed pride, hatred, self-hatred, low self-esteem, and idolatry – false idolatry.

The Poem:

There is beauty in peace,
There is beauty in serenity,
There is beauty in dignity,
As well as there is beauty in integrity—

There is beauty in kindness,

There is beauty in gentleness,
There is beauty in selflessness,
As well as there is in forgiveness—

There is beauty in love,
There is beauty in Heaven above,
There is beauty in the flight of a dove,
As well as there is in every preceding verse thereof—

For Man, in his very creation, is beauty:
For we are all a creation of beauty—

Regardless of race, creed, or nationality,
We are all a creation of beauty—

And every one of us is somebody.

The Poet's Commentary

There is no such person as a "nobody." Every man, and every woman, having been made by the hand of the Lord thy God, is somebody.

There is no such thing as "irrelevance" where it concerns any given human being: for the very existence of Mankind is relevant, as those of us who live play witness to that almighty power by which we've come to exist.

Weighed together, we are lighter than air. For indeed, we, as a human race, live today and are cut down tomorrow, that the Earth shall no longer provide for us a place upon its surface.

Self-love. It's a beautiful thing.

"The Longsuffering"

Genre: Narrative

The Synopsis

This production of the written word, in poetic form, intends to reflect a human spirit that remains unbroken despite oppression.

The Poem:

Despite her maniacal history,
I still love my city:

The city of Chicago...

Despite her inability to form an affinity,
I still love my city:

The city of Chicago...

Despite her second-class mentality
And her segregation of citizenry,
I still love my city:

The city of Chicago...

The city of Chicago: for she is indisputable—
Even the only city I know,
Who can have both eyes blackened
And still, be beautiful—

The city of Chicago: for she is indisputable—
Even the only city I know,
Who can have a busted lip
With a bloodied nose,
And still, be beautiful—

Despite her corruptibility,
I still love my city:

The city of Chicago...

Despite her neglect of poverty,
I still love my city:

The city of Chicago.

The Poet's Commentary

As the old saying goes, 'It's not where you live, it's how you live.' And where it regards the inspiration for *The Long-suffering*, that timeless adage is once again proven as truth.

LIKE OIL AND WATER.

In my beloved city of Chicago, where her physical beauty remains unmatched, even to this day, the spirits in many of her children—both the native and the adoptee alike—continue to spoil and rot in the scorching heat of political corruption and law-enforcement corruption - not to mention racism, street-gang violence, illegal drugs, prostitution, senseless crime, etc.

I love my city, but I do hate the godless ways of many of her children. And this would include both the Jew and the Gentile. These are my fellow Chicagoans, but many do evil. And they're tempted to do evil for sport.
Now am I banging down a gavel in judgment against any single individual? No, of course not; that's not my place. But I speak what I know. And I know my own because I come from them.

Chicago has always been a gawjus, albeit hard-nosed, town. And I love her with everything I have in me: for she is the only city in the Earth realm able to arouse so deep a love within me. And I could never be ashamed of her, nor of my having been born from the womb of her. But historically, many of her offspring have proven themselves to be quite atrocious. And in short, that had been the point of the production.

"The King of Glory"
Genre: Narrative

The Synopsis

This production of the written word, in poetic form, intends to render a testimony of one's trials and tribulations as a faithful servant of the Most-High God and the public persecutions inflicted upon him or her as a result of such faith.

The Poem:

The enemy wars against me—
Because I refuse to renounce You,
The King of Glory—

Because I refuse to renounce You,

The King of Glory,
Therefore the enemy wars against me—

For Your name,
I am—forever—defamed:
For Your name,
I bear the cross of shame—

The enemy wars against me—
Because I refuse to renounce You,
The King of Glory—

Because I refuse to renounce You,
The King of Glory,
Therefore the enemy wars against me.

The Poet's Commentary

I have said it before, and I will say it once more: I don't conform well.

REFERENCES OF TRUTH.

Truths:

"Yes, and all who desire to live godly in Christ Jesus will suffer persecution."
—II Timothy 3:12

"If the world hates you, you know that it hated me before it hated you.

If you were of the world, the world would love its own. Yet because you are not of the world, but I chose you out of the world, therefore the world hates you."
—John 15:18-19

I'm not here to preach, only to state facts so that the people may get a good understanding.

And this is understanding:

No matter who you are—Jew or Gentile, well-known or unknown, rich and wealthy or poor and needy—if you find that you're the constant target of unprovoked anger from people in the world, be they familiar persons or strangers, there is a good chance the Lord may be calling you. And the spirits in the world can detect the "light" within you.

My advice to you? Answer that spiritual phone and bid the troublers adieu.

MY (PERSONAL) TESTIMONY.

There was a time, during which I was lost in the world, that I noticed something. Wherever I went, I perceived hatred directed towards me from people out there in society. The hate towards me had not been from *everybody*, no, that would be an over-exaggeration, but there were many people. It didn't matter their race, nationality, or gender. They were just hateful towards me without just cause. Perhaps it had been my free-spirited nature? Or maybe my sense of style showcased by my wardrobe, or my height, or my hairstyles, or my cosmetic application, or my natural ability to immediately hit it off with other people whether I had known them or not, or just me being myself. Whatever the case had been, I received a lot of hate.

Such an experience isn't unique, as millions of people in the world can attest to my witness. Because they, too, are the recipients of similar treatment from both the stranger and the familiar person alike.

Being "excluded" or "alienated" from among the "crowd pleasers" was one thing when I was a young woman of the world many years ago. But on the day that I finally decided to answer that spiritual phone—which had been ringing off and on over several years—the hatred directed towards me from countless people in the world grew worse. And though it took time, I eventually learned why: the Lord was calling me. And Satan had been hatin' (through worldly people) because he knew it: the one of darkness could see the Spirit of Light on me.

WISDOM CONTINUES TO SPEAK.

"If I were of the world, the world would love its own."
—John 15:19

But there is no true love in the world, only hatred disguised as false love.

What that quote derived from the Holy Scriptures means is this. Those who are of the world are similar spiritually, and they move as a body to war against those who are not part of the evil world system. Lest anyone should seek to confuse the matter, the war-at-hand has never been physical, only spiritual. And I would rather be hated by the world for being a Pentecostal Christian woman, particularly an African-American woman of the Pentecostal faith, than a lost soul in the world system who is falsely loved (and *accepted*) by a bunch of strangers for being a practicing sinner.

Therefore, I do not receive my blessings from the hands of men but the hand of my Lord.
And His hand ain't ever short.

"A Declaration of Independence"

Genre: Free Verse

The Synopsis

This production of the written word, in poetic form, intends to witness the blessedness of independence - and of how one did not need to bow before men to receive any honor on the Earth.

The Poem:

They did not make me;
Therefore, they cannot break me—

They did not bless me;
Therefore, they cannot curse me—

They did not educate me;
Therefore, they cannot make a dummy,
They cannot make a dummy out of me—

They did not give me honor;
Therefore, they cannot disgrace me,
They cannot disgrace me with dishonor—

They did not make me;
Therefore, they cannot break me—

They did not feed me;
Therefore, they cannot starve me—

They did not clothe me;
Therefore, they cannot uncover me—

They did not give me my fame;
Therefore, they cannot take credit,
They cannot take credit for my name—

They did not make me;
Therefore, they cannot break me—

They did not make me wealthy;
Therefore, they cannot bring me to poverty—

They did not exalt me;
Therefore, they cannot humble me—

They did not make me;
Therefore, they cannot break me.

The Poet's Commentary

For it is He, the King of Kings, who has made me.
It is He, the King of Kings, who has made me—C.E.

And I render Him the praise of which He is entirely worthy.

NATURAL BORN MAVERICK.

The poetic testimony which you, my dearest reader, have
just read may appear *"preachy"* enough, but it is not so
much preachy as it is *"righteously indignant."*

If I must admit it, I utterly hate the idea of anyone trying to
control me. Seriously, just the thought of it kindles burning
anger within me. I am not keen on the idea of being swayed
by other people, period. But the world in which we live is
full of individuals who covet power and to have control over
others, even if they must use money or their authoritative
positions in society to do so.
Unfortunately, many people have weak faith. And I don't
judge them because of it: some people hate to wait.
Whatever the case may be, too many people have allowed
themselves to fall into subjection to other human beings.
And in many instances, those other human beings are in
positions to control their lives.

Here is where you get the master/slave scenario:

People get told what to do and how to do it. They get told what to say and how to say it. What not to say. What to eat and what not to eat. They get told what to wear and what not to wear. Who to love and who not to love. Whose party or event to attend and whose party or event not to attend. They get told how they should look and how they should not look. They are always under scrutiny: who to appease and who not to appease - and who they should ignore. All such actions lead the one in subjection down a path of destructive anger, rage, hatred (towards themselves and others), bitterness, and self-hatred.

PUBLIC PERSECUTIONS.

Understand that those hateful men and women—under whose thumbs such people exist—are the same ones who do evil on Earth, thereby being an evil trial unto others, especially to those who find themselves in their "debt." Moreover, these same types of people despise *anyone* not under their control, pretending to ignore the targeted person but keeping a watchful eye on him or her nonetheless. And because I can't bring myself to run in the same flood of dissipation with them, therefore many are tempted to speak evil of me as a public figure.

"How come she ain't like us?" They utter among themselves.

"Who the fuck that Black bitch think she is?" They utter among themselves.

"Cat just looks like she thinks her shit don't stank." They utter among themselves.

"God, she is just so fucking narcissistic and arrogant!" They utter among themselves.

"That bitch acts like she's next to God. Ol' self-righteous ass bitch." They utter among themselves.

"I'on like no-muhhfuckin-body who thank thay betta'dan me. An'is bitch ack like she thank she betta'dan otha niggas." They utter among themselves.

"Shiiid, she got her shit, all her achievements 'n shit. But she ain't throwin' shit to no other muthafucka." They utter among themselves.

"Arrogant Black bitch!" They utter among themselves.

"Who let that nigger bitch in? Who gave her the freedom to own and operate all of those fuckin' companies in the entertainment industry? Who let that bitch in?!" They utter among themselves.

"Ain't no White-owned corporations overseeing her black ass? They ain't controlling her black ass like they control my black (or white) ass? She's just free to do what the hell she wants to do? Damn! Who allowed that? They don't own her rights 'n shit—like they own all ours?" They utter among themselves.

"If she ain't writin' shit for Bey and Cardi B and Taylor and Katy cat and Rih Rih and 'em, we don't know her." They utter among themselves.

50

"If she didn't get the seal of approval from Ellen, and the White people in the mainstream media don't mention her in their magazines and newspapers, she ain't important." They utter among themselves.

"She doesn't support the Kardashians and kiss their asses and validate them? Who the hell is she? Errbody else do it." They utter among themselves.

"Does she think she's better just because she's a so-called songwriter and casting director and author? Does she think she's better than the rest of us?" They utter among themselves.

"Why doesn't she support what we endorse? Why doesn't she support the LGBTQ? What's wrong with her?" They utter among themselves.

Get understanding, my dear men and women. I'm from the South Side of Chicago, even its innermost parts. And there ain't a man or a woman alive—be he or she gay or straight—who can say *anything* that's going to shock me. Neither is there even one who can out-cuss me or brandish a verbal sword bearing a double edge sharper than that of my own.

Indeed, I was living life with a bunch of hell-raising (and wig-snatchin') "dykes" and "fairies" on Chicago's South Side way before homosexuality became an *acceptable (and somewhat celebrated)* lifestyle in this here society. And I

love my men and my women. I am not ashamed of them.
No, not even one of them.

There were no *"respectable"* LGBTQ organizations back then. No one was fighting for the *"gay rights"* of my gay family members. No, my loved ones had to suffer it to be so. They were called "fags" and "bulldaggits" daily, especially on the South Side of Chicago where Black folks—in mass numbers—didn't approve of the *"alternative lifestyle"* then, and where Black folks—in mass numbers—don't approve of the *"alternative lifestyle"* now.

Back then, *"Gay pride"* didn't exist. There were no yearly *"parades"* organized either. And the only "rainbow" we knew was *Rainbow Push*—founded, of course, by the Reverend Jesse L. Jackson, Sr., respectively.

Faggot-ass muthafuckas and bulldaggit-ass bitches.

Those were some of the only words my gay relatives had ever heard spoken concerning them.

My men and my women went through the shit—way before the LGBTQ came into existence. And regardless of all the hate and persecutions they continuously endured, I, nevertheless, continued to cherish my loved ones. So do not ever falsely accuse me of fostering prejudice against anyone based on their *sexual orientation.*

Understand that I, Cat Ellington, was the original fag hag. *I* was the first person that ever used the term (in 1989), though I have never received any credit for it—being that I had only been a member of the general public during that era and not yet a public figure in the arts. Get understanding.

AS FOR THE OTHERS...

My reply to every other hateful word uttered against me is this:

My lips don't do ass. They never have, and I don't reckon that they soon ever will. I am who I am. Take me or leave me.

As commanded, I will commence doing the work of my Lord as a creative artist in the arts & entertainment industry. And know for a certainty that not even one will be allowed to shoo me away. Nevermind them taking offense to the hue of my flesh and the Spirit of Truth in me.

Indeed, I come from a long line of fighters. And I intend to stand my ground.

Trust, my dear and women, that I do not believe myself as being better than (or as good as) anyone else. I just like my coffee the way I like my coffee: sometimes black, sometimes creamy, but always sweet.
I have to do things in the way I like. And not in the way that someone else wants me to do them. Especially where it concerns my contributions to the arts & entertainment industry.

WISDOM. GET IT WHILE YOU CAN.

Absorb this wisdom, my dear men and women. It is the Lord who gives one the power to get wealth. And only the Lord can make one's name great, not people. Do not ever get it twisted. A great name and mere fame are two different things: fame is fleeting, but a great name will stand, even until the end of time. Therefore a great name is to be desired.

Should fame seek to associate itself with anyone, there ought to be a legitimate reason why. Understand that false fame is lazy, without honor, and seeks its (own) kind with which to associate. But genuine fame—and the legitimate recognition it inevitably brings—is partial to those whose hands have toiled long and hard in his or her respective fields and crafts.

To reiterate, only the Lord God has the power to make someone's name great and to command wealth to acquaint itself with him or her, and not people. People do not have that kind of power. Only the Lord can make it possible. Only He has the power to bless people with (great) gifts, talents, and abilities. For this, His name is worthy of praise. And from my mouth, *it will be praised*.

And I thank God every day for blessing me to nurture my (creative) independence. For were it not for his blessing, I would be homeless, poverty-stricken, and hungry while waiting to be recognized - and supported - by a bunch of faithless, hateful, and self-hating people who despise both Him and me.

"The Black Diamond"

Genre: Dramatic

The Synopsis

This production of the written word, in poetic form, intends to exhibit a healthy level of self-confidence, self-esteem, and self-love short of narcissism.

The Poem:

Like a black diamond,
I shine ever so brightly.

Like a black diamond,
Brilliantly cut,
With pristine clarity—

I am a rarity—

Like a black diamond,
I shine ever so brightly.

The Poet's Commentary

She is,
She is like a black diamond:
Dark in physical hue,
Mysterious in nature,
Multifaceted in creativity,
Precious - in the vein of an uncommon jewel,
Unique,
And one of a kind.

That's me, baby.

Part Two

"The Unwavering Soul"

Genre: Dramatic

The Synopsis

This production of the written word, in poetic form, intends to proclaim one's devotion to the Lord thy God, regardless of public persecution and exclusion.

The Poem:

I will stand in my faith in Thee:
I will stand in my faith, despite the hate:
I will stand in Thee—

Despite their hate for me,
I will stand in Thee:

I will stand,
I will stand in Thee...

From my eye,
There may be many tears shed,
But I?
I will not be misled:

I will stand in Thee,
Despite their hate for me:
I will stand in Thee.

The Poet's Commentary

Here lies the conviction when one makes up his or her mind
to do it right.

The Unwavering Soul serves as the conclusion to *The King
of Glory*.

A FINAL WORD.

Stand for something lest you fall for anything, my dear men
and women.
Stand for something lest you fall for anything.

"Inspired by Imitation of Life"

Genre: Satirical

The Synopsis

This production of the written word, in poetic form, intends to witness a real-life struggle with one's racial identity, particularly within the African-American culture in modern-day society—reminiscent of the fictitious "Sara Jane Johnson."

The Poem:

I see you—to yourself being untrue:

Deceiving and being deceived,
Draggin' your manicured fingers
Through your stringy, blonde-haired weave:

I see you—to yourself being untrue:

Shameful and debased;
Fraudulently encased;
A blubbery shell of what you ate;
A pitiful embodiment of pride and self-hate:

I see you—to yourself being untrue:

In that lyin' Caste System reflection,
Passin'—with your near-White complexion:

I see you—to yourself being untrue:

Pretendin' to be one of the Caucasian persuasion,
When in fact, you know you're Black:

I see you—to yourself being untrue.

The Poet's Commentary

If there is one thing I cannot stand in life, it is self-denial,
especially when it rears its ugly head in "High Yella"
African-American people who are light-complected enough
to "pass" for White.

EXAMPLES OF SELF-RESPECT.

The late and legendary Lena Horne was fair-skinned enough to pass, but she never did. And she persevered through a much-greater hardship than those of a similar hue today.

The lovely actress, Lonette McKee, is fair-skinned enough to pass, but she never has. And she endured much worse in her time.

The beautiful actress, Jasmine Guy, is fair-skinned enough to pass, but she never has. And she had been subjected to much worse during the height of her fame.

The sexy R&B diva, Faith Evans, is fair-skinned enough to pass, but she never has, even when she could have for "mainstream acceptance."

The pretty and extremely talented Alicia Keys is fair-skinned enough to pass, but she never has, not even throughout her entire entertainment career.

And so on, and so on.

A HISTORY LESSON IN SPIRITUAL WARFARE.

Worse than self-denial (which stems from self-hatred) is cowardice (which stems from fear). Decades ago, when the world had been a different place for the oppressed in this society, namely African Americans, many light-skinned Blacks with so-called keen/European features were tempted to buckle to what was/is commonly known as the White Caste System.

A (demonic) practice enforced (and perpetuated) by human beings around the world, the Caste System serves one self-destructive purpose: to tempt people to sell their souls (or sell out) by catering to the needs and desires of Satan. This type of spiritual warfare operates through the people in the world who occupy the (ungodly) position of the oppressor, particularly those of European descent.

Satan's intention (through the evil Caste System) is to use divide-and-conquer tactics against human beings based on the flesh. Not the spirit, but the flesh. His job is to wage war against Mankind by way of the flesh. In this way, he tempts human beings to sell their souls to him in exchange for all the things in the world—based on the preferably lighter hue of their flesh. And unfortunately, countless numbers of people—the world over—have fallen for the wicked and destructive lie hook, line, and sinker: for they preferred the liar to the Spirit of Truth. And many, many generations have fallen into condemnation because of their error.

No one has ever been able to defeat spiritual forces with a carnal mind. To obtain victory in spiritual warfare, one must battle back with a spiritual-mind. It is all set in the mind. That is where the battle starts. And if oppressed people have been told—even for hundreds of years—that they are beneath someone else or the lesser, just based on the skin they were born in, those people are sure to become conditioned in their *minds*.
And Satan knows this. He knew it from the beginning, and he, the evil spirit that he is, knows it now. For he is still at war with all of Mankind. But in the country called America, he uses race. That and economics.

Because the Lord God called the oppressed people—in mass numbers—to a newfound faith in Pentecostal Christianity, it is for this reason that the devil hates and seeks to destroy people through the flesh.

One such weapon of usage in his demonic arsenal is the spirit called self-hatred. Once he can penetrate a human mind with self-hatred, he already has his war on that human won.

And whenever you see anyone—be he or she Jew or Gentile—denigrating themselves and destroying themselves to try and look like another race of people other than themselves, know for a certainty that such people are full of self-hatred.

I am not talking about hairstyling. That does not apply here. Because women, especially Black women, love to change their hair for variety. So I am not addressing various styles of hair design. I am talking about people bleaching their skins or having surgery to obtain physical attributes they were not born with: butt injections, collagen injections, rib removal (to achieve the hourglass look), cheek implants, and every other procedure of the like.

Women are paying big money, even going broke, for vanity purposes – desperate to look like someone else who they are not because of the demons called self-hatred and low self-esteem.

A Black woman will never be a White woman, and neither will a White woman ever be a Black woman. All such confusion stems from spiritual warfare - in the human mind.

Worse than a White woman pretending to act and look like a Black woman (by paying for surgical procedures to obtain those physical attributes found naturally on a Black woman) is a woman, born a very light-skinned Black, pretending to be a White woman. Such people pass for White and shamefully conduct themselves in the hope of monetary gain and acceptance in the world. And there goes self-hatred.

UNDERSTANDING IS THE NEW HEALING.

Simply telling people to love themselves and to be themselves is always easier said than done. Because the weapons of spiritual warfare have pierced too deep for far too long, and it is going to take Divine intervention to free them from their enslavement.

The fictional character by whom the production of poetry was inspired fell prey to the same spiritual forces of evil, as does the individual about whom the poem speaks.
Get wisdom. And while you are at it, grab hold of some knowledge and understanding, too.

You are who you are. And you are what you are, period. God created beauty, not ugliness. And it will be well for you to understand that you are a magnificent and unique beauty—whomever you may be.
Learn to love yourself. Learn to love yourselves.

"The Testimony of Cat Ellington"
Genre: Narrative

The Synopsis

This production of the written word, in poetic form, intends to render the author's (personal) testimony to the reader – which reveals how my past dead worldly lifestyle succumbed to a new life in Christ Jesus.

The Poem:

The queen of revelry,
Who engaged in the Trois and orgy?
Oh, how it was me:
Destitute, spiritually—

Through the looking glass of homosexuality,

I frolicked with gay empathy:
Oh, how it was me:
Destitute, spiritually—

The scoffer of marriage,
And a bosom buddy of adultery?
Oh, how it was me:
Destitute, spiritually—

Blowing my nose in the "snow,"
While diving in the sewage
Of my wickedly-frightful destiny?
Oh, how it was me:
Destitute, spiritually.

The Poet's Commentary

Indeed, everyone has a past. And the production is a revelation of mine. Yes, I have moved on in life and gotten older. But the days of my youth were wild and eccentric ones inspired by my unconventional upbringing.

PERFECTION ELUDES ME.

I am not a perfect individual by any measure, and I've never presented myself as such. I'll be the first one to testify about my flaws—physical and otherwise—without shame.

As human beings, we all fall short. Not one of us gets it right all the time, and none of us ever will. We have all succumbed to something. We have all been slaves to something of sinful nature. And for this reason, not one of us can stand in judgment of another. We can speak by way of observation, sure, but not as judges.

STATING MY CASE.

What is an example of observation? One might ask.

Well, let's take a few of my productions, for instance. *The Falsifier, The Proverbial Diva,* and *Inspired by Imitation of Life* are all witnesses based on *spiritual observation* and not judgment.
They were inspired by what I had been *observing* in certain peoples' lives and actions. The works are not (meant to be) judgmental, but only to shed light on perversities based upon what I had been observing from a personal standpoint.

If it quacks like a duck, it's a duck. And people will address it accordingly. If it barks like a dog, it's a dog. And people will call it as such. If it growls like a bear, it's a bear. And you'll know it by its fruits.
The same scenarios apply here. You're not judging either creature; you're only referring to them by what they are, based on their characteristics.
The Testimony of Cat Ellington is a condensed account of my (personal) witness.
It reveals only a small portion of what my life had once been like when I lived it like a wild young woman of the world. It is not something that I gleefully endorse, but it was what it was. And I do not live with regret in the present because I cannot go back in time and change anything. Furthermore, I

believe that my former life had to be what it was yesterday for me to be the woman—in Christ—that I am today.

I do not point my index finger at anyone, lest my thumb should direct itself back towards me. But know this, that before I speak about *anything* concerning another person's trials, I will most definitely snatch the curtain back to reveal my own first. Always remember that. Because a hypocrite I have never been, nor ever will be. And I'm proud of that fact.

"The Windows Have Eyes"

Genre: Dark

The Synopsis

This production of the written word, in poetic form, intends to witness the subject's descent into the deep throes of severe depression and a yearning for death by suicide.

Here, the eyes are the windows of a tormented soul; the downpour rain is the tear of scalding-hot emotional pain; and the house, the physical body of entrapment.

The Poem:

The hellish abyss,
Dark and cold,
It bargains with time,

To lay hold on my eternal soul—

Every day, I battle with the shadows,
With things unseen:
Misery is consuming me,
Like the maggot on a corpse
That is my inner being—

Behind the velvet face,
There lies only moth-eaten decay:
O let death finally come,
Let it come,
I solemnly pray—

From the windows of my house,
There is a torrential downpour of rain—
Yet there is no one
Who can comprehend my inner pain?

I groan all alone—
And this hand I have been dealt?
I detest and bemoan—

Thoughts of self-destruction corrode me;
They corrode every layer of my hopeless psyche—

Lonely is my pitiable place;
No one cares about me—
Worse is that I'm awake:
Oh, how I wish that I could sleep—

If only I could fall asleep,

Then my soul would be free—
Free from the burden
That is my tormented body—

Behind the velvet face
There lies only moth-eaten decay:
O let death finally come,
Let it come,
I solemnly pray—

The hellish abyss,
Dark and cold,
It bargains with time,
To lay hold on my eternal soul.

The Poet's Commentary

Low self-esteem, self-hatred, self-pity, depression, hatred, anger, impatience, frustration, and irritation: they all may sound like simple words, but they're anything but simple.

THE (SPIRITUAL) EMANCIPATION OF ME.

They are *demons*. And they are real. And their primary purpose is to trouble the mind by tempting human beings to absolutely hate their own lives, to absolutely hate themselves, and to absolutely hate others. No one man, woman, or child possesses a monopoly on any of these as their spiritual warfare on human beings is universal. These tempt and trouble the minds of people all around the world – of every tongue, tribe, and nation. And they're dangerous.

I had fallen prey to the vicious (spiritual) assaults waged on my mind by these demons in my life once. And it took me many years to learn how to battle back against them (by way of divine rebuke).
For they had nearly cost me my life on several occasions, and I know each one of them quite well.

The Living Word is Truth:

"Resist the devil, and he will flee from you."
—James 4:7

Rebuke him in the name of Jesus, my dear men and women. And he'll get off of you. Trust me, I know.

Stay in hope, stay in faith, and stay in love. Keep your joy.

"The Proverbial Diva"
Genre: Satirical

The Synopsis

This production of the written word, in poetic form, intends to witness the great proverb of how hastily received inheritances come to nothing in the end. And of how pride will always precede a great fall.

The Poem:

Before her downfall,

She'd come into great means—
Because fame came quickly,
She'd come into great means...

Oh, she'd had it all—

Before her downfall,

She sang like a lovely dream—
The epitome of renown and esteem,
She sang like a lovely dream...

Oh, she'd had it all—

Before her downfall,

She'd reigned supreme—
A first-rate, world-class celebrity,
She'd reigned supreme...

Oh, she'd had it all—

Before her downfall,

The world had been at her "well-heeled" feet—
In a shameful display of false idolatry,
And unfathomable sycophancy,
The world had been at her "well-heeled" feet...

Oh, she'd had it all—

Before her downfall,

She'd arrogantly scoffed at humility—
Enveloped in the festivity of drunken revelry,
She'd arrogantly scoffed at humility,
And shunned the great Deity of Divinity...

Oh, she'd done it all—

Before her downfall.

The Poet's Commentary

The Proverbial Diva is my "You're So Vain".

Read into the piece whatsoever you will, dear reader.
Read into the piece whatsoever you will.

Part Three

"Enemy Centered"
Genre: Prose

The Synopsis

This production of the written word, in poetic form, intends to witness an evil trial of malicious hostility inflicted upon the subject—resulting from hatred, anger, racism, bigotry, and revenge.
Here, the "little birdie" serves to represent callous and embittered people.

The Poem:

You're gonna fly away, little birdie:
One of these days, little birdie,
One of these days, little birdie,
You're gonna fly away from me—

For you, little birdie, are of an adversarial coop;
Yes, you, little birdie, are of an adversarial coop—

But you're gonna fly away, little birdie:
One of these days, little birdie,
One of these days, little birdie,
You're gonna fly away from me—

(Chirp, Chirp)
You peck at me—
(Chirp, Chirp)
You're an evil trial, little birdie—
(Chirp, Chirp)
But one of these days, little birdie,
(Chirp, Chirp)
You're gonna fly away from me—

You're gonna fly away, little birdie:
One of these days, little birdie,
One of these days, little birdie,
You're gonna fly away from me.

The Poet's Commentary

The production was inspired by me enduring over seven
years of hell on a popular social media platform.

THEY PECK WITH THEIR BEAKS.

This social media platform subjected me—without just cause—to nothing but anger, hatred, malice, racism, bigotry, covetousness, envy, jealousy, lust, spite, stalking, and harassment - from the top (the head of the company) on down through the lower ranks of said platform and out into the general public.

WHY I HAVEN'T FLOWN THE COOP.

I remained on this platform because I had every right to use it for networking purposes – just like everyone else does. It is a public social network. And during my time on it, I have never done anything deserving of the hatred that I have gotten. You know, from the people who control the site. My only offense—as far as these people are concerned—is the fact that I exist and that I can exist without having to kiss their asses or conform to what *they* believe I should be. I did my very best to make the most of my time on the social network in question since I signed up in 2012. But God, it has been an awful experience.

I say this because it had not been the platform itself, but rather the *people* thereon. The site is just that, a site. It could not harm. But the people operating it? *They* are the problem. The people utilizing it? *They* are the problem. The idiotic and self-loathing ass man serving as that company's CEO? *He*, especially, is the problem.

EXPOSING THE STUPIDITY.

The social network about which I speak is truly representative of a vile and perverse culture - brimming with all manner of confusion and madness. A loathsome social network chock full of hateful and ugly-spirited people: both the Jew and Gentile alike; both the well-known and unknown.

Using this particular social media platform has been nothing short of a terrible experience for me. And should the Lord allow me to live to 100 years of age, I will still be testifying about it. Not ever will I grow weary of testifying about it. Not ever. It has been a horrible experience with horrible people.

The social media platform about which I speak? It is a desperate place. And it crawls with desperate people who clamor too much. And for what? Pitiful and pathetic people who covet notability for doing absolutely nothing. Awful and bothersome and perverse people who jockey all over the damn place, trying in vain to grab hold of something for nothing. Lazy people who refuse to put in the hard-ass work one must do to acquire *LEGITIMATE* recognition and who can't help but hate (and envy) those that do: everyday people who shame themselves in desperate attempts to compete with PROFESSIONALS in the arts & entertainment industry.

It's just madness, what this pathetic system that needs to fuel the sorry ass engines of low self-esteem and self-hatred. Madness. I honestly cannot think of any other term to describe it.

And my personal experience with such madness over seven *long* years was just terrible. The social media platform about which I speak has been nothing short of unkind to several people—both renowned and unknown—so I am not the only one. But I needed to testify here concerning my (personal) experience on the site. It has also involved the "shadowing" of my name in my Mentions on the site, including several accounts claiming to be named *Ellington* when I know they're not. These are the same lying-ass people who deliberately tag the word "*cat*" in their posts so that they can have an excuse to troll the Mentions under my name. And the (hostile) people who operate the site have continuously denied me the option to "filter" my Mentions in the Settings feature.

Why? One might ask. Well, because a certain man at the company is also involved in the trolling. The CEO—with his nutty, obsessed, and troubled ass.

EXPOSING THE STUPIDITY FURTHER.

Now one might also ask: Cat, what has this man done that's so offensive?
'Quite a bit' would be my answer to the person.

As I mentioned earlier, the people who run the platform allow trolling because they, too, have become partakers in it. But the CEO? He is perhaps the worst one of them all. The man has gone so far as to use different variations of my name to create false accounts on the site to stalk and harass me. This repulsive man—out of unwarranted spite—also refuses to unlock my original username (inactive since 2012), so that I may be at liberty to reclaim it.

Moreover, my account on the site is still not verified because I refuse to kiss his skinny ass, validate his weak ass manhood, treat him as if he were my man (which he will never be), and pay him my hard-earned money for it.
When I joined this triflin' social network in 2012, ASCAP, Harry Fox Agency, and the Art Institute of Chicago had been three of the first accounts that I followed. That's how I know they were all there before me. And two-thirds of these profiles are *still* not verified? But many of these damn *YouTubers*—and nearly every one of these so-called "Reality Show personalities"—are?
Something is seriously wrong with that.
That is not hatred or envy speaking; it's the truth.
Something is seriously wrong with that.

People (and organizations), such as those mentioned above, should not have to pay for account verification on ANY social network - while illegitimate people dubbed as *Web stars* or *Internet famous* sit on these sites with unpaid ticks following their truly unknown names.

Are you reading these written words, Mr. CEO? Good, if you are. Because now you have a valid reason to call me *arrogant* and *narcissistic,* whereas you didn't before. You hateful, self-hating, angry, bitter, pathetic, abusive, power-hungry, and disturbed ass man you.
I know good-and-damn well you couldn't be that fuckin' enthralled with people like Lauryn Hill, Beyoncé, Kanye West, and Kendrick Lamar while you sittin' on yo' skinny, one-meal-a-day-eatin' ass throwing hate at me for no reason. If you're hostile (without cause) towards me, I know damn well you hate them because they're my people. We share a

culture. You're full of shit, you're a damn liar, and the truth
ain't nowhere near you.

You didn't win a friend in me; you only made an enemy of
me. You keep that in mind. I sought to show kindness and
friendship to you, but you couldn't even receive it because
you're so damn full of fear, confusion, and self-hatred.
Therefore, I withdrew my hand from you. And I will not
extend it to you again. Now glare and frown at *that*,
muthafucka. Don't seek an enemy in me, and you won't find
one.

RESTATING.

Now, concerning my prior statements (regarding Payola for
account verification), I feel like this. I have worked my ass
off—as a creative writer—for decades. And whatever I'm
blessed to receive on this Earth (as a result of my work), I
want to be able to say that I genuinely EARNED—and
NOT BOUGHT—it. And I do mean that with everything I
have in me.

I have not worked in my craft, that is (creative) writing, for
nearly 40 years of my life (building a catalog of work) to
have muthafuckas—strangers at that—treating me as though
I'm nothing, when I know good-and-damn well I am
something. I know what my Lord has given me on this Earth
of *His*. Therefore I will not bend and subject myself to the
whims of a bunch of sorry-ass people. And neither should
anyone else, be they public figures or members of the
general public.

I have testified, time and again, about the hateful (and malicious) treatment I have endured as a member of the social network about which I speak. So the words spoken here are not foreign to those familiar with my postings at the *Boutique Domain* – the same that shed a bit of light on the situation. And because this personal trial of mine (spanning over seven years now) has been so unusually peculiar, I elected to compose a quick work of poetry in response to it; hence, *Enemy-Centered*.

ENCOURAGING OTHERS.

Many readers are sure to find this production highly relatable as they, too, might be encountering a similar experience, if not on a social media platform such as the one that inspired this work in some other area of their lives. Their troublers might be bosses or co-workers or schoolmates or even people with whom they live.
Whatever the situation, they're being given a hard time in their lives by self-hating and malicious people. But always remember this, that nothing lasts forever, not even your problems.

My dear men and women, here is a little bit of advice from me to you. When you see a storm coming towards you, don't turn and run away from it because it'll catch up with you in the same path. But when you see a storm coming towards you, run right through it. Because when you dare to run through a storm, it will eventually pass over you. It will pass over you, the sun will come out again, and your faith will be stronger for it. Always remember that, my dear men and women.

Stand in your faith.

God gotcha. Stand in your faith.

And also remember this, that God is. He has assigned every (human) dog his and her special day. And each one's day will be the most brutal. Always remember that. People will reap what they sow, be it for good or for evil. And the same outcome applies in every scenario of life. So be encouraged.

Nothing lasts forever.

Nothing.

Oh, and one more thing. In case some of you might be wondering why I cuss like I do, being as that I'm a Christian, pay heed:

While I may often cuss—in heated earthly-indignation, I am relentless in my obedience to the will of my Lord on this Earth. Indeed, I would run the soles off of my feet to obey my Lord's commandments. And He, in His almighty firmament, knows it. Should He command me to walk through a valley of deadly vipers, I would do so in a heartbeat because I know that He will not allow the venomous fangs of even one to strike me. But if hateful and evil-minded people allow themselves to break forth upon me, that they should mistreat me without cause, know for a certainty that I will cut their asses up with the verbal sword truth. And. I. Will. Not. Hesitate. *Not even for a moment.*

That is my answer to you.

You: But what about turning the other cheek, Cat?

Me: I have. That's why I ain't got no damn assault and
     battery charges hangin' over my head.

"The Falsifier"
Genre: Satirical

The Synopsis

This production of the written word, in poetic form, intends to expose hypocrisy in those confessing to be members of the household of faith but whose actions are quite contrary to their spoken words.

The Poem:

I know of such a man:

His mouth speaks of Pentecostal Christianity,
But his actions expose the truth,
Which is worldly-minded immorality—

I know of such a man:

His mouth speaks of self-respect and unity,
But his actions expose the truth,
Which are self-deprecation
And partiality—

I know of such a man:

His mouth speaks of peer praise,
And God-fearing modesty,
But his actions expose the truth,
Which are backbiting
And impropriety—

I know of such a man:

His mouth speaks of cultural harmony,
And gracious piety,
But his actions expose the truth,
Which includes selfish infighting,
And a blatant obsession with his celebrity—

I know of such a man:

His mouth speaks of holy devotion,
And fervent love,
But his actions expose the truth:

It is only the world he truly desires to be a part of—

Yes,

I know of such a man.

The Poet's Commentary

Falsifiers. They exist all over the world. But the sole
individual who serves as the inspiration for my production,
The Falsifier, is one of whom we all know publicly.
Regardless of his Pentecostal Christian faith, the individual is
allowing evil to tempt him. And he's not rebuking it.

FACEBOOK ~~FRIENDS~~ ENEMIES.

The person about whom I speak is being tempted in his silly
mind to "backslide," if you will. The enemy tempts this
individual to hate himself. He is also tempting him to hate his
life in Christ and to hate his spiritual calling. This man has
become malicious and hateful in his actions towards other
people, including those who supported his career. This man
has come to hate his community. He is also coveting love,
approval, and acceptance from the people in the world: for
he has become loathsome.
This man, the same man about whom I speak, is desperate to
be perceived as a worldly celebrity rather than as a servant of
God—first and foremost. Do not believe his lip service.

This man has shamed himself in the public eye and, most
importantly, in the sight of the Lord. I know this because I
once fell prey to his anger and hatred back in 2012/2013.
And it, too, had been a most loathsome and evil situation.

The succeeding witness explains what the enemy tempted
him to do to me.

While I managed a Facebook profile back in late 2012, early
2013, I subscribed to an industry page for a television
program hosted by this man. He was also the moderator of
the game show fan page at the time. And while I haven't
been an avid viewer of the game show since its earlier years
on TV, particularly during the early to mid-1980s, I had,
however, been a great admirer of the man, himself, and only
subscribed to the page for that (singular) reason. I said I had
been. I had been a great admirer of the man about whom I
speak until he allowed the enemy to tempt him to carry out
an evil action against me in due course.

To engage both his and the game show's fan base, this man
presented a question to his subscribers and asked them to
give the most popular answer coinciding with a survey poll.
And I dared to offer my unique answer to the
question—which it had been my right to do in the first place.
As far as I was concerned, it was only a friggin' game show
poll, and it was supposed to have been good fun. But when
you're dealing with self-hating people—be they public
figures or members of the general public—their malice
towards others will always get exposed eventually. And the
man about whom I speak is one of such types, what
self-hating. This man is full of self-hatred, not to mention
hatred, anger, malice, and revenge towards other people.
And he is being tempted to use his precious *celebrity* as a
pathetic ass clutch. But when he ran his country-fried ass
into me, he ran into the wrong woman.

The Wrong Woman. That sounds like it could be the title of a Lifetime Movies movie. Doesn't it?

Speaking of Lifetime Movies—formerly known as LMN—the legendary cable network is one of my most beloved channels - ever. And I have never been shy about voicing it publicly. By now, many of you know how much I adore the film projects that air on the Lifetime Movies network. And my passionate love for these films nearly got my Facebook account suspended all those years ago. Because I had the nerve to find joy in something, a certain someone sought to do what was evil to me. Indeed, his feet—clad in those ugly ass shoes of his—swiftly ran to do evil. And not once did his stupid ass stop to consider the consequences. You know, regardless of his tired-ass celebrity status, this individual is one of the miserable ones. He is a hateful and vindictive man who comes from a past of wretchedness. And he, despite the divine mercy that the Lord has shown him, has never forgotten it.

I will now make my point.

While I do not remember the question asked verbatim, it had gone along the following lines:

Ladies, other than his old age, name a reason you would want to marry a rich man?

The answers poured in. And mine had pertained to something that included LMN (the acronymic identity of the network at that time). No harm meant on my part. I was only having a little fun with my answer. But two days later, after signing in to my Facebook account, I returned to the game show page (to which I subscribed), saw another question asked, and typed out my answer. But when I clicked Post to share it to the thread, I was immediately greeted with the following bulletin: *You have been reported for spam.*

The dark pink notification threw me for a loop because (1) I did not know what the hell spam was, and (2) I could not think of any deliberate offense that I had committed against any other Facebook user. But after it settled in, the Holy Spirit immediately showed me who it was that had contacted Facebook to bring the spiteful charge against me: the game show host.

And the Holy Spirit, the Spirit of Truth in whom there is no lie found, did not make a mistake. This man had allowed himself to carry out a lowdown action against me out of spite. And why? Well, because I had spoken what I thought were words of encouragement to his ol' country, boxy suits-wearin' ass only a few days before I replied to the fateful question on the game show page. And I guess he didn't like what he heard, seeing that he was already acting like a rebellious backslider anyway. So he went behind my back and sought an opportunity to be vindictive towards me. And contacting Facebook to have my account flagged had been his chance.

What he did to me was lowdown. And if the Lord ever allows me to see his veneers-wearin' ass up close, I'm sure gonna tell him as much – straight to his face.

What he did to me, I could never have done to anyone and been able to sleep. My conscience would have eaten me up. But his ol' baldheaded, droopy-eyed ass slept, even after he did what was evil. He did what he did because he believed that his celebrity somehow made him immune.

Being new to the Internet and its social networks at that time, I had no understanding of what spam was, so I went into research mode. It was my job to know what it was that had accusations brought against me. And I spent the next four hours of that day reading through every page of the company's Policies and Guidelines. I even visited its forums to learn as much as I could about this thing called spam. And by the time I completed my research, I knew everything I needed to know.

Under the circumstances of my reply to the game show's original question, I had not committed any offense; nevertheless, I had offended the triflin' ass game show host, personally. And he contacted the company to utter a lie on me – in the hope that he would get my account suspended.

My account never suffered a suspension, but I learned a lot about the true nature of people. And in this case, the knowledge I gained had been from that of a well-known public figure who puts on his "God-fearing" airs in the faces of his "adoring" public, while his private actions are a blatant contradiction to the lip service he renders.

But one who sows shall also reap, whether for good or evil. And that goes for every one of us.

IMPATIENTLY WAITING.

No one is perfect. We all fall short. But when one knows better, the penalty for that person will be more severe than for people who do not know any better. And the man about whom I speak knew better. His ol' loud, black ass knew better. But he acted lowdown anyway. And I cannot wait for the opportunity to finally see his Uncle-Tomin ass up close so that I may be at liberty to tell him as much.

Now, it is not my intention to get physically violent with the man; I will not put my hands on anyone. But I am going to tell him how I felt about his lowdown-ass actions against me. *That*, I am going to do.

His public claim is this: *God has given me all that heart could wish*. But he sure doesn't act like it. Ain't no humility in his ignorant ass, only vindictiveness. And trust that I will most definitely tell him the same to his goofy-ass face the minute I see him up close and personal. Lord knows that day ain't comin' fast enough.

"Welcome to Springtime"

Genre: Minnesang

The Synopsis

This production of the written word, in poetic form, intends to pay tribute to what has to be the greatest affection known to Mankind, even that which is love.
Here, the subject joyously expresses its rapture.

The Poem:

I'm just smilin'...

I'm so happy,
I'm just smilin'...

I feel so blessed,

So wonderfully blessed—
So blessed, Oh, yes,
So blessed by the best—

And ah, the joy,
The beautiful joy—
Oh boy, oh boy,
I'm so full of joy—

You wanna know why?
You wanna know why?
Good gosh, oh my,
I'm tellin' you why—

It's 'cause I'm in love,
I'm madly in love—
I'm glowin' because
I'm madly in love—

This very first time,
My life is just fine—
Thank Heaven above;
I'm madly in love—

I'm happy and giddy and joyful,
Because—it's happened to me,
I'm madly in love—

I'm just smilin'...

I'm so happy,
I'm just smilin'.

The Poet's Commentary

And there you have it, folks. There is simply something amazingly gorgeous about the power of love. Love. It's a beautiful thing. And falling head over heels in it? Well, that's even more wonderful. Stay in love, and you'll stay empowered. Stay in love (and not in hate), my dearest men and women.

"The Golden Goose"

Genre: Satirical

The Synopsis

This production of the written word, in poetic form, intends to personally testify of one's own loathsome experience with those motivated by greed and covetousness, even the same who flatter to the face in the hope of gain.

The Poem:

Meet the woman who has great possessions:

I can do no wrong, no wrong at all,
And those around me are at my every beck and call—

Whatever I say or do, even if crooked and untrue,

They all love it
Because they all covet—

At every one of my stale jokes, they all laugh—
They all laugh because they covet what they do not have—

Meet the woman who has great possessions:

Seeking favoritism, they compete to tickle my ears:
Eagerly speaking to me only what I may desire to hear—
For these are a loathsome and miserable lot,
Who secretly plot to receive what I've got—

Meet the woman who has great possessions:

Yea, their flatteries to my face will eventually give way—
To bitter hearts filled with rot and decay—
But lest there shall befall me extreme economic plight,
I will continue to shine,
Within their ravenous eyes,
Radiantly bright—

Meet the woman who has great possessions.

The Poet's Commentary

Trust, my dearest reader, that you will know true friendship when you happen upon it. But beware of those who flatter to the face in the hope of gain.

Beware of the man-pleaser and the sycophant. And remember this wisdom:

100

The first person who will stick a knife in your back is an ass-kisser, considering that they are already (positioned) behind you.

"The Hour of Trial"
Genre: Dark

The Synopsis

This production of the written word—in poetic form—intends to witness severe depression, anguish, distress, frustration, rage, and self-loathing plaguing the author as she wallows in a sea of self-pity during her hour of intense, spiritual trial.
Here, she takes the plea of repentance before the Lord thy God while the reader bears witness.

THE SPIRIT OF DEPRESSION WROTE THIS:

When the human spirit gets broken, hopelessness appears to rejoice. I had once dared to lament in the wallowing of my pitiful descent. My soul is pulling away from me like death at harvest. For even it has waxed wary of the stranger that I have come to be.

This life You have given me, I have come to hate. And the people You made, I have come to hate. What has become of me? For I am deathly and sickly: open your mouth, Earth, and swallow me.

The Poem:

What has become of me?
What happened to the person that I used to be?

The free spirit is no longer;
For it too has bid me adieu—

Now, I am only a hardened shell:
A shell laid along the endless shores of a living hell.

What has become of me?
What happened to the person that I used to be?

The free spirit is no longer;
For it too has bid me adieu—

Now, I am only a hardened shell:
A shell laid out along the endless shores of a living hell.

An embittered soul, unloving and cold,
I search for the warmth of a lost love from of old—

What has become of me?

What happened to the person that I used to be?

The free spirit is no longer;
For it too has bid me adieu.

The Poet's Commentary

Trust, my dearest reader, that this has been (or will be) the lamentation of every brand new creature in Christ Jesus on the face of this great Earth.

THE FAITH TEST.

In the wake of making the born-again confession, there is always this thing called the bliss period. But once that bliss period ends and trials and tribulations begin, that is when people find out who they are. That's when Old Scratch is allowed to attack one's faith in God.

Are you going to remain faithful? Or are you going to turn back like Lot's wife?

A person will either stand in his or her faith in God—despite the growing opposition from Satan through ungodly people in the world system—or he or she will be defeated in (spiritual) battle and give up.

Me? I elected to stand in my faith and obey the Lord and His commandments. Because I wanted to be a true warrior, and I wanted to get the victory, and I wanted to receive the promise, and I wanted to see my dreams—even the ones I have had since the time that I was a very young child—become a reality. Therefore, I held on and fought against the old temptations that troubled me when I had been another lost soul plugged into the Matrix of the world system.

Those early years were rough, yes, but boot camp training will - in all due time - strengthen any soldier, including the spiritual boot-camp training designed for soldiers in Christ. Take off the old (man), and put on the new man. Take off the old (man), and put on the new man. It takes practice, but practice makes perfect.

Therefore, stand. And after having done all, stand.

Part Four

"The Adorable Rufus Hunter"

Genre: Friendship

The Synopsis

This production of the written word, in poetic form, intends to pay an affectionate tribute to a special friend and fellow Sagittarian, namely Rufus "Big Ru" Hunter.
Psst! You mah boy, Ru.

The Poem:

I adore you, Big Ru,
I adore you, I do—

You remind me of,
You remind me of a ray of sunshine:
The kind of sunshine that gleams,
The kind of sunshine that is bright,

The kind of sunshine that pries into the depths,
The depths of my dusky brown eyes—

I adore you, Big Ru,
I adore you, I do—

You remind me of,
You remind me of a warm, gentle breeze:
The kind of warm, gentle breeze that is carefree,
The kind of warm, gentle breeze that flees,
The kind of warm, gentle breeze that blows
With sweetly-succulent and effervescent ease—

I adore you, Big Ru.
I adore you, I do—

You remind me of,
You remind me of a peaceful night's sleep:
The kind of peaceful night's sleep that is tranquil,
The kind of peaceful night's sleep that is deep,
The kind of peaceful night's sleep that is rejuvenating
And serene,
Even to the inner core of the physical being—

I adore you, Big Ru.
I adore you, I do—

You remind me of,
You remind me of a smooth jazz melody:
The kind of smooth jazz melody that is sexy,
The kind of smooth jazz melody that is groovy,

The kind of smooth jazz melody that is mellow and moody—
You feelin' me, cutie?

Jazz—with all that pizzazz
To you from me—in a spirit of sultry sensuality—

I adore you, Big Ru.
I adore you, I do.

The Poet's Commentary

And I do love you, Ru. Thank you for being a friend.
Sagittarius forever, baby. Sagittarius forever!

"Mother Chicago"
Genre: Lyric

The Synopsis

This production of the written word, in poetic form, intends to witness the woes of a beautiful American city in horror. *Mother Chicago* was inspired by CNN's *Chicagoland*.

The Poem:

Mother Chicago,
You need to heed!
Embrace true wisdom,
And get understanding—

Mother Chicago,
You're draped in disgrace:
Your wounds are bleeding all over the place—

Mother Chicago,
It's time to erase,
It's time to erase every scar from your face—

Mother Chicago,
You need to heed!
Embrace true wisdom,
And get understanding...

Mother Chicago,
It's not yet okay,
You're losing your children to crime every day—

Mother Chicago,
You need to heed!
Embrace true wisdom,
And get understanding—

Mother Chicago,
Your prayers are a sin,
Your houses are laid-up with bloodthirsty men—

Mother Chicago,
The wicked endorse it,
They have no regard,
And they shun law enforcement—

Mother Chicago,
You need to heed!
Embrace true wisdom,

And get understanding...

Mother Chicago,
I want you to hear me,
I want you to hear me,
I love you so dearly—

Mother Chicago,
You need to heed!
Embrace true wisdom,
And get understanding.

The Poet's Commentary

Where's mine?
The corruption motto of Chicago—since 1869

Debilitating cancer eats away at its core, and it did not develop overnight. And one work of poetry is not a surefire way to make it alright. It takes an entire community to rebuke a culture of iniquity. And only one faithful chance to take a life-changing stance.

Need I say more?

"I Call the Wind Mariah Carey"
Genre: Lyric

The Synopsis

This production of the written word, in poetic form, intends
to witness the great faith of the author in a long-awaited
divine prophecy. A lyrical piece, this work graciously
expresses her undying love for the one prophetic, even the
inimitable Mariah Carey.

The Poem:

From her throat,
There came a musical sound.
'Twas a great wind that caused astound.
This ode to her is one most honorary.
I call the wind ... Mariah Carey.

You and I are prophesied
And highly favored in His eyes—
By the Lord, we were ordained
Kindred spirits in His name—
I love you with everything,
With everything within my being—
There has never been a day,
When through my mind, you didn't sway—

This is you,
I speak of you,
And from a spirit just and true—

This is you,
I speak of you,
My sister from another womb...

For many years I have been waiting,
Waiting and anticipating,
For us two, yes, me and you,
To be bonded through-and-through—
By the Lord, we were ordained
Kindred spirits in His name—
And His will I wish to do,
I am not ashamed of you—

This is you,
I speak of you,
And from a spirit just and true—

This is you,
I speak of you,

My sister from another womb...

You are now within my heart,
And from it, you will never part—
Trust His word will come to pass,
And we will be an everlast—

This is you,
I speak of you,
And from a spirit just and true—

This is you,
I speak of you,
My sister from another womb.

From her throat,
There came a musical sound.
'Twas a great wind that caused astound.
This ode to her is one most honorary.
I call the wind ... Mariah Carey.

The Poet's Commentary

God gives wisdom, even to the unlearned. One of whom I
had been way back in 1990, the year that He sent to me the
first vision concerning her.

Yeah, I had a vision, too. And it was a beautiful vision that,
to this very day, I still believe, even with everything I have in
me.

I still believe.

CHRISTMAS EVE, 1990.

I sat on the king-size bed in the luxury hotel room that I shared with one of my exes, "Mr. Saks Fifth Avenue," watching a rerun of the *Arsenio Hall Show* and eating imported cheese. My beloved ex, "Mr. Saks Fifth Avenue," was given that playful moniker because he was a Saks man. All of his tailored suits (quite a few) were Saks Label. And he took great pride in them: Mr. Saks Fifth Avenue took great pride in everything he had. He was just that type of guy: he worked hard, and he played hard. And I loved his soul.

Anyway, finally making time for a little R&R, he booked us a suite at the Radisson. We were going to spend the entire Holiday week just chilling out and eating and drinking and watching TV and being lazy and doing all of the other extracurricular activities that we enjoyed. Indeed, we were going to have a good time. And while I watched a commercial on our large TV, he prepared to order up more room service. We first discussed the menu items that we were going to order, and then he made the call. And it was while he placed our orders with RS that Arsenio resumed. The dearly beloved (and legendary) comedian/late-night show host was introducing his next guest, a new songstress named Mariah Carey - who was about to perform her popular debut single, "Vision Of Love." And it may have been while she was belting out the second verse that the

Holy Spirit spoke the following words into my mind: *She is going to be like a sister to you one day, Cat.*
My internal response to that? *Oh, okay.*

Though spoken loud and clear in the spirit, the words—about this woman from New York whom I knew not—fell on deaf ears as I couldn't care less. And being the self-absorbed girl that I was during that time, I moved on with the evening, not once considering the thought that had entered my mind earlier any further: for I floated in my own orbit and didn't want anyone else in my space.

THE SANDS OF TIME.

The Lord would speak to me about the slim and curly-haired girl again and again as time progressed. Over three decades later, He would still be talking about the pretty gal via divine prophecies and visions. And that is the truth. The Lord has never ceased to speak to me about this woman. He has chosen her to be a part of my life. For according to His words, which will surely come to pass, she is my kindred spirit and my sister from another mother.

At the time of this writing, it has been nearly 30 years since the first vision was shown to me on that fateful night in the hotel room. And over time, I became compelled to believe every prophetic utterance, no matter how long each prophecy seemed to be taking to come to pass. That is called faith, my dearest men and women. Real faith. And my faith has had no other choice but to grow over the years. While she is still *eternally 12,* I have gotten a lot older, spiritually. And because no one who is blind can lead the blind — lest they should both stumble over into a ditch — it was I who had to mature first, considering that I was converted to Pentecostal Christianity ahead of her.

THE UNUSUAL INTRODUCTION.

In April of 2012, about a month after I joined the Internet, I was guided by the Spirit to reach out to Mariah by way of an old social network outlet. The outlet about which I speak allowed its users to send text messages to other users to start a conversation thread. So here is what I did. I mustered up the courage (I was a nervous wreck at the time, y'all) and started a conversation with Mariah, typing out a short message and introducing myself. And as I received notification of each message sent, I typed out a few more, gaining more courage with each new letter. I was initially nervous because we were not face-to-face: I had only been communing with her via text messages. And I did not want her to think that I was some crazy whack job, you know? Everything was new to me then, the usage of the Internet. But thankfully, I'm a quick learner.

The text conversations lasted until April of 2014. I know this because I have every one of my letters to her copied on paper today and safely stored away in a binder. And if I might say as much, I gained a new fan in the woman named Mariah Carey during that time. But I am not surprised by that. Because she is an Aries, you know? And the Aries? Well, the Aries can't help but be fascinated with the Sagittarius.

(Laughs)

All good-natured jokes aside, know that I speak the truth, dearest reader. The woman named Mariah Carey is my number one fan. And I? Her biggest inspiration.

THE AFTERMATH.

Full of pride, ego, arrogance, and rebelliousness, she acted ugly in her ways and showed her ass on me for the first few years. And I had to inform her of my bullshit intolerance online, particularly at the Boutique Domain, via published postings. But despite our bumping heads due to any number of our differences, I love Mariah Carey more than any word in the English vocabulary can express. And I would go down fighting for her in a heartbeat if push came to shove. But I will not tolerate her infamous ass Divatude. *Not even for a split second.*

So, there you have it, my dearest men and women, what a summary of the events that inspired the production, *I Call the Wind Mariah Carey.*

And as for you, Ms. Carey? Get it real:

The Earth is spacious enough for both of us. And there is more than enough air for the two of us to share.

"I Am Cat Ellington"

Genre: Dramatic

The Synopsis

This production of the written word, in poetic form, intends to witness glory ascribed to the one and only Jehovah and His Christ through the declarative statement made by His deaconess, even the same called to be a creative artist on the Earth. That is I, Cat Ellington.

The Poem:

The one who has created me
From the dust of the Earth?
It is He whom I serve:

The one who has given unto me
The ability to speak wisdom
Through the written word?

It is He whom I serve:

The one who has brought me forth
To utilize me from within—
Like a double-edged sword?
It is He whom I serve:

Forever.

In the names of this Holy One
And of His only begotten Son?

I am— Cat Ellington.

The Poet's Commentary

Saturday, July 16, 1994

It was the day that I made up my mind to do things the right way. And my life has not been the same since.

Liberated.

"Wonderment"

Genre: Narrative

The Synopsis

This production of the written word, in poetic form, intends to witness the author, though alive and well, being treated as if dead by various people, but who, nevertheless, remains a challenge to ignore.

The Poem:

Here is what I perceive in my reality;
Here is what I perceive my reality—to be:

Why do they fear me?
Why do they not endear me?
Do they hate because they cannot relate?

Is it because I contradict their stereotypes?
Is it because I depict an original prototype?

Why do they fear me?
Why do they not endear me?
Do they hate because they cannot relate?

Ah, let the ear hear:

They hate—because they cannot relate—

Awe baffles the mind,
And the eye lays in its socket:

See—

In baffled awe,
They continue to watch me—

The muted mouth does not speak,
But the liquid eye can see,
The liquid eye can see me—

From afar, their actions are quite bizarre—

Here is what I perceive in my reality.
Here is what I perceive my reality—to be.

The Poet's Commentary

My dearest men and women, I felt compelled to testify about this for three specific reasons: to testify regarding my spiritual trial, to expose the lies, bigotry, racism, hatred, self-hatred, and vile hypocrisy in the world, and to speak to those experiencing a similar treatment in the world, so that they may be encouraged to continue onward in endurance and perseverance.

THE CULT OF ~~PERSONALITY~~ POPULARITY.

While the silly childishness and self-hatred of many of those who engage in social media activities on the Internet show themselves disapproved daily, I have elected not to participate in the madness with them. Because I know who I am. And thankfully, I do not need any of these people in the world to tell me who I am.

Get understanding, my dearest men and women. Once upon a time, worldly popularity and I had been quite close. Both it and I were well-acquainted, especially during my teen years into the era of my twenties. Indeed, wherever I ventured on land, popularity had its rightful place alongside me as we were inseparable. But on the day that I made the good confession and formed a new bond of friendship with the Divine Trinity, worldly popularity and I parted ways as it was inevitable. And while it still seeks to keep up with me today, even if only from a great distance, worldly popularity and I will never again be as close as we once were. And that is just as well as it carries the bulky weight of too many conditions.

I have to be me. That is just the way it is. And not everyone is going to be understanding of that. I have to be who I am and not who others want me to be. I have always been this way, but that has never stopped popularity from seeking me out, even to this very day. Unfortunately, the same is not the case for many people who covet popularity on social media platforms – seeing it as a cheap means to compensate for their low self-esteem. For example, lots of *Likes* equates to being *liked* by a lot of people, particularly strangers. While having lots of *Followers* equates to having a false sense of fame. For such people foster a desperate desire to receive honor and notability without producing any creative works. And lest I forget, photoshopped photos. These only serve to cater to a delusional mindset that tells many everyday people they are members of some professional industry—most likely entertainment or fashion—when in reality, they are anything but: for there lies the spirit of madness. And it will drive people to insanity if they find themselves void of understanding.

I do not need to strive for social media popularity. It simply is not that important to me. Because I already know popularity, it is not unfamiliar to me. As a young girl of only seventeen, I had my very own phone word. That is how closely associated with popularity I had been. It. Is. Not. New. To. Me.

As a (professional) creative artist in the arts & entertainment industry, I do not receive money based on likes and followers on social media platforms. As a (professional) creative writer in literature, I do not get money based on follower counts on social media platforms.

I see social media for what it is: networking, nothing more, nothing less. But if people view social media platforms as anything other than what they are or use them to obtain some false (and delusional) sense of renown—otherwise known as fame—something is wrong with that. And trust that low self-esteem, self-hatred, desperation, bitter envy towards others, racism, jealousy, greed, covetousness, idolatry, laziness, and hopelessness are all acting as the maniacal culprits.

A WOMAN WHO DARES TO BE CONFIDENT.

I am who I am, and I do what I do, even professionally. And I was who I am and doing my professional work long before there was such a thing as social media. And when this miserable and pathetic era dissolves into a new and much better era, I will still be who I am and doing what I do, even professionally.
Always remember that.

Time. It will most certainly reveal.

BE YOU. DO YOU.

My dearest men and women, peace, self-love, and contentment with oneself do not happen overnight. They are hard-won. And if I may suggest anything to you, it would be for you to have faith in God. Believe in yourselves. Love yourselves. Be at peace with others. And embrace the unique talents that you have. Work on developing your skills. And mind what is on your plate and not that of someone else. Do this, and you will be at peace.

Any lawn of grass can be lush, healthy, and a gorgeous shade of Kelly green if it is well cared for; therefore, you should nurture your abilities and be at peace. Because once people start comparing their own lives to the lives of others, hostilities are sure to arise, especially if they feel inferior or inadequate in comparison to the target of their envy.

Believe in yourself. And do not keep your dreams waiting lest they move on without you.

Rebuke fear. Conquer fear.

Part Five

"A Test of Character"
Genre: Prose

The Synopsis

This production of the written word, in poetic form, intends
to witness the author coming down to the end of her fiery
trials and tribulations.
Here, the spirit of the piece reflects humility, maturity,
gratitude, and reverence.

The Poem (Part I):

As I trek through this wilderness,
My heart comes to know the spirit of bitterness:

Am I not all alone?
Am I not all alone?

To Thy command to rebuke,
I have not been mute,
Nor have I given in to grumble
And refute—

Am I not all alone?
Am I not all alone?

Am I not cold?
And with each passing hour,
Am I not becoming a new day old?
Am I not in distress?
Am I not in distress—
As I trek through this wilderness?

Am I not all alone?
Am I not all alone?

Before Thee,
I have been humble;
And not a word against Thee
Have I ever mumbled:

For to Thee,
I have been obedient,
Lest Thou would not have been lenient...
With me—

The Witness (Part II):

For Thou had concealed me from the rain,
And relieved me of my emotional pain:

For Thou had sheltered me from the wicked storm.

Thou hast provided me with love from above,
And kept me warm in the storm:
For I had become distressed in the wilderness.

That every eye should see,
After Thou hast delivered me,
The great honor and mercy
Thou hast bestowed upon me—

Then there will be no more distress.

The Poet's Commentary

Trials and tribulations are no sunshine day at the park. Trust
me when I tell you that, my dearest men and women. One to
whom much is given, much is required. And I have been
chosen to do a prolific work on the Earth – both spiritually
and creatively; therefore, my spiritual trial had to be
extended over several years, that my mind should be
well-trained and equipped for service in honor of the King.
For this prolific work that I am ordained to do is not my will
but that of the Lord. And I must do His will to the best of my
human ability.

My dearest reader, I composed *A Test of Character* while I
had been going through a very rough period in my life and
felt like my spirit was at the point of breaking altogether.
And although that chapter of my life has ended, many others
are currently in the training stage. And I want to encourage

everyone to remain at their posts and complete their (spiritual) training. Because I have been there and know what the barracks are like, I encourage you to stand your ground, soldiers. Rebuke the enemy away from you in the name of Jesus, and stand in your faith. Conquer the old (man) and overtake him with the new man. Stay in that spiritual school and do not drop out. Pass those faith tests and earn your honors. Get. Your. Blessings! Do you understand me? Get your blessings!

The enemy will do everything he can to tempt you to drop out, but you better not drop out. You stay in the boot camp, complete your spiritual training, and open your mouth wide so that the Lord may fill it with blessings you shall not have room enough to receive. Stay in the Faith. Trials do not last forever. It only seems that way while you're going through them. Always remember that.
Stand in your faith. And be of good courage. It will be over before you know it. And you'll look back at the trial and laugh. Trust me, I know. Stand in your faith. And be blessed. I love y'all.

"Luxury"
Gogyohka

The Synopsis

This production of the written word, in the subgenre of micropoetry, intends to witness the peaceful state of contentment.

The Poem:

The warmth of your arms
Wrapped around me?
I liken them to this:
A gentle cashmere sweater
That comforts me in the winter.

The Poet's Commentary

Although *Luxury* is not one of my favorite works, I decided to include it in this book anyway. After all, it was (partially) inspired by one of my favorite cashmere sweaters, a cute little V-neck number in a lovely plum shade. The piece—centered around a lover's embrace—was also composed on a whim: I scribbled the very first words that came to mind.

But regardless of how I feel about the work, my dearest readers, I hope you all will find some enjoyment in it.

"Beastial"

Gogyohka

The Synopsis

This production of the written word, in the subgenre of micropoetry, intends to witness ruthlessness among men.

The Poem:

They break forth
Upon men
Like lions
Full of bloodthirst,
Annihilating their prey.

The Poet's Commentary

The truth follows.

A BREAKDOWN OF SORTS.

Now, this is what happens when people hate other people.
But before they can hate others, they must first hate
themselves. Worse is when such people are in positions of
power, authority, and influence. Indeed, they become
abusive to others - and a terror to themselves: for such
people are open wells filled up with all manner of evil and
ungodliness. There is not even one man, woman, or child on
Earth who has not encountered the "wrath" of these people
at some point in their lives. Wicked people—such as the
ones about whom I speak—never last long though, it only
appears that way. But while they're awake—meaning
alive—they pose themselves as an evil trial unto other
human beings with no qualms. However, in the very hour of
their perishing, the people will rejoice.

These are great bywords - even great examples of how one
must not live his or her life on Earth, what being a wicked
hindrance unto others through systemic oppression, financial
warfare, physical violation, dishonest scales, discriminatory
practices, etc. These are weights with which wicked people
burden the poor, the working-class, the needy, the fatherless,
and the widow: for theirs is the law of the evil one, and it is
his bidding that they eagerly do. But only for a season. For a
little while, they are allowed to fester in their wickedness
before they're cut down and diminished forever. And if one

so desires to search out their place, he or she shall not be able to locate any place for them.

For the way of such wicked individuals is eternal death. And the spirit therein is *Beastial*.

"Hot and Humid"
Tanka

The Synopsis

This production of the written word, in the subgenre of micropoetry, intends to witness erotica.

The Poem:

He drips profusely:
His manhood inside of me,
Stretching and filling
My wide-opened cavity—
He whispers to me, saying...

The Poet's Commentary

There is simply no art better than that of lovemaking: for it is indeed my most undeniable pleasure. and in it, I take great solace.

Erotic pleasure. One of the most delectable pastimes of life.

"We Love You!"
Senryu

The Synopsis

This production of the written word, in the subgenre of micropoetry, intends to refer to the blazing glare of the media and the harsh cutty public eye reminiscent of the adage, *They build you up to tear you down.*

The Poem:

The lens of bitterness
Is an eye of hate:
It cuts through the mind and soul.

The Poet's Commentary

More truth.

THINKING BACK.

I can remember reading an interview that a writer for *Ebony* magazine had done with the late, great Whitney Houston many years ago – in which Whitney shared a little bit of wisdom that had been passed down to her by her legendary mother, Cissy. Those words of wisdom had pertained to the following:

'Nippy, the perfume is only meant to be smelled, not drunk.'

Whitney went on to interpret the meaning of her mother's advice, telling the interviewer—in so many words—that they pertained to both the spotlight of fame, the media, and the general public – whose sugar-coated sweetness in the beginning often turns sour like vinegar in the end. The clear-cut meaning of the parabolic advice that Cissy Houston shared with her beloved daughter? *'They build you up to tear you down.'*
I don't know about anyone else who may have read that fascinating interview from the late 1980s, but I took those words of wisdom to heart—literally—as if they had been spoken to me by my mother, a wise woman in her own right. And they're still written on the tablet of my heart today, even after all these years.

Only smell the perfume, don't drink it.

When one is doing work in public, especially if that work is considered high-profile, it's best to keep a level head and remember who you are as the ego is a natural trait common to all people. And in the case of those wise words, the incomparable Cissy Houston spoke to her equally storied daughter, Whitney: ego had been the trait to whom she referred.

We still see it today, the exaltation of celebrated people from both the media and public-at-large. Everything floats along just fine until the celebrity makes the mistake of being human and says or does one little "offensive" thing. From there, the media—as a collective body—goes to work churning the instigation machine to sway public opinion about that person to the negative side of the fence. And before long, down he or she goes. Because the public is fickle and very rarely is true loyalty found in them.

In a nutshell, that was the point of my short piece, the same being *We Love You!*

Thank you, Mrs. Houston, for speaking the truth to your child. Because when she repeated those words publicly, they went on to be a great blessing to others, including myself, as I have never forgotten them.

Part Six

"The Heavy Load"
Senryu

The Synopsis

This production of the written word, in the subgenre of micropoetry, intends to witness the hopelessness of a weary human soul.

The Poem:

In the depths of grief,
The spirit faints:
Here, it swelters in depression.

The Poet's Commentary

This piece takes its inspiration from my battle with depression and suicidal tendencies.

I'M A SURVIVOR.

While *The Heavy Load* was originally a fuller piece (written when I was 15), I elected to shorten the work and publish it as micropoetry in 2013. I believed that the composition, in its edited form, would be enough to serve its purpose. And I hope that it has.

To those of you out there who can relate to my witness, I say be of good courage and overcome. You are going to be okay, and you are going to make it. Believe that. You are going to do just fine. Believe me. All you have to do is reel in that pride and put it in subjection to you. Let go of it and let God handle it; because you cannot change one hair on your head. So just let all of that old mess go and live. Do you understand me? Let that old mess go and thrive. Let it all go and stay alive. Get yourself back in the race, run it, and win it!

"Jeer"
Gogyohka

The Synopsis

This production of the written word, in the subgenre of micropoetry, intends to witness hate-filled spirits of contempt.

The Poem:

The serpent
Uncoils itself,
Then slithers up
To hiss from
Throats of scoffers.

The Poet's Commentary

The scoffer and the wise are not the same.

DIFFERENTIATING THE TWO.

While a wise man will love you for supplying him with a cold drink of sound wisdom, that he should become wiser - a scoffer, on the other hand, will gnash his teeth at the truth and hate the one bearing it. Indeed, we have all had our share of encounters with the scoffer, even with one who is entirely faithless and whose throat is a well of strife. And if you desire to understand, you should know that it is written, 'Do not give what is holy to the dogs, nor cast your pearls before swine, lest they trample them under their feet, and turn and tear you in pieces.'

My dearest men and women, whenever you encounter an angry and contentious person in denial, trust that you have happened upon folly. Bite your tongue and go your way in peace lest you be scorched and consumed by the kindled flames of their self-destruction.

"That Stuff"
Genre: Dramatic

The Synopsis

This production of the written word, in poetic form, intends
to witness an emotional testimony concerning my beloved
mother and her battle with the demon called drug abuse.

The Poem:

She was a mighty dainty dame.
How was it that she began to lose her way?

That stuff is gon' kill her;
Lord, rebuke her dealer!
That stuff is sho gon' kill her;
Lord, rebuke her dealer!

I fear for her—

That stuff?
It took away her beauty—
That stuff?
It stole away her dignity—
That stuff?
It hindered all her ability—
That stuff?
It even drove her to poverty—

Dear Mama,

You're breaking my heart:

That monkey, dear Mama,
It's gon' tear us apart—

You need me, dear Mama,
And I need you—
But if you leave me, dear Mama,
What the hell am I gonna do?

Dear Mama—

The Poet's Commentary

I wrote this piece about my mother during her struggle with
crack cocaine addiction in 2004. She spent time in rehab,
and she is now well – both spiritually and physically.

Thank you, Lord God.

THAT'S MY MAMA.

Thank you, Mama, for allowing me to share your personal experience, in brief, with my reading public. Because it is for a certainty that others will be able to relate, even wholeheartedly, to our witness. I love you, Mama. And I am proud of you. You got the faith back, and I am so very proud of you. You are still a mighty dainty dame. And I love you all the same.

I got my Mama back. :)

"That Which Is Never Full"
Gogyohka

The Synopsis

This production of the written word, in the subgenre of micropoetry, intends to witness the symbolic terror of eternal destruction.

The Poem:

That which feeds
Into the mouth
Of the fiery pit
Is the main course
Of the lost soul.

The Poet's Commentary

The path of the wicked: it guides their crooked feet over the
cliffs of Sheol.

THE PATH OF THE UNJUST.

Today they live, eat, drink and make merry while they inflict
suffering upon others. But tomorrow, you will search out
their places on Earth and not be able to find them anywhere:
for theirs is a spiritual escalator that goes straight down into
the spiritual realm.
See, preceding them were those of their generations before
them. And know for a certainty that following them will be
those of their lineage after them.

The piece, *That Which Is Never Full*, is intended to shed
light on the way of the damned.

Live on this Earth long enough, and you will start to notice a
pattern: there is always a price to pay when people do evil
and be evil. And that goes for every man and woman of
every tongue, tribe, and nation.
Get wisdom, my dearest men and women. Get wisdom.

"From One End to the Other"
Gogyohka

The Synopsis

This production of the written word, in the subgenre of micropoetry, intends to witness the double-minded.

The Poem:

These are the perverse:
Who shun and spurn
As they sway to,
And who flatter and cajole
As they sway fro.

The Poet's Commentary

I have always had the following mottos: (1) If you can't speak to me all the time, don't speak to me at all, and (2) If one is not willing to eat beans with you, the same is not worthy to eat steak with you.

These are my mottos, even ones that I have tended to live by since I was old enough to remember. And I have never faltered in my beliefs.

THE REAL DEAL.

When dealing with people, regardless of whomever they may be, I have always dealt with them straightforwardly. With me, what you see is what you get because I do not put on airs. And I am not a very good liar. If I like you, I will tell you as much. And I will tell you exactly why I do. I will not beat around the bush with you. But if I do not like you, trust that I will inform you of as much. And I will tell you exactly why I do not. I will not beat around the bush with you. That is the way I live my life, what straightforwardly. But not all share my level of bluntness.

IF I KNEW BACK THEN WHAT I KNOW NOW.

As a professional in the arts and entertainment industry, I finally decided to join a few social media platforms in 2012. I wanted to connect: with not only those members of the general public but also those of fellow creatives in the industry. And by the time of this writing, regret would still be gnawing at me because of that decision. For had I known then what I know now, I would never have reached out to any of them. But it had to happen. It had to be. Because I learned a valuable lesson from it: I had to be allowed to see people for who they (truly) are: a bunch of self-hating, miserable, bitter, angry, malicious, vindictive, faithless, hopeless, envious, and jealous-hearted people.

A BLUNT INSTRUMENT.

Here is something you all should know about me. After I have extended my hand in a spirit of kindness to anyone, and that person regards my hand with spite and hatred, I will never again offer my hand to the same person. Never again. I will leave them alone and let them be. Because they did not do it to me, they did it to the Lord, considering that I am His servant. Therefore, they do not have to answer me. But they will have to answer to Him. And He does not play with human beings that He made from dust – be they well-known human beings or unknown human beings. The Lord does not play with people who allow themselves to act hatefully. Trust me, I know.

When people—especially those who know better—allow themselves to heed the lies of the enemy rather than rebuking those lies away from their minds, it will not be good for them. And quite a few of the individuals to whom I reached out and got shunned know better. But sadly, they refused to do better.

Those about whom I testify are the same who claim to be members of one Body, even that of Christ. But they were tempted to act perverse and worldly-minded, thinking that their actions were going unnoticed. And rather than showing themselves approved, they preferred to settle in their ugly ways by engaging in partiality towards me, thereby conducting themselves like judges with evil thoughts. With their lips, they praise the name of the Lord before the people, but their hearts are full of bile. And though I may strongly desire to do so, I will refrain from mentioning any of their well-known names lest they should deny my witness and accuse me of slander. But they know who they are. And *I* know who they are. And one day, when desperation drives them to the other end of the spectrum, and they jockey to seek me out, so will you, my dearest reader. I will make sure of it.

HUMBLE YOURSELVES.

I am not willing to kiss the ass of anyone, and I do not expect anyone to kiss mine (and Lord knows I got way more ass than every one of 'em), but it would have been pleasing had they exhibited a little bit of self-respect while showing the same to others.

The people about whom I speak are not deities. They are only creative people who work in the entertainment industry. That is all. But many are delusional. They see their status in society as being anything other than what it truly is: a job. And when people start treating the job as though it is a false idol in which they put their faith, the same people are already on the wrong road.

It is just a job. And you folks do not have to act shitty with other people as a result of your either having—or having had—that job because I work in the same industry. I am a member of various guilds and societies in the industry, too. And just because I am not seated at the same table with you breaking bread does not make me nonexistent or unimportant. If you pay attention, you will find out that the truth is the exact opposite. It just has not been revealed yet.

So watch yourselves because you may need me for something one day. And I will bet good money on the odds that most of you will.

Humble yourselves.

ONE FINAL JOLT.

That is the folly with people, you see? They know where they have been but do not know where they're going. They can remember what happened yesterday, but they don't know what's going to happen tomorrow. Be careful of nothing.

Part Seven

"The Bout"

Genre: Narrative

The Synopsis

This production of the written word, in poetic form, intends to witness a spiritual battle with the enemy, cast here as an "Opponent" in the symbolic setting of a boxing match. Here, great faith is what sustains the witness.

The Poem:

My opponent tries to beat me,
My opponent tries to defeat me,
My opponent tries to delete me,
My opponent tries to retreat me—

My opponent tries it all,

But to no avail—
Because my Trainer?
My Trainer has trained me well—

Even when the bell sounds,
Ding, ding, ding—
I'm still standing on both feet,
I'm still standing in the ring—

Even when the bell sounds,
Ding, ding, ding—
I still elude defeat,
I'm still standing in the ring—

Even after every round,
My opponent still can't keep me down—
Even after every uppercut,
I'm still standing up—
Even after every low blow,
My opponent still can't get a TKO—

I elude defeat,
I'm still standing on both feet—
I elude defeat,
I'm still standing on both feet—

My opponent fails to beat me,
My opponent fails to defeat me,
My opponent fails to delete me,
My opponent fails to retreat me.

The Poet's Commentary

In this order: humble yourself, repent of your sins, accept the Lord Jesus Christ as your personal Lord and Savior, receive the Holy Spirit of God in His name, make the Good Confession, take up your cross, and let the trials, tribulations, and public persecutions begin. Get the victory!

A GOOD TESTIMONY.

The Bout is my witness, respectively. And it was inspired by over 25 years of my membership in the Body of Christ. Dear fellow brethren, always remember this one thing while undergoing your spiritual trials: the enemy will throw everything he has at you until he uses up all of his evil tools, and you get the victory in the name of Jesus.
As the timeless song lyrics go, *The battle is not yours. It's the Lord's.*
And He has already won it. So be of good courage.

"And Now A Word From Chicago's South Side"

Genre: Narrative/Dramatic

The Synopsis

This production of the written word—in poetic form—intends to witness the author embodying a particular geographical location.

Here, if the South Side of Chicago could talk, it would say:

The Poem:

There is a mission to condition your minds against me:

You always hear about my so-called curse—
Because they have made it a habit
To only show me at my worst—

But you never get to see my beauty—
Because all they want to show you is my ugly...

There is a mission to condition your minds against me:

You always hear about my economic pain—
Because they have made it a habit
To only shine the spotlight on my maim—
And while they focus on my trepidation,
Never do they take the time to recognize
My great education...

There is a mission to condition your minds against me:

You never see my luxurious homes and condos—
Because they have made it a habit
To only publicize my crime-ridden ghettos;
And because I am—always—shown at my worse,
I am—forever—regarded among the scourge of the Earth...

There is a mission to condition your minds against me:

You never get to see my God-fearin'—
Because they have made it a habit
To only showcase those who're my wicked churen;
And though there be within me wisdom
That is second to none—
According to their witness,
All of my children are coming undone...

There is a mission to condition your minds against me:

You always hear about my so-called curse—
Because they have made it a habit
To only show me at my worst—
But you never get to see my beauty—
Because all they want to show you is my ugly...

And why?
So that you might be susceptible
To perceive me through the eye of a lie—

There is a mission to condition your minds against me.

The Poet's Commentary

From her, there is much Godly praise. And both she and her
children? Well, they see many joyful days. Indeed, within
her, there is tremendous hope. But is anyone ever allowed to
hear about it? Nope.

WHY DO THEY HATE THE SOUTH SIDE OF CHICAGO SO MUCH?

Judged and spat at, pissed on, pooped on, and ridiculed: that
is the South Side of Chicago. Mocked and excluded,
ignored, scoffed at, lied about, and singled out: that is the
South Side Of Chicago. Demonized and looked down,
denigrated, redlined, and always used as a scapegoat: the
South Side of Chicago.

But even still, she keeps going.

Despite the lack of a positive spotlight on her, even still, she shines. And although many feet ache from all the work they put in stomping her down, the Lord blesses her to keep rising. Because contrary to the lies they prefer to believe about her, God is for her. And He is with her. Because many, not all, but many of her children continue to stand in their faith in Him. And they have not bent the knee to the spirit of error in the world: for this reason, Satan, who operates through ungodly people, has waged war against her and her predominantly Black children, whom, by the way, just so happen to embrace Pentecostal Christianity in mass numbers: for the people are monolithic and unified in that regard.

Therefore, a (spiritual) war wages against them. And it manifests itself in the godless and oppressive treatment that it inflicts upon them.

PREACH, GIRL!

The war has never been so much about the physical than it is about the spiritual. It was always a spiritual battle, even from day one: because the people chose to put their faith and trust in God, not in Man. And there lies the rage – operating through racism and economics.

Everyone is not asleep. Satan only tries to make it look that way.
Not all are lost. Satan only tries to make it look that way.
Not all are down and out. Satan only tries to make it look that way.
Not everyone is getting shot to death. Satan only tries to make it look that way.

Not all are broke and struggling. Satan only tries to make it look that way.
Not every neighborhood is dilapidated. Satan only tries to make it look that way.
Not every young Black man is a thug or gangbanger. Satan only tries to make it look that way.
Not every young Black girl is popping babies out of her ass at an alarming rate. Satan only tries to make it look that way.
Not every sidewalk is cracked up and caved in. Satan only tries to make it look that way.
And he uses many evil-minded people in the world—particularly in both politics and the media—to perpetuate his evil lies. For it was spoken concerning him, 'He is a liar and the father of it.' For the devil tempts those people—whose minds are open to his lies—to only seek out the worst in others, particularly in those who are African American.

By the way, whenever you hear someone say, *In the South Side* rather than *On the South Side*, know for a certainty that the same is an ignorant-ass outsider who does not know what the hell he or she is talking about: it's not *In* the South Side, dumb-asses, it's *On* the South Side.

Oh, and another thing. Contrary to popular belief, we have beautiful flowers, living trees, and green grass, too. We also have gorgeous parks, lovely bookstores, state-of-the-art libraries, fascinating museums, stunning art galleries, and cozy cafés.
We have beautifully decorated homes, and apartments, and high-end vehicles, too.

We have youth centers that cater to the advancements of our
children, too.
You might not hear about them, but we do.

Be ye not deceived, my dearest men and women.
Be ye not deceived.

"This Womanhood"

Genre: Dramatic

The Synopsis

This production of the written word, in poetic form, intends to witness both the social struggles and spiritual triumphs of the Black woman in America.

Inspired by over four centuries of integrity.

The Poem:

We are strength...to the furthest extent;
We are queens—
Who descended from kings:

We have swam

In the oceans of hate—
Through the whip,
Through the branding and rape—
We withstood
Every torture and ache
From the ones who decided our fate—
We have suffered many wages of sin,
But survived
And we stood by our men—
We have borne many children in plight,
Swung the rod,
So they knew wrong from right—
We are blessed,
We don't settle for less—
How do we do it?
Well, that's anyone's guess—

We are strength...to the furthest extent;
We are queens—
Who descended from kings:

We have cried
Bitter tears from our eyes;
We were judged,
And subjected to lies—
We had learned
How to read and to write,
And we fought,
Yes, with all of our might—
We are fierce:
We're like steel; we don't pierce—

We were faithful
Through the toughest of years—
We have earned every honor and grace,
As we've come from a mighty long way—
This is true,
And my tribute to you,
You, my sisters
Of the ebony hue—

We are strength...to the furthest extent;
We are queens—
Who descended from kings.

The Poet's Commentary

I see the lady,
I see the lady I call my Nana.
I see the lady,
I see the lady I call my Mama.
I see the lady,
I see the lady I call my sister.
I see the lady,
I see the lady I call my daughter.
I see the lady,
I see the lady who is me.

I see the lady,
I see the lady who has withstood the trial and tribulation of a
ruthless generational history.

Not of her own accord has the Black woman withstood, but only by the tender mercy of the Lord has the Black woman: breathing into life the past, present, and future of the ugly, the bad, and the good,
I present to every one of you ... *This Womanhood*.

"Operation imPlantation"

Genre: Tanka

The Synopsis

This production of the written word, in the subgenre of micropoetry, intends to witness the wicked workings of Satan through those human operatives in the world that occupy its leading branches of Science and Technology.

The Poem:

They're already damned:
Those who have received the "Chip"
In their heads and hands:
Slaves to man's technology;
Doomed for all eternity.

The Poet's Commentary

IT IS A MAN'S NUMBER.

A cashless society? Do not trust it. Fear tactics? Trust them not. Lies told to disguise the truth? Believe them not. The Class Structure in Society - used as a weapon to attack one's self-esteem? Surrender not to it.

All of the above are the main components used to lead the impressionable—and perhaps even unlearned—individual astray. These have one common purpose, and that is to shove impressionable—and even unlearned—men, women, and children right over the edge into a deep valley of complete and utter self-destruction.
Microchipping, particularly of humans, is the ultimate evil. It is the most atrocious (and inhumane) technology there is, and no one should be deceived—or forced by fear tactics—into undergoing its invasive processes. No, not even one. Because of its sudden growth in worldwide popularity, I felt compelled to compose *Operation imPlantation* in rapid-fire response. And it is my sincerest hope that all of you will open your minds to sound wisdom: for it will save your life, even your eternal soul.

No one needs to penetrate your bodies with any form of invasive technology, regardless of what anyone says. One need not be paranoid, only vigilant to abstain yourselves from such a vicious raping of your bodies.

Be faithful, be at peace, and watch out for yourselves. You don't need to have a damn microchip implanted in your hand to open a door. All you need to do is grab hold of the doorknob or door handle and open it yourself. If you can't be issued a key or a keycard, you don't need it.

Do not allow anyone to lie to you and deceive you into self-destruction using "convenience" as an excuse to give in. Because that is what it will be: a lie.

Watch out for yourselves.

"Dance, Nigger, Dance"
Genre: Satirical

The Synopsis

This production of the written word, in poetic form, intends to witness the fiery wiles of spiritual warfare on those who continuously cower to subserviency and self-denigration – despite being released from a culture of oppression and societal enslavement.

Here, spiritual warfare is all in one's mind; hence, the *Conditioned Negro.*

The Poem:

Watch the nigger:

Watch the nigger as he does his jungle dance,
Before the face of the White man—

Watch the nigger:

Watch the nigger play the lesser
To his European oppressor—

Watch the nigger:

Watch the nigger disown his own
For the White man's dollar;
Watch the nigger get overthrown
In a way that makes me wanna holler—

Watch the nigger:

Watch the nigger shuck and jive
To keep the stereotypical folklore alive—

Watch the nigger:

Watch the nigger on display in his symbolic cage;
Watch the nigger as he implodes from hopelessness
In his self-destructive rage—

Watch the nigger:

Watch the nigger as he hustles to please;
Watch the nigger as he bustles to appease—

Watch the nigger:

Watch the nigger on display in his symbolic cage;
Watch the nigger as he continues to coon and buffoon,
Even in this very day and age—

Watch the nigger.

The Poet's Commentary

"My people are destroyed for lack of knowledge."
—Hosea 4:6

THE MODERN-DAY MINSTREL.

To this very day, such men refuse to leave the plantations of their minds. To this day, such men still believe that they are inferior, particularly to the ones of European descent. To this very day, such men hate not only their outward reflection but also those who share it. To this day, such men put their faith in a long-dead Massa rather than in Father God, who lives forever. To this very day, such men give away their power to others, particularly those who hate them. To this day, such men are those who, instead of building their own companies, prefer to play the sickening role of the subservient and begging fool within companies founded by others. To this very day, such men disregard the immense power of economics, electing to toss their resources into the coffers of those who blatantly hate them. To this day, such men subject themselves to much humiliation and disregard at the expense of their integrity.
To. This. Very. Day.

Indeed, such men would be willing to bullwhip themselves—to save their modern-day oppressors the trouble of having to do it for them. Indeed, such men will kick themselves in the ass—to make sure their modern-day oppressors do not have to go to the trouble of doing it for them. Like the children of Israel in the days of old are such men. For such modern men long to return to the various enslavements of their oppressors. As the men of old had been, so are they. Like the (rebellious) men of old, these also groan and grumble in the sight of God about their newfound liberation: for in this modern-day (wannabe ancient) Egypt, such men desire to be beaten into subjection and stomped down beneath the leaden feet its false Pharaohs.

This illness is what happens when one has had a conditioned mind for over four-hundred years. Rather than treating themselves to the filet mignon of life, such people seek out the scraps in life. Not because they prefer the least, but only because they keep getting told that the least is all they're worth.
All they know is the same old song and dance. And they've perfected the dance. They've perfected the dance, and Satan—operating through flesh-and-blood humans—has perfected the tune to which they dance. And as surely as the sun rises and sets, the enemy of all Mankind will continue to spin that tired-ass record until someone finally breaks it, that it should be played—and danced to—no more.

SHOW HIM YOUR FAITH, NOT YOUR WORKS.

My dearest men and women? Obedience—to God—is better than sacrifice. Learn to obey Him, and He'll make you the head, not the tail. Always remember that.

Here, the man was the focus because the man is before the woman; therefore, the man has the greater shame.

Bonus Material

"The Black Girl"

Genre: Lyric/Dramatic

The Synopsis

This production of the written word, in poetic form, is a literary adaptation of an original composition from the Cat Ellington song catalog.

The Poem/Song:

I'm a Black girl,
And I was born into this world of divisions—
To a mother who was all shuffled up
In the world system—
You know, a Black girl,
A Black girl ain't much welcome
In this hateful culture of contentions—

The system failed the Black girl
In this world—

I'm a Black girl,
And I was raised on the South Side of Chicago...
In the ghetto—
We received public aid,
And I attended a public school:
I was in the "class" of the poor—
I wore the same ol' clothes over and over,
'Cause new ones, we couldn't afford—

The system failed the Black girl In this world—
The system failed the Black girl In this world—

Black girl—
Black girl—
Black girl—

Black girl—
Black girl—
Black girl—

Just say no
To the status quo—
Just say no
To the status quo—

Black girl?
Where you at in this world?
Just say no

To the status quo—

Black girl?
Where you at in this world?
Just say no
To the status quo—

The Poet's Commentary

THE LEGACY OF THE BLACK GIRL.

One of my most cherished works from the Cat Ellington song catalog is *The Black Girl*. The piece is a passionate anthem inspired by my childhood. The poem/song comes from my upbringing in some of the most legendary (and historic) communities on the South Side of Chicago, including Kenwood/Hyde Park, Washington Park, Jackson Park, Bronzeville, and Douglas.

A proud product of the inner-city, I wrote *The Black Girl* as a personal tribute to my life and education - as well as my community's subjection to the city's culture of racism and segregation.

Originally written as a basic structure (of words) in 1983, I soon arranged a simple musical composition, and *The Black Girl* was born as a song. Ironically, the piece was also a mutation of poetry; hence its "crossover" into a literary adaptation.

While I would not have done so under other circumstances, my love for my friends and mentors, Dorothy Luckett, Melvin Gaynor, and Gary Martin, helped with my decision to include *The Black Girl* on these pages.

Here's to ya!

"The Black Girl"
Words by Cat Ellington
©2019 The Black Jaguar Music Company (ASCAP)

Pardon the intrusion,
But you are now at the conclusion.

Ha!
Now that's a rhythmic fusion!

Coming November 2019

Memoirs in Gogyohka: A Book of Short Poems and
Memoirs
Imprint: Quill Pen Ink Publishing
Cover Tint: Mandarin

About the Author

Cat Ellington is an American songwriter, casting director, poet, author, and entrepreneur from Chicago, IL. She is best known for her creative contributions to the diverse industries and fields of music, movies, art, and literature.

Cat Ellington's professional credits list a collection of nonfiction books, including the Reviews by Cat Ellington series, The Making of Dual Mania, More Imaginative Than Ordinary Speech, Memoirs in Gogyohka, and You Can Quote Me On That. In film and music, Ellington's credentials include her work on the psychological thriller, "Dual Mania," and its soundtrack—on which she wrote five original songs: "The Book of Us," "I'm Still in Love," "Something in Your Eyes," "Gett Out," and "I Do."

Outside of her professional element, the award-winning creative enjoys reading, listening to music, cooking, collecting vintage and modern charm bracelets, watching movies and classic TV shows, sailing, jet-skiing, playing tennis, and eating frozen yogurt – lots of it.

Cat Ellington on Amazon: Books, Biography, Blog, Audiobooks, Kindle

Cat Ellington at the Award-Winning Boutique Domain

Cat Ellington at The Review Period with Cat Ellington

Cat Ellington at IMDb

Cat Ellington at Goodreads

Memoirs in Gogyohka

A Book of Short Poems and Memoirs

BY CAT ELLINGTON

A Book of Short Poems and Memoirs

MEMOIRS
IN GOGYOHKA

Inspired by the Diaries of Cat Ellington

FROM THE
Cat Ellington
LITERARY COLLECTION

Memoirs in Gogyohka

Books by Cat Ellington

REVIEWS BY CAT ELLINGTON: THE COMPLETE
ANTHOLOGY, VOL. 1

REVIEWS BY CAT ELLINGTON: THE COMPLETE
ANTHOLOGY, VOL. 2

THE MAKING OF DUAL MANIA: FILMMAKING
CHICAGO STYLE

REVIEWS BY CAT ELLINGTON - THE COMPLETE
ANTHOLOGY LIMITED EDITION HOLIDAY GIFT
SET (BOOKS 1 & 2)

REVIEWS BY CAT ELLINGTON: THE COMPLETE
ANTHOLOGY, VOL. 3

MORE IMAGINATIVE THAN ORDINARY SPEECH:
THE POETRY OF CAT ELLINGTON

REVIEWS BY CAT ELLINGTON: A TRILOGY OF
UNIQUE CRITIQUES #1

MEMOIRS IN GOGYOHKA: A BOOK OF SHORT
POEMS AND MEMOIRS

Memoirs in Gogyohka

A Book of Short Poems and Memoirs

Cat Ellington

Quill Pen Ink Publishing

THE BEAUTY OF EXPRESSION™

CHICAGO

PAPERBACK ISBN-10: 173344212X
PAPERBACK ISBN-13: 978-1-7334421-2-1

Library of Congress Control Number: 2022362738

Published by Quill Pen Ink Publishing
Chicago, Illinois, USA

Quill Pen Ink Publishing, 2019
The Cat Ellington Poetry Collection
The Cat Ellington Literary Collection
The Cat Ellington Diaries

Cover design: Tommie Mondell for Quill Pen Ink Publishing
Flower art: Watercolors by Ateli
Cover tint: Mandarin

Watercolors by Ateli appear courtesy of Quill Pen Ink Publishing

QPIP | Books: The Boutique Domain

This is a work of creative nonfiction. All of the events in this memoir are true to the best of the author's memory. Some

Dedication

To Mama, RaVan, baby James, and aunt JoAnn—
I love y'all

Preface

My dearest reader, the succeeding effort has been a very long time in the making. And I am so excited to say that it's finally here. I love it when my creative juices begin to flow. And as I was looking through the pages of some of my old diaries over the last five years, an exciting idea came to mind: *Cat, why not create a series of Gogyohka micropoetry to coincide with some of your diary entries?*
Yeah, I thought in response. *Why not? It'll be fun!*

Five years later, and here we are.

I bought my very first diary at a Chinatown basement store in 1982. And I've been recording day-by-day accounts about my life in them ever since. I love diaries. They are the record books of life. And I genuinely believe that everyone should have at least one (or maybe even two) in their possession. Because as life moves forward, so many different experiences are happening. And one will never be able to get those parts of their life back: but if he or she makes time to keep a journal, as time progresses, they can always go back to every special moment and relish those memories, whether those memories consisted of circumstances that tested their faith or rewarded it.
It's always good to remember the past to understand both your present and future. And my dearest readers, I cordially invite all of you to play witness to those random selections of my own life story on the proceeding pages of *Memoirs in Gogyohka*.

Although my (featured) entries reflect actual events, some names and identifying details in this book were changed to protect the privacy of the people involved.

Thank you for your support of my creative efforts in literature. And I do hope that you will enjoy *Memoirs in Gogyohka*.

Acknowledgments

I ascribe all glory to my Lord God for His extraordinary blessings: for the (earthly) work that You have blessed me to do, I am unequivocally grateful. And I thank you for everything.

Thank you to my husband, Joseph Strickland, and our three gorgeous children Nathaniel, Nairobi, and Naras. Thank you for your continued love and support. I love you all wholly and dearly.

Freddie and Maurice, thank you both for everything. Over the years, you guys have been nothing short of a great blessing to me. And for your many kind deeds, I will love you forever.

Thank you, Jessica Zillhart, for marrying us into the St. Paul Public Library family. We appreciate you.

Thank you, my dear Tammy, for your many kind words and encouragement throughout the roller coaster years of my early teens. For much like me, you truly believed. And I will always love you.

Thank you, my most beloved Anita, for your unconditional friendship and tireless conversation. For you were a great blessing to me throughout many a year, and I will forever cherish the bond we share(d).

Thank you to all of my readers who take great pleasure in my contributions to the field of literature.

And a very special thank you to Jenny Wang, who encouraged me to purchase my first diary in February of 1982.

Contents

A Stiff-necked Rebel
She Flew In On Her Broom
The Evolution of Life
The Muffin Top

The Fourth Stage:

Single Black Female
Slippery
Wind Chill Advisory
The Orgy
The Girl on the Red Line

The Fifth Stage:

It Happened at Buckingham Fountain
Snake Eyes
It Can't Be
Misery Loves Company
Blessed Are You

The Sixth Stage:

The Whisperer
The Bitch Called Karma
Looks Can Be Deceiving
Talkin' 'Bout My Generation X
Amazon Women on the Earth
For Old Times' Sake

The Seventh Stage:

The Artist and His Subject (My First Lover)
The Low-End Legends

The Private Investigator
Motivated by Hate
The Attorney
Deflated Balloons
Serenaded by Kenny G

Introduction

Gogyohka
/go-gee-Yoh-Kuh/

Noun

Translation: five-line poem or song.

The art of Gogyohka poetry was created by Japanese poet Enta Kusakabe in Japan in 1983 - pioneering the five rules of five-line, freestyle poetry. Unlike its counterpart, Tanka (a five-line structure differentiated into *31* syllables: first line (5), the second line (7), third line (5), fourth line (7), and the 5th line (7)), Gogyohka is intended to allow the writer a bit of leeway in syllable count; nevertheless, the traditional style generally consists of *24* syllables: first line (5), the second line (4), third line (4), fourth line (7), and the fifth line (4).

I learned this form of the Gogyohka structure years ago, and I tend to stick to it in my literary compositions.

In this particular form of Japanese style poetry (Gogyohka), each line should represent one phrase - such as is found in standard Western poetry. And for my presentation here, I have elected to compose each of the 40 poems that precede my diary entries in the traditional Gogyohka form of five-line, 24-syllable structures, primarily because I love and enjoy the creativity of the method so much.

I had way too much fun writing *Memoirs in Gogyohka,* and I loathed to see the creative process come to an end. But it had to, unfortunately, and now I must let it go. And while I am sad that I will not be able to play with it any longer in the creative stage, I am ecstatic that you will have the opportunity to get to know me and various parts of my life a little better because of it.

Comprising over three dozen entries selected at random from my diaries, *Memoirs in Gogyohka* serves as the appetizer before the main course of my biographical works. And I am delighted to share them with all of you. Of course, I don't plan to write my autobiography, but I *was* at liberty to compose my memoirs. And it is my sincerest hope that you will view them with wisdom, knowledge, empathy, and understanding, as well as in a spirit of enjoyment, my dearest readers.

Based on a collection of true stories, I now present to you ... *Memoirs in Gogyohka.*

All my love,

Cat Ellington

The First Stage

"My First Diary, c. 1982"

THE POEM:

This small book of mine?
It holds the lock
And the brass key
To my eventful annals
And memories.

THE ENTRY:

10th February 1982, WEDNESDAY
4:35 p.m.

Dear Diary,

*H*i! My name is Kimberly, but my friends call me Cat. I live with my Mama Linda, my big brother RaVan, my godmother JoAnn, my baby brother James, and our cat, Spot. James is my godmother's beautiful son, and we call him "baby James." I'm eleven and I go to Haines School. I'm in the 6th grade, in Ms. Soo Hoo's class. And this is my first entry.

You're my very first diary. And I bought you at the Basement Store after school today. My friend Peaches told me that Jenny Wang had a diary in Ms. Bramlet's class, and I got excited. So I went to ask Jenny about it and she told me that I should get one, too, because I'm a writer. And I told her that that was a good idea. When I asked Jenny where she bought her diary, she whispered in my ear that she got it from the "Basement Store," which is a store in Chinatown that Mr. Moy operates out of his basement. Jenny told me in my ear because she didn't want anybody else to know. So I kept it to myself. I asked Jenny how much it cost and she told me $4.99. That was good because I had nine dollars on me that I took out of my savings. I was going to use the money at the Snack Shop tomorrow and Friday, but I bought you instead. And I'm happy I did. I was so excited when I got to the "Basement Store" and found you because you were the diary that I had hoped to find: you have a lock and key just like the one Jenny has. And you're special because you were the last one that the store had with a lock and key. None of the other diaries had locks and keys. And I like your cover, too, because it's cushiony with pretty pink and white flowers all over it. And it reminds me of me because I love beautiful things.

Jenny showed me how to write a diary entry on a sheet of paper, and I will never forget how to do it. Jenny told me that Ms. Lau taught her how to do it.
I was so happy about buying my first diary today, that I bought a big bag of Funyuns to celebrate. When I get to school tomorrow, I'm gonna give Jenny a hug and say thank you.

WBBM-FM is playing one of my favorite songs, "Magic," by Olivia Newton-John. One of these days, people are going to say that my songs are beautiful like "Magic" is. And they're gonna say that I'm a great songwriter, too, like John Farrar. That's what I wanna be, dear Diary, a great songwriter. And God is gonna bless me to be a famous songwriter because it's my dream. And that's what mama said. My dream is to join ASCAP like all of the best songwriters and to have a star on the Walk of Fame in Hollywood like all of the great people. And God is going to make it happen. Watch. I'm gonna be a songwriter in ASCAP like Stevie Wonder, Elton John, Billy Joel, and Lionel Richie. Watch. Watch me. Dear Diary, I love music and writing.

My Mama is cooking fried chicken, rice, and gravy for dinner. And it smells good.

Now they're playing "Love Is In Control" by one of my favorite women, Donna Summer. I love Donna Summer. I also love Barbra Streisand, Grace Jones, Diana Ross, Chaka

Khan, Bette Midler, Olivia Newton-John, Suzanne Somers, Nell Carter, Dionne Warwick, and Shirley Hemphill.

Well, that's all for now. I'm gonna write to you every day until I run out of pages. And when I do, I'm going to buy another diary and keep writing.

Love,

Cat

"Aloha"

THE POEM:

In the wee hours,
The Hawk swooped in
And woke me,
Asking me to fly with him
To Waikiki.

THE ENTRY:

28th March 1990, WEDNESDAY
5:51 a.m.

I was in the deepest of sleep when my ringing phone jolted me out of it. Groggy, I opened my eyes to see that the bright blue LED display on my bedside clock read 3:09 a.m. It was the Hawk calling me. I could hear his voice, but it sounded as though he were calling me from far away as I had been trying to return to the natural world from the dream world. I had fallen asleep with my stereo on a low volume — as is my routine — and Janet was on the dial singing "Escapade." By the time I picked up the phone and said, "Hello," Janet was telling the subject of her affection how they'll break the rules as they go along.

Hawk asked, "Ellie, you up?"
"I am now," I answered in a practical whisper. "What's going on, Mac? Why are you calling me so early?" I asked worriedly.
"Nothin', baby, I was just thinking about you," he responded, then quickly added, "I wanted to hear your voice. It's been a while... Ellie, get up. I need to talk to you."
"Okay," I obliged.

Hawk MacAlister, my on-again, off-again, calls me "Ellie" as a short variation of "Ellington," and I call him "Mac" as a short variation of "MacAlister."

I sat up and stretched, then turned on my bedside lamp and reached for my cigarette case and lighter. With the phone receiver cradled between my right ear and shoulder, I lit my first cigarette of the new day and asked him what it was that he needed to talk to me about so early in the morning. He started by asking me how I'm doing and then apologizing to me for the last fight we had, saying that he'd simply lost his

214

temper, "Because you were being such a bitch, Ellie," blah, blah, blah. And he had no sooner said it than I wanted to say Fuck you, Mac!, and hung up, but I reeled it in. He went on with his sincere apology speech, and in time, I forgave him and apologized, too.

We talked a little longer, catching up on everything we've missed during our break-up. And I told Mac that I have been keeping up with all of his games on TV and that he looks good. After we got up to speed, he started talking about the off-season and what his plans were for it. And knowing him, I figured that it would be something exciting. Well, as I soon learned, it is. He wants to go to Waikiki for a week or so — to recuperate after the long season — and he asked me if I wanted to go with him. I was at a loss for words initially. But I eventually spoke again and told him that I would have to think about it. I already know that my answer will be yes. I just want to watch him squirm for a while.

Yep. That's the *bitch* in me.

(Smiling)

The beautiful Isle of Waikiki. It sounds like it's gonna be a lot of fun. But what on Earth will I pack to wear? I need to go shopping for— wait, I already have a few tunics, so I don't need to buy any more of those, but I do need to buy a new swimsuit, or two, or maybe even three. No, three will be too many. One or two will suffice. And I have plenty of oversized floppy hats and giant, movie star sunglasses, so that's covered.

(Thinking)

I need to change the musical atmosphere in this room. I'm in
the mood to hear Nicolette Larson singing "Lotta Love."
Yeah, that would sound really good right now. Hold on, dear
Diary. I need to get my 70s soundtrack going...

(Pausing to change the music selection)

(30 minutes later)

Okay, dear Diary, I'm back. After I got my 70s hits on the
cassette deck, I had to pee. Then I went downstairs to get
some coffee brewing. I can forget about going back to sleep
now. I'm up. Nicky Larson sang "Lotta Love." And now,
the Jackson 5 are performing "Mama's Pearl."

Before Hawk's and my conversation ended, he asked me if I
wanted to have dinner with him this weekend, and I told him
that that would be fine. Hey, you can't fault a man for trying
to make it alright, right? I didn't tell Mac during our
conversation, but maybe I will when we go out. I needed to
let him know about that man I saw at Ridgedale who'd
asked me if I wanted to sell him the signed jersey I was
wearing: the same sweater that Hawk and all of his
teammates signed for me the day he and I met. It was one of
two identical jerseys that I took along with me to have
signed at the Outlet: the other sweater was a birthday gift for
my dear buddy, Brent Kartak. Anyway, the jersey is
stunning. And I can understand why the man wanted to buy
it right off my back. But I just couldn't sell it to him because
it's my own special keepsake.

(Sighing)

What am I gonna do today? Knowing me? Nada. Temps are expected to be in the 50s, and I have nowhere that I need to be. I *will* do some writing, though. Yeah, I'll just write until the fatigue of my right hand motivates me to stop. Frankie Valli's voice is coming out of my speakers now singing "Grease," and it sounds so good. "Grease" is one of my favorite songs ever, and there is absolutely no one who can sing it the way Frankie Valli does. Nope, not even one. I love that movie, and I especially love that song. I swear, I could listen to it over and over all day long.
See, I'm already rhyming. Now, how's *that* for good timing?

(Smiling again)

I'll give the Hawk my answer this weekend about going to Hawaii with him in the off-season. For now, though, I need coffee… And an extra-large blueberry muffin.

Love,

Cat

"Puppy Love"

THE POEM:

I remember him,
A handsome boy
Of seventeen.
Like the color of the sea
Were his jade eyes.

Cat's Prologue:

I do declare. The heart of one of Central High's most
greatly-desired sophomores belongs only to me.

And they called it … *Puppy Love.*

12th May 1989, FRIDAY
8:32 p.m.

Dear Diary,

*T*here is this boy with whom I work named Trevor
McGuinn. And he's a rather beautiful fella that would put
one in the mind of a young Tom Cruise or a teenage Rob
Lowe. Actually, he's a perfect combination of both,
depending upon whom you ask. My best friend Nessa thinks
he favors Lowe, but me? I think he looks more like Cruise.
Anyway, I found out about his crush on me today. And you
won't believe who the purveyor of the news was. Are you
ready? Kleo. Yes, Kleo, a bastard, was there ever one. How
did Kleo know? Well, because Trevor told him first (I swear,
I'll never understand why Trev is so damn enthralled with
Klee's silly ass) and then begged him to tell me, which Klee
did. At first, I thought it was another one of Klee's
adolescent ass jokes until I heard Trevor yell out to him,
"Tell her what I said, Kleo!" After that, there was no more
room for doubt. And because Trevor is so damn giddy in -
puppy - love, he made sure that everyone else in our
workplace knew about his feelings for me as well. But I just
don't have a good feeling about any of this; because I can
already smell the stench of teasing surfing the wind in our
direction.

While I'm flattered by Trevor's crush on me, I'm not interested in him romantically. And I'll tell you why later. For now, though, how about I just provide you with a short bio on Mr. Trevor McGuinn?

Tall and very athletic (he plays hockey and baseball), Trevor is a Scorpio boy who is one year younger than me. At Country Club Market, a popular grocery store chain here in St. Paul for which we both work, Trevor's duties include bagging groceries and stocking the store's shelves. While mine revolves around cashiering and bookkeeping. And despite his being a Scorpio and I a Sagittarius, we get along great: Trev and I have a ton of fun working together with friends and enjoying all the perks that working in a supermarket has to offer: free food (including deli (my personal favorite)), free drinks, free snacks, employee discounts, etc. We have too much fun - and I love the whole gang, especially my babies, Willy and Big G, who manage to make every shift a riotous blast.

Naturally, there are days that I wish would never end and other days that I would sooner see obliterated into Hell forever. But for what it's worth, we're doing alright.

Somewhere along the course of our working together, Trevor (I call him *"Twitch"* because of a twitching condition in his right eye that resulted from a hockey puck injury) has developed this wild crush on me. But I can't be bothered because (1) he's a year younger than me (he's 17, and I'm 18), and (2) I don't believe in dating co-workers.

Now someone would probably ask, "Whaddaya mean he's *'One year younger,'* Cat? What's one year?" And I would understand their point of view, sure, but I would also want that person to know that I prefer older men. That's right, *older* men. I like my men "well-seasoned," if you will, meaning with a little bit of "salt and pepper" sprinkled in their hairy parts. Yeah, yeah, yeah, some people will probably conclude that I have a "father-figure" fixation, but they would be wrong.

While it's true that my father wasn't in the home, I have not set out to fill the void he left. I just desire mature men in relationships. That's all. I happen to be a mature girl for my age, and I feel that I need to have mature partners in my life. Besides, girls mature faster than boys do anyway. It's true, and everyone knows it. It's a universally known fact that girls are seven years ahead of boys on the maturity scale. And I am way ahead of Trevor in understanding on all levels as it is so blatantly obvious; nevertheless, that doesn't stop me from loving him, even if only platonically. I love Trevor more than words can say. I love him in much the same way that I do Gary and every other associate who has secured a place in my life. And because he's so beautiful to behold (seriously, the boy is easy on the eyes), I had to honor him with an entry within my precious diary today. Plus, I didn't have anything better to do at the moment.

Love,

Cat

Cat's Epilogue:

The preceding Gogyohka, *Puppy Love*, was written during a very special time in my life about a very special friend: for if nothing else came of us (intimately speaking), said work did.

I love you, Twitch. And I always will.

"He Called Me 'Baby Golden'"

THE POEM:

When I looked at him
My heart skipped beats,
My loins moistened,
My spirit fluttered with love,
And the stars blazed.

Cat's Prologue:

*T*he gorgeous year was 1988. Rick Astley was on the radio singing his hit song "Never Gonna Give You Up." Whitney

Houston's powerful vocals belted out her top 10 hits, "So Emotional" and "Where Do Broken Hearts Go." The cute and auburn-haired Tiffany was on fire with "Could've Been." George Michael sat atop the Billboard charts with "Faith." Eddie Murphy and Arsenio Hall were cracking us up in the timeless masterpiece, "Coming to America." Bruce Willis was killing it as "John McClane" in the blockbuster hit "Die Hard." Tom Cruise and Dustin Hoffman were winning our hearts in "Rain Man." Kevin Costner and Susan Sarandon were French-kissing in the romantic comedy "Bull Durham." And I was a seventeen-year-old waitress working the dining room at a Wendy's restaurant in St. Paul, Minnesota.

THE ENTRY:

11th July 1988, MONDAY
10:15 p.m.

Dear Diary,

I saw him for the first time today. It was during the lunch rush that he walked into the restaurant and robbed me of my breath. His name is Terry Salerno, and he's hot as Hell. He looks exactly like Scott Baio's "Chachi," shoulder-length hair and all. He even has the same flair and personality as the fictive character. My clit immediately started throbbing at the sight of him: as fate would have it, Millie knew him from her days working as a dancer at the Kittie Lynx Club. And she introduced us.

224

I never knew that my mind could do flips: but at the sight of Terry, my psyche proceeded to turn over an elegant somersault while my mouth took on a dry spell. I was in love at first glimpse, which is uncharacteristic for me, considering that I am not the type of girl who often drools over any member of the opposite sex. However, in this case, I did. I drooled, not literally but figuratively. And I knew that I had to have him. But first, I had to get to know him. My tongue was eager to speak, but no words wanted to oblige. And I just stood there in my spot next to the salad bar staring at him. I felt my knees go weak, but I couldn't sit down. And my entire body suddenly felt warm as though I'd been given a dosage of intravenous fluid at room temperature. My heart skipped to a giddy beat as my ears refused to hear anything save his voice when he placed his order. And it was a distinct order that I will never forget: *"Two singles everything, no onion, no mustard."* I learned that it's his trademark, the way he prefers his burgers. And it is a trademark with which I will forever be familiar.

When the words finally tired of tormenting my tongue, I was able to speak. And it was only to Millie that I was able to pour out the contents of my heart concerning him in the wake of his departure. Good ol' Millie, she has promised to relay my message to him.

19th July 1988, TUESDAY
(One Week Later)
1:10 a.m.

Dear Diary,

I couldn't get my time card punched fast enough today! After our shift started, I was on Millie like black on tar: I needed to know what Terry's response was when she told him the news about my interest in him. And what she told me he said in response nearly brought me to collapse. According to Millie, he spoke the following words: "That's a cute little girl, Mills. Tell her I said hi."

His words flew in circles around my head like swans at twilight: *That's a cute little girl, Mills... That's a cute little girl, Mills... That's a cute little girl, Mills...*

I'm cute!! I'm cute!! He said I'm cuuuute!!!!

I pretty much leapt through the workday like a ballerina, marinating in his words. I was high on the fumes of lust and excitement, and it took a long time for me to come down from that high. He's my ultimate desire, and I will tell him as much no sooner than I can muster up the courage. I promise. With that, it's almost 2:00 a.m. and time for me to go beddy-bye.

Try to stay dry in my wet dreams, Mr. Tall, Dark, and (fabulously) Handsome.

14th September 1988, WEDNESDAY
(Two Months Later)
9:47 p.m.

Dear Diary,

By now, Terry and I have bonded. Over the next few weeks after our initial meeting, I would eventually tell His Hotness how I felt about him myself. And as is natural, we got underway as friends first and then gradually evolved into something more, growing closer with each passing day. We're close in more ways than one, what with his workplace being right across the street from the restaurant. And because the dining room's windows are so sprawling, we're provided with a clear view of our customers' comings and goings, including his. So whenever we look out and see Terry approaching, our line crew gets to work handling their business. And by the time he sets foot in our clean and comfortable abode, his two singles, layered with everything, save onions and mustard, are already bagged and ready to go.
Indeed, we've got ourselves a groovy system. And I love it.

I am not ashamed to admit that I'm falling in love with Terry Salerno. I pulled him into the bathroom while I was at work tonight to hug him, to kiss him, to check out his package - which is nice, by the way - and to let him know that my vulva is now his for the taking.
Laughing, he kissed me and said, "You're too bold." And I purred in reply, "You're absolutely right."

20th September 1988, TUESDAY
(One Week Later)
6:39 p.m.

Dear Diary,

The Lord has shown great mercy on the man named Terry Salerno, as his loins are not merely for the repressively faint! Our intimate trysts are now underway. And our musky scent of passion is seeping out from the air vents of my respective workplace like that of hamburger grease. Indeed, my Sagittarian fire is kindled, evaporating all the water out of his Scorpio. And whithersoever we can locate a place in which to fuck like rabbits, it is there, in that place, that we fuck like rabbits: the bathroom at the restaurant, outside in his car, the woods during the daytime, the parks at night, my bedroom (whenever my mother is out), his apartment (whenever his estranged girlfriend is out), at the Dunes, etc.

27th September 1988, WEDNESDAY
(One Week Later)
11:46 p.m.

Dear Diary,

Terry and I made man-eating love in the back seat of his so-called Batmobile today. After driving all over the city sightseeing just for the hell of it, he took me to SuperAmerica for coffee and snacks, and then he took us downtown to our secret hideaway in the woods. We love the location because it's discreet and daring (just like us), and we tend to spend a lot of time there. We drank our coffees and talked shit about a lot of people we know, including Jake

"Jakie" Goss, Terry's archenemy. We laughed and talked until our eyes locked and our passions started to rise. And when that happened, no one else mattered. Not Jakie, not Krista, not that Madonna-look-alike Angel, not Shane Conley, not anyone. It was just him and me. We were one another's for the taking. The entire world had stopped spinning around us. Everything still went just like it always does when we're together. And after he adjusted his seat and pulled me into his lap, one kiss led to another, and then to another, until he soon took me.

He's seen my body before, but he still complimented it telling me how pretty it is: and because I love to play in his hair, I filled my hands with it and pulled his beautiful mouth to mine again. Our heated breaths fogged up the windows, but it was just as well, as there was absolutely no erotic passion similar to that of our own. Fire tested our limits, and calming waters cooled us down once we reached them. Together, Terry and I were like nitroglycerine. And when we became one, we became one in paradise.

He loved my pussy - he kept telling me how tight and wet it was. And when he went down to suck it, he became gluttonous, eating both it and my ass as though they were two singles with everything, no onion, no mustard. He fucked me and sucked my hardened nipples at the same time, causing my love to come down in Earth-shattering orgasms. And at the tender mercy of his dominating dick — a full ten inches in length — I could only scream at the top of my lungs with ear-piercing pleasure.

He was sweating all over me, salty and manly perspiration that I opened my mouth to swallow down. And panting heavily in my right ear, he kept telling me how much he loves me: "*I love you, Cat, I love you, Cat, I love you, baby. I love you. I love you...*"

Taking heavy breaths in boiling lust, I asked him what he was trying to do to me, and he answered in a whisper, "I'm trying to make you feel good." And he was. He was making me feel like a stick of dynamite waiting to explode. He was exceptional.

My right hand was all tangled in his soft brown hair as my left arm wrapped around him as tightly as it could. And nowhere near done, he soon turned me over and fucked my asshole deep, filling it up with the entire contents of his majestic ejaculation. I cried out in primal passion because I love getting fucked in the ass as it is the most intense feeling in the world. I came, again and again, floating to a new height with each climax, as he shot me up with hit after hit of his aromatic sexual heroin. And I can still feel it right now, even after all these hours. I can still feel the remnants of Terry's warm cum oozing out of my asshole. And it's making me hot all over again.

God, I need to masturbate to relieve some of this sexual pressure. I want to fuck again, and so very badly. I want my asshole fucked, and my pussy sucked, all over again. And I'm tempted to call Terry at work and ask him to come over here afterward.

Speaking of which, he almost didn't make it in on time today because as we were driving out of the woods, he steered into a swamp of mud, and we got stuck. Seriously, we got stuck in the fucking mud: Terry got out of the Batmobile to push us out, but the car wouldn't budge. And when I offered to help, he said no, because he didn't want my boots and clothes to get ruined from the muddy mess. He, on the other hand, had been wearing a pair of jeans and sneakers. So it was okay for him to get all dirty and shit.

(Laughing now)

I got behind the wheel and followed his instructions on what to do to help free us from the mud pit. He pushed the car as I stepped on the gas pedal, but the car still wouldn't move. So after a few minutes, we saw a pickup truck heading our way, and Terry flagged the driver down, explaining our dilemma.
The man was out of his pickup in seconds, surveying the scene. He then got back in his pickup, pulled out in front of us, attached his hitch to Terry's car, got back in the driver's seat of his pickup, and towed us out. Ta-da! We were free!

(Laughing again)

But Ter was muddy as fuck, and so was the Batmobile. We drove to the nearest car wash to get both him and the car cleaned up, and afterward, he brought me home – with only forty-five minutes remaining before he had to be at work. He came inside, jumped in the shower, got out, dried off, kissed me good-bye, drove to his apartment (which is only a hop, skip, and jump from mine) to change clothes, and made it into work three minutes before his shift started. I know this because he called me right before it did and told me. And I could only chuckle in response.
Damn, we're good!

Today was an adventure, and I loved it! And I love Terry because he makes me feel so fucking good. Honestly, I don't think that I'm ever going to be able to let this go.

(Yawning)

I feel like calling Nessa to tell her about my day, but I know we'll end up talking for over an hour, and I'm sleepy now. So I'll have to tell her tomorrow.

Phil Collins (one of my favorite people alive) is on the radio singing "Groovy Kind Of Love." And as I listen to the lyrics, I think, *That's what Terry and I have. A groovy kind of love.*

Terry calls his cock "The Italian Stallion," and for a good reason. He's blessed, and he knows it. And on this day in history, "The Italian Stallion" gave my heart-shaped ass a "standing ovation."

Love,

Cat

Cat's Epilogue:

We were wild in our day, Terry and I. And I will never forget those old times or him. By the way, Terry is the same man from whom I got the nickname, "Baby Golden." He told me one night, as we lay naked on the back seat of the Batmobile, that he got the name from the lyrics of one of his favorite songs. And because the song had reminded him of me, he decided to grace me with the new moniker. And I love it because I think it's very special.

From that night forth, the nickname had only continued to grow on me, and it has never changed in all these years. To this day, Terry Salerno still calls me "Baby Golden," and I still call him "Night Rider." Indeed, our given monikers are set in stone. And if truth be told, they always will be.

The Gogyohka, *He Called Me 'Baby Golden,'* is the result of an initial fantasy that eventually found its way into reality. From the moment I saw him enter the old Wendy's, I knew that I had to have Terry Salerno in my life. And he was allowed to have a special place in my life. Our history is colorful as we had a good time back in the day. And I will always cherish him and every memory that we share.
Always.

I love you, Night Rider.

"How to Love a White Man"

THE POEM:

It's clear what they loathe:
You're loving me
And holding me;
Ebony and Ivory,
Eternally.

Cat's Prologue:

During my coming of age in Minnesota, I had an opportunity to meet new people of various cultures and ethnicities. And unlike my nativity of Chicago — where decades of segregation served to divide its people and its communities — St. Paul, Minnesota was a hub of racial integration and liberty. And I fell in love with its spirit because I've always loved people and genuinely believe that people have a right to connect without having to worry about various forms of hatred in a society seeking to rip them apart. There is absolutely nothing wrong with people of different races being friends or lovers or neighbors or co-workers or whatever. But because we live on this Earth and the divider is allowed to roam among us, we have to suffer the evil trial of racial divisions in society that results from the flesh. I do not like to see divisions among human beings that I know stem from the divide-and-conquer tactics used against them, but many others prefer to fall prey to such. They need to hate because it makes them feel more powerful. And they need to hate to have an enemy upon which to focus. However, they get played every time because (1) hatred is a sign of weakness, not strength, and (2) they fail to see their real enemy because he is a spiritual being and not physical.

The enemy's attacks on the mind are designed to tear down and destroy, not to unify and build. And we, as humans, need to always be aware of that.

I believe that people should strive to make love and not war. But for some strange reason, when it comes to intimacy between selected individuals, the enraged divider suddenly rises to lash out in anger and bitterness.
Case in point: interracial relationships, especially where they involve white men and black women.

THE ENTRY:

21st August 1990, TUESDAY
5:18 p.m.

Dear Diary,

Why do some black men and some white women take (so much) offense to my relationships? Why am I always being called a bunch of "white boy lovers" and "whores?" Why are my relationships (be they platonic or intimate) with men — who just so happen to be white — having such an adverse effect on certain types of black men and white women? Why? These two groups seem to take serious offense to romantic involvements between white men and black women, whereas when there is a romantic bonding between a black man and a white woman, they don't seem to mind as much.

It angers me because it's hypocrisy. I *hate* hypocrisy.

Even though the city of St. Paul - hell, the entire state of Minnesota, for that matter - crawls with white women who lust, ravenously, after the loins of black men, for some odd reason, it bothers these same types of women to see a black woman on the arm of a white man. It gets worse if that white man is highly educated and financially prosperous. And while those black men who eagerly feed into such "taboo lusts" number many, the same hate to see a black woman on the arm of a white man, especially if she's a black woman like me.

That's called hypocrisy. I *hate* hypocrisy.

These two specific groups, black men and white women, have sought to make my life a living hell because of my love interests, who just so happen to be men of the Caucasian persuasion.
If I am not a white boy lover, according to the *brothas*, I am a whore according to many white women who, for some odd reason, need to believe the lie that I am taking their men away from them.

All of this nonsense stems from fear and ignorance. And I cannot stand it. I hate fear. I cannot stand ignorance - because these two divide people. And I hate one-sided ass people, too, because they are liars. Liars that make me sick to my stomach! I understand what is going on. I do. I am a black woman, respectively. And being a black woman, I represent everything such people fear and hate in society: for the contents of such fear and hatred have been under pressure for centuries in this country.

I'm able to love others because I love myself, period. And I'll continue this conversation with you later, dear Diary, as my hot bath awaits.
Also, I need to rest my hand.

Love,

Cat

22nd August 1990, WEDNESDAY

Dear Diary,

I spent last night meditating about a lot of things. After a long phone chat with Nita, we both came to agree on the following:

Before anyone can love another, they must first love themselves. Before anyone can appreciate others, they must first appreciate themselves. Before anyone can respect another, they must first respect themselves; and before anyone can understand another, they must first understand themselves. That is common sense. But we do not see a lot of common sense in society. Instead, we play witness to the exact opposite.
The world is full of self-hating people who hate not only their own lives but also the lives of others. And therein lies the discontent.

To date, I have only dated three white men, including Terry. But according to some, I am just out there whippin' my (black) pussy on every Caucasian cock large enough to fill it up. I am sick of these judgmental and jealous-hearted ass people. I am. I am not a white *boy lover* or whore; I am simply a young woman enjoying her life while she has it to live. And though they fail to notice, that also includes relationships (both platonic and intimate) with black men.

Men are men, be they Jewish men or Gentile men. I both respect and love them all equally. When it comes to my love life, I do not take race, creed, color, nationality, or origin into consideration. I only love and respect others as I do myself: it is because of this outlook that I can (genuinely) love the men in my life, no matter their culture. In truth, I had to understand and respect my cultural history before I could even begin to understand and respect theirs. And it has never been a challenge for me.

For me, it has never been so much about lust as it has been about true love. Because by the grace of God, I do not need a self-esteem boost. I know who I am. Nor do I need any of *their* money as I have plenty of access to means of my own.

Here is my written truth as I stand to gain nothing from a lie.

Love,

Cat

Cat's Epilogue:

The preceding (and personal) witness had been the inspiration behind the Gogyohka, *How to Love a White Man*. It's all about self-love, self-respect, respect for others, and truth garnished with understanding, not sexual taboos. Because sexual taboos are just what they are, sexual taboos. And no real love will ever be found in such - as they have their origins in empty lust.

In brief, this entry will conclude in the succeeding Gogyohka, *The Ol' Double Standard*.

"The Ol' Double Standard"

THE POEM:

Why you, but not me?
Your bigotry?
It's plain to see;
And for your hypocrisy,
I will slap you.

THE ENTRY:

25th August 1990, SATURDAY
2:39 p.m.

Dear Diary,

Worldly and bigoted white women — such as those types mentioned in *How to Love a White Man* — need the "Mandingos" to run their black dicks in and out of their weak, nasty, and repressed asses to feel good about themselves. Because their self-esteem is bottomless. And for centuries, black men have only been perceived as wild sexual beasts who can bring them into submission to their own sexuality, considering that they're so damn out of touch with their own bodies.
For as it is written, in the first chapter of Romans: "They forsook the natural for the unnatural."
It is for this reason that they hate their own bodies - as well as themselves as women. Hence their sexual covetousness towards black men, in particular.

And as for those worldly and ignorant ass black men who keep spitting in my face the words *white boy lover*, I am also familiar with their fucked up mindsets: for these have no faith in God and are being tempted to covet the white man's "position" in this ass-backward society; hence *their* sexual covetousness towards a bunch of hateful and self-hating ass white women who can't stand the sight of their own fuckin' bodies in the mirror.

They deserve each other because both are miserable, pitiful, and pathetic.

Now "whore" and "white boy lover" *that*, you ignorant and worthless ass bitches and muthafuckas!

You're a whore, bitch, not me. *You're* the one in need, muthafucka, not me.

You hateful ass women don't mind laying up with black men - to validate your bottomless self-esteem. But you hate to see one like you, according to the flesh, embracing women like me in beds of peace; therefore, I returned to the scene, that I would be allowed to rebuke you and your godless hypocrisy, fiercely, through the Spirit of Truth; hence the "slap."

Thank you for the therapy, dear Diary.

Love,

Cat

"A Cut Through Bone and Marrow"

THE POEM:

You were in my drink,
Spoiling its taste
And enjoyment—
Until I swallowed it down,
And ended you.

THE ENTRY:

10th March 1994, THURSDAY
7:05 p.m.

Dear Diary,

I need to vent. I have all of this righteous anger bottled up inside of me, and I need to vent it out. May I? Oh, what the hell am I doing? I don't need your permission to rage. That's what you're here for, what to provide me with a blank canvas of pages on which to obliterate my muthafuckin' enemies, even every single one of 'em.

Because murder is unlawful and I won't be allowed to enter into the kingdom of Heaven should I commit it, I'm gonna need for you, my dear journal, to double as a dartboard on which I can paste that fat ass face belonging to the bitch from my job. Is that okay, dear journal? I knew it would be. I will now render my entry. But before I do, it should be known that I got those bitches today: for written here is the conclusion of them versus me.

7:22 p.m.
(17 Minutes Later)

You didn't think I forgot about you, did you, Tonia? I didn't forget about you, you hateful ass bitch. I didn't forget about you or your damn cohorts. And you didn't forget about me either, did you? Even after you and your tack-headed ass girlfriends did what was evil to me — without just cause — your low-wage and ghetto-entrenched ass brain still had my image embossed on it, now did it not? Well, of course, it did, you desperate and covetous ass bitch you.

You couldn't take me on alone, could you? No, of course, you couldn't; you needed others to assist you. You sat on your average ass and talked a whole lotta shit, but in the end, you needed help, because you knew that I would have skinned your limp ass alive, didn't you? Didn't you?! Yes, of course, you did, you skank ass bitch. At first sight, you were tempted to despise me because you already despised yourself. And as my days of having to be near you slithered into weeks, and the weeks inched along into months, I became a most troubling obsession for you, even inspiring frown lines between your hard-ass eyes, and a few gray hairs on your silky weave-wearing ass head.

You — with a little help from your backup bitches — did everything you could in an effort to break me, but the Lord didn't allow it, did He? No, of course, He didn't. Instead, he broke *you*. He took your legs right out from under you, didn't He? And once that task was completed, he threw your dumpy ass down for all to see. Moreover, He put His sword in my mouth and granted me the right to cut your ass clean through audibly. And when the verbal slaughter had reached its end, you and yours were done.

In the wake of the throwdown, peace and I rekindled our companionship. And in my newfound absence, you plopped your rejected ass down on the spot I had once occupied, took up the makeshift mantle, and pretended to be me. And because you had nothing else, you self-loathing ass bitch, I let you have your pathetic ass fantasy.

You've been given over to a delusion but you will never be me in reality, nor will the cavity of your nasty ass pussy ever be filled with the loins of my man.

It is finished. Thank you, dear Diary. Once again, you've been extraordinarily therapeutic.

Love,

Cat

The Second Stage

"The Iceman"

THE POEM:

I look at the ice:
Cold, like his heart;
Hard, like his loins;
White, like his manly body;
Brittle, like us.

Cat's Prologue:

*T*he sport of hockey shall never be permitted to know another one like him. For his fish had simply been too large to flop on the frozen ponds of the NHL; therefore, it bid him farewell. But my heart has never abandoned him. My soul, yes, but never has my heart. True love? It once dwelled in our midst, but when it could no longer pay its fair share, he motioned to evict it from us. That was the night his right palm made contact with my left cheek. Not the left cheek of my ass - as was its natural place, but the left cheek of my face: for he so loved the softness that both had to offer, but I hated the rigidity of his aggression.

Even if I awoke to find him in Ontario, the stars would not be willing to offer us a second chance because they're too dim to shine upon us anymore; therefore, ours will slowly become history like the ancients.

I wrote a song about us, though. Yes, I most certainly did. And it is a beautiful work made up of powerful lyrics and a delicate melody reminiscent of our passive/aggressive unification.

The rugged Hawk MacAlister. I was his *"Ellie"* and he swore by me. But his infamous machismo simply would not leave him to be.

It simply would not leave us to be.

THE ENTRY:

12th January 1990, FRIDAY
8:46 p.m.

("Mr. Tambourine Man" by The Byrds plays softly on
KQRS-FM in the background)...

Dear Diary,

Apparently, I am all that I have left. So why am I just sitting
here? There's a great big world beyond these beautifully
painted walls just waiting to meet me, right? So why am I
just sitting here? Fuck this, I can move on with my life. I
have no obligations to anyone, including him. Fuck him.
Fuck. Him!
Fuck him, fuck him, fuck him, fuck him, fuck him...

Whenever I start thinking that way, I remember his dick,
hard and slathered with my pussy cream; and his face,
distorted in savage passion. I remember his grimacing mouth
missing several of its teeth... And his battle scars.

The moon had whined like a big baby at the sight of his
greatly endowed manhood, and my vaginal lips quivered in
contemplation of its entry - parting like the Red Sea to allow
its passage.
Throughout the blackness of night, I had been made privy to
his sweet nothings of erotic wisdom. And with one fierce
slapshot, he scored my soul.

The love we made had a peaceful spirit that contrasted,
sharply, with the way we fought. But sometimes I knew him
better than he knew himself. He knew that after a bad fight, I
would want to be fucked silly; and I knew that after a bad
fight, he would make it up to me by taking another woman's
ass in a different city. Whenever he does that, I get

250

something new to add to my massive collection of nearly everything else. Like the new silver fox fur trapper hat and matching scarf set, for instance. On the night he handed me the gift box containing the gorgeous pair, I knew that he had left home again. And much like a bitter Canadian winter easing into the month of May, we came to an end.

I'll keep the stick that he left here in my bedroom in loving memory of him. And the tape wrapped around its blade will age and fray with the dawning of each new day.

Love,

Cat

Cat's Epilogue:

Time will judge us accordingly. And one day I will make amends with the native son of Ms. Ontario. For now, though, I'll just sit here on my brass bed and watch him as he plays the game of his nativity on my television screen. And by the end of the third period, his once-powerful carbonation will have suddenly gone flat in my mind.

"Lying and Denying"

THE POEM:

You fear the "Black hole,"
So you deny
Your desire,
And repress your horny loins.
You're a pity.

Cat's Prologue:

*B*e yet another man of weakness today, and suffer the bitter comeuppance of regret tomorrow.

THE ENTRY:

16th April 1989, SUNDAY
3:14 p.m.

Dear Diary,

Paddy O'Shea. His yearnings call me by name, but his fears
quickly quiet them, that they should be able to go on spoiling
the wealth of his mind. What his body wants to do, his mind
rebels against. And so he goes, being pulled from one end to
the other in the Herculean tug-of-war of his fears and
desires.

Lest he become perverse in his way, he must break free. He
must break free from the chains that bind him, and he must
break free from the chains that link the hard-boiled words of
his many naysayers.
So what if those idiots call us "Tom and Helen Willis?" We
should run with it! We should turn it all around on their
envious asses and piss 'em off the more so!

(Sighing)

Why couldn't Paddy be more like me? Why does he feel so
obligated to give a damn to the poor and needy of mind?
Why? Well, because when his shadow says "Boo!" he
jumps, that's why. Oh, what a pity.

I could've sucked you in and slowly spewed you out into
another dimension, you cowardly Irish bloke, but you

couldn't handle the atmospheric pressure; therefore, pleasure your eyes upon my flesh only, but touch it not: for your boyish cowardice is not worthy of my womanly courage.

(Sighing again)

Nessa was right about him. His fantasies are more stimulating than his reality.
And if I know anything at all about Patrick O'Shea, it's that he's only Superman in the private channels of his own mind; but in the real world, he's all wimp. No wonder he likes to call me a "Maneater."

Tsk, tsk, tsk, whiskey, whiskey, whiskey...
Oh, well. Another day, another diary entry.

Love,

Cat

Cat's Epilogue:

While you're asleep, Mr. Paddy O, I'll be rendering a dazzling performance in your troubled dreams. And upon your awakening, you'll be compelled to applaud it forever.

"The Revelers"

THE POEM:

Fruity and tannic:
It was the city.
We drank its wine,
Wet and overpowering;
And we were free.

THE ENTRY:

13th October 1990, SATURDAY
1:05 p.m.

Dear Diary,

*T*he private eye and I went out to paint the town burgundy red last night. Burgundy red like the Pinot Noir that we drank; burgundy red like the shade of my hair, lips, and nails; burgundy red like the shade of your hardcover; burgundy red like the color of the Cabernet I'm sipping with my cheese and Triscuits as I compose this entry.

The world is most definitely our oyster! It is a place where everybody knows our names, and where our drinks are always on the house. The nightlife is like a colt to which we are sire and dam, and the dusky dens that drip sin like moss serve as our sacred hideaways.

We owned the night, dear Diary. The air around us giggled with the scent of his Aramis mingled with my Norell, and his private eyes watched me with daring intent. In a lip-lock of passion, our tongues dueled for dominance, and the dance floor preceded our feet to the edge of weariness. Laughing at the dying energy of a drowsy night, and sneering our displeasure at the well-rested awakening of the judgmental dawn, we wined and dined at Rudolph's in the Galtier Plaza (their Caesar salads and cheesecake are to salivate for), and then we gave in to the kinder temptation of his Sealy Posturepedic.

Too famished to "dance" in erotica, I kissed his bald spot and complimented the salt & pepper in the hairs of his mustache before I fell asleep on him for the second time since we first met by phone back in July.

My dearest Diary, the evening whimpered as we went about our way: for it loathed to see us go, and secretly envied the next evening that would play host to our debaucherous affairs.

The man named Behr Rossi, otherwise known as "Mr. Saks Fifth Avenue," is now the head of this young woman here. And I'm incredibly honored.
While our love is still relatively brand new, we shall continue to command our pleasures and make the most of them.

Love,

Cat

"Take This Bitter Pill"

THE POEM:

The embittered asks:
"How's she happy?"
"Why is she loved?"
Infected with jealousy,
They hate my life.

Cat's Prologue:

Someone once told me that women are catty. And it's true,
they are. But not one of them is cattier than myself; hence

my nickname, *Cat*: for the same has been given to me for a legitimate reason.

THE ENTRY:

11th October 1991, FRIDAY
4:56 p.m.

Dear Diary,

Everywhere I go, I have to put up with a bunch of bitter ass women. No wonder I get along better with men. Women can make you hate them, I swear. Because they're so damn angry with themselves, which in turn causes them to take it out on other women, especially if the other women represent certain types.

Women. They can never get ahead in life because they're too damn busy holding one another back and clawing each other up. And I just can't stand faithless and self-hating women, such as the ones with whom I currently live: the hot-combin' hypocrite, her two crabs-in-a-barrel-minded ass daughters, and her nappy-headed ass niece. Together, these four are a lot of misery, and they are completely representative of everything my mother had ever told me about women like them: miserable, self-loathing, envious, jealous-hearted, and a dime a dozen.

Women can be something else, I tell ya. If another woman has a pair of shoes more than them, it's a blow to their self-esteem. If another woman has a dress more than them, it's a blow to their self-esteem. If another woman has a bottle of perfume or a tube of lipstick more than them, it's a blow to their self-esteem. If another woman has a bigger house than theirs or a more beautifully designed apartment than their own, it's a blow to their self-esteem. If they see another woman with a bigger ass than their own, it's a blow to their self-esteem. If another woman attracts more attention from the opposite sex than they do, it's a blow to their self-esteem.

That's how fragile women are. And I don't buy the "Sisterhood" and "Women's Lib" bullshit for one second. I cannot stand weak, jealous-hearted, and self-loathing women. Because women like them have always tried to make life just that much harder for women like me.

I have been the target of such women for as long as I can remember now. Even without just cause, they had always lifted their arms to swing on me in hatred, anger, and frustration. But when I got tired of being a fuckin' punching bag, I started swingin' back on their asses. I have yet to miss one target.
Now, I tend to be a woman who harbors her peace. But should it become necessary for me to strike back, I most certainly will, and in the most venomous fashion.

Having been born a free spirit, there is no one with whom I can't get along. Just ask anyone who knows me, and they'll tell you the same. But unfortunately, there are also those of the miserable lot who need to hate. And where people like me are to be regarded, the former can be highly susceptible to the wicked gremlins of anger, rage, and even murderous intentions concerning the latter.

Triflin' women, like the ones with whom I temporarily live, are no different. They not only harbor resentment against me themselves but also desire to see it directed towards me from others. And while they are always allowed to sway a few to their enemy-minded ways of thinking, they are never able to win over everyone. And that both troubles them and eats them up like cancer.

Although my life is moving forward, it's as if I'm still living in the era of my high school years (where many of the girls had the same queries concerning me), or on jobs that I've worked where any number of my female co-workers wanted to know the same. And while many of these women don't even know one another, it's as if they were (and are) reciting words from the same script: "Why does everybody like her so much?" "I can't stand that tall bitch because she thinks she's better than me." "If I could, I'd whoop her ass!" "I wish somebody would just fuck her up." Blah, blah, blah; blah, blah, blah, blah.

The aforementioned talked a whole lotta shit and spoke great swelling words concerning me. But for all the shit they talked behind my back, not even one of them ever showed enough courage to voice their queries to my face. I had to always hear about their hostile inquiries and opinions concerning both my likability and so-called "ego" by way of the grapevine. And the Lord knows I would've exhibited greater respect for their dumb, enemy-minded asses in the event they had shown a bit mo' moxie.

My retort to each woman has always been the following: "Why do *you* hate me so much?" It was an honest question to which I never got a straight answer because they were too busy chickening out. And to be completely honest, I really didn't expect one. Because I already knew the truth, what that such women were always tempted to absolutely hate themselves as women; ergo hatred, envy, and jealousy towards other women, especially towards those women whom they believed were just "gliding through life, getting everything they wanted," while less fortunate women, particularly in the area of physical beauty, suffer want and go lacking in their own lives.

Sadly, such women will be that way until the end of time. Because they have no faith in God, or in themselves.

Speaking of time, it's 12:45 a.m. and I need to hit the sack. Until my next entry, dear Diary?

Love,

Cat

Cat's Epilogue:

Wisdom is lovely in all her array. And people ought to allow themselves to embrace her while they have a chance. Because once people learn to love themselves, it will be quite easy for them to love others.

"Right Back Atcha"

THE POEM:

You ripped into me
Out of envy.
You spoke amiss;
You showed out for all to see
Your misery.

Cat's Prologue:

As I strutted along the pathway of my life, financial destitution stuck out its bunioned foot and tripped me, causing me to stumble and then tumble downward. And while I rested on my knees surveying my scrapes and bruises, she ushered up to stand over my head, finally able to peer down at me for once. For she had waited a long time to spit in my face the following words: "My, how the mighty have fallen."

She brandished her fat, flat ass and proceeded to moon me in my time of economic misfortune.

THE ENTRY:

15th October 1991, TUESDAY
12:50 a.m.

Dear Diary,

> "*N*aked I came from my mother's womb,
> And naked shall I return there.
> The Lord gave, and the Lord has taken away…"
> —Job 1:21

While I am nowhere near Job in the area of great faith, it is to his words that I can wholeheartedly relate, especially now.

> "But God *is* the Judge:
> He puts down one
> And exalts another."
> —Psalm 75:7

To those words, I can also relate.

My beautiful mother raised me on the finest values of faith
that she knew, as she had been brought forth from many
wise men and women. And when I came of age, she put the
Holy Bible in my hand and instructed me to always have it
in my possession wherever I went in life: "Always carry this
with you, baby, and God will watch over you," my Mama
had said.

Indeed, the Lord had given, and then He chose to take away.
And who am I to question the living God, the Father of all
creation?
I have been newly humbled by my former place of
exaltation. And maybe it serves me right.

CHICAGO — I have been back home, in my native
Chicago, for exactly 5 months now. I'm burning through my
savings. Times have hit me as hard as they could with a
sledgehammer, and I am now living here in this
God-forsaken house with these miserable ass women and a
covetous ass man — who's being tempted to lust after me —
in this neighborhood called Englewood. My life has fallen
apart but I'm alive, thank God, and I'm still healthy and
afloat. I wanted to be back home in Chicago, but not like
this. I wanted my dream condo on the lakefront, not this. I
wanted my money to keep growing, not depleting. I wanted
to be free, not trapped. What the hell has my life come to?
How did I go from there to here so fast? Did I really leave
Kemba — the Nigerian attorney — for this? I should've just
stayed in Minnesota with him and grown our brand new
relationship, but I wanted my dream more. I had every
reason to believe that my city was exactly where I needed to
be to achieve my lifelong dream of becoming a published

songwriter and writer. And I'm determined to stay here and find it, despite the tightness of my finances.

I currently have a little over eight thousand dollars stashed away in my accounts. And while it's a whole lot less than what I used to have, it's something. I'm pretty much living on my Chase Manhattan Visa and Discover cards, so I don't have to burn through too much more of it, especially not now that I've found a new job. It's a receptionist job in an office building downtown on Wabash, one of my most beloved avenues in the city. And although it pays less than nine dollars an hour, it'll suffice for now. I can use the extra money that I'll be earning there to pay for both my monthly invoices and my storage container. All of my personal belongings are safely tucked away in storage, which is where they should be, considering their value. I hate it that I have to wait until February to move into my new apartment, but the place is worth the wait because it's rent-controlled. I just have to be patient, and I'll make it. I know that everything is going to be just fine because not only am I a survivor but God is with me.

Even still, I can't stop thinking about Kemba. I can't stop thinking about anything that pertains to how my life had once been. Was I living too fast? Did the Lord allow this hardship to come upon me, that I should learn humility? Was I flying too high? Did I have too much? Is the Lord paying me back for the affair? What happened to my life? I used to be so happy, but now I'm not anymore. Well, I'm happy to be back home in Chicago, but not here in this God-forsaken house.

If only I had known then what I've come to know now. If only I had known…

While I had initially planned to live in the Holiday Inn until February, some old friends of the family would eventually offer me a place to lodge until that time. I had thought it was a win-win, considering that I've pretty much known them my entire life. But although we all share a long history, we have not seen one another in many years. And as I've come to realize, the course of time can change people, although in some instances not for the good. And had I known that these people would get me here only to do what is evil to me, I would have stayed right where I was. Because at least peace dwelled there, and not strife.

After I got settled in, I called them on the phone and we agreed to meet up. My "play cousins," KeKe and DiDi Greene, met me at the bus stop on 63rd Street and brought me here to see Poochie, the mother of KeKe and her sister Chub, and the aunt of DiDi. I also address Poochie as "aunt" because an aunt is what she had always been like to me. We chatted about old times and caught up on the new times. And KeKe begged her mother to let me live here with them until my place was ready. And though I could tell by her expression that Poochie had not been too crazy about the idea at first, she eventually gave in and decided to honor her youngest daughter's incessant request. Me? I didn't care either way, but I secretly liked the idea of being able to save more money and rebuild my financial house.

It wasn't that I couldn't pay my way (I most certainly could), it was the fact that I am no longer the morbidly obese girl with the crooked teeth and acne-prone skin they once knew. And some couldn't handle the new me.

That was two months ago in August.

Just when I thought I had gotten away from a bunch of enemy-minded ass women, I had to drop in here. I have known these people nearly my entire life and I love them like family, but the living arrangement has become hostile and intolerable beyond what I can stand any longer. And while I'm tempted to skip out, I don't want to waste my extra money on hotel rooms; therefore, it's best for me to just lay low, eat the damn crow, and keep adding more of my earnings to the existing foundation of my cash flow. That's the wisest thing for me to do right now.
But they don't need to know that. No one needs to know my next move. And they definitely don't need to know about what I have accumulated in both material and monetary assets.

Thank God for my new job. Because having it provides me with a little economic leeway, meaning that I'll be able to add more money to my savings without having to sell off some of my jewelry and handbags. I may have material wealth, but my monetary assets are much less. And if I can just stick it out for four more months, I'll be home free. And I will never have to see these miserable people again.

Mariah was on V103 singing "Emotions" when the angry and embittered cow, nicknamed Chub, called me downstairs to interrogate me about twenty dollars. No sooner had I reached the base of the stairs than she asked me, "Cat, did you steal 20 dollars out of my mother's bedroom today?"

And when I told her that I had not, she pretended to disbelieve me, even though she knew I had been telling her the truth. And rather than further investigating the mystery of the missing money, she elected to tear me down in front of everyone present, including her idiotic and hypocritical ass mother, her slow ass sister, her dumb ass cousin, her tired, broke, and covetous ass stepfather — if you could even call him that — and her crackheaded ass aunt, whom, by the way, just so happens to be the real thief. They all stood around looking at me accusingly as though I were the one who'd taken the money and sat there lying about it. But every one of them *knew* I hadn't stolen it. They knew I hadn't taken it, they just needed an excuse — even if that excuse was bogus — to go off on me. And being accused of doing something that I had not done enraged me. They knew I was innocent of any crime; nevertheless, they desired to tear my morale down anyway because of their envy and jealousy towards me.

The cow knew better, but she was tempted to take all of her misery, anger, and frustrations about her own worthless life out on me. She read me the riot act, preaching about their false integrity and a bunch of other bullshit. And it was during her adrenalized teardown of my character that the bloated bitch, along with her dysfunctional ass family unit, failed to remember my history.

Twenty dollars ain't shit to me. I have tubes of lipstick right here in my Dior makeup case that set me back twenty dollars or more apiece. And they know it. I don't wear cheap shit, I wear the best. I'm used to the best, and I'll spend good money to have the best. *That,* they failed to remember. And needless to say, I took the liberty — when I was able to get a word in — to remind their wretched asses, which only caused the self-hating muthafuckas to blow up the more so. But it didn't surprise me, because I know that the truth is one painful ass bullet wound to the head.

Another thing they fail to remember is the fact that *they* begged me to stay here with them until my apartment cleared. *I* did not ask them to let me stay here. And while such accommodation stood to eat into a larger chunk of my finances, I would have gladly stayed put at the Holiday Inn until February. But I just couldn't see the future then.

I swear, if I had known then that they would soon unravel on me like this, I would never have agreed to stay here. Where the fuck do they get off accusing me of some shit like that? They know better.

I can't stand these muthafuckas because I detest self-hating ass people. It's not my fault their lives are all fucked up and shit. They made their own decisions in life, and I was not here (in this city) to influence them in any of those decisions; I was in the state of Minnesota. Their irresponsible actions are what caused them to be in the predicament they're in. And if Chub kept fucking without protection and had two kids at a young age, that's her damn fault. Her lazy ass hypocrite of a mother should've had her on some damn birth control pills — as my mother had me on them so that I wouldn't be bringing any babies in her house — but she didn't. And that's on *them*, not me. But I seem to be the only one they seek to take all of their anger and hatred and regrets and shit out on. And they were (and are) in the wrong. They're wrong as two left shoes.

Not to be outdone — where falsely accusing me had been concerned — Poochies's idiotic ass had the nerve to ask me if I had taken a pair of Chub's panties. This was on top of the accusation about the money. Apparently, her fat ass daughter had some panties from her "thinner days" that have gone missing, and she assumed that I had taken them. And I honestly couldn't be more offended.

As I'm composing this entry, I have a storage container housing all of my personal belongings. And one of my boxes in that storage container has the word "Intimates" written on it in black marker. The box includes over 40 bra and panty sets from such top brands as Bali, Maidenform, and Olga, just to name a few.
While working in retail, I built a considerable collection of intimate apparel by way of Lerner New York and T.J. Maxx. And what I didn't acquire through my dear employers, I purchased from Dayton's as I had a Dayton charge and could accumulate items for my wardrobe as I so desired. The best lingerie that money can buy has a box of its own in my storage container among my other personal belongings, and these muthafuckas sittin' in here accusing me of stealing some tired ass panties that they bought at Woolworths down the street on 63rd and Ashland?! Ain't that a bitch?! Ain't nothin' wrong with Woolworths, I buy my Noxzema, Caress, and some of my other personal care items there, but damn.

In the first place, even if I wanted to wear her muthafuckin' panties, I couldn't. Because both she and I have two completely different body types. I got way more ass and hips than that bitch and her damn panties wouldn't even fit me; they'd be too fuckin' tight! And here's something else to consider. Why would I need to steal another woman's panties when I have a wallet full of credit cards and can go out and buy my own? Damn, are they just stupid? I mean, really.

Having found a job, I don't have to worry about going into default on any of my cards, I can pay my monthly minimum balances. But that was not so much the point as them accusing me of something as petty as stealing a pair of panties (of all things) in the first damn place. They must be out of their dumb-ass minds.

We ain't got the same taste in undergarments no muthafuckin' way. I wouldn't be caught dead in that tired, frumpy ass shit that bitch be wearin' unless my damn period was on.

Ooh, I can't wait to call my Mama and tell her about this shit in the morning. But then again, that may not be the wisest thing to do. Because knowin' my Mama, she'd get on a plane and be back here on the South Side of Chicago within 45 minutes fuckin' these people up. For real, I know my biological women. My Mama would burn this whole house down around their asses about mistreating me. And that's the truth. So rather than involving my dear mother, I will just have to move into a hotel and stay there for the next four months. Because by then, or maybe even before then, my apartment will be ready for me to take up residence in.

I didn't want to waste any extra money that I could use as I progress forward in re-establishing my citizenship in this city, but fuck it. I'll just have to make it up. Anything will be better than continuing to stay here. Because while I once knew these people, much has changed over the years. And they have a lot of shit that they need to evacuate out of the bowels of their lives.

I swear, I did not know that it was going to turn into this when Keke begged me to stay here with them. But now, it's time for me to go. Maybe I should've kept some of the details about my personal life to myself, but how was I to know? I would leave now but it's too late, it's after one in the morning. So I'll rest tonight and make a move tomorrow.

Love,

Cat

16th October 1991, WEDNESDAY
(The Next Day)
11:15 a.m.

Dear Diary,

Even though I'm not a morning person, I was up bright and early on the phone. First, I enjoyed the pleasure of speaking with Kemba (he'd called to say hello and ask how I'm doing), then I called the Holiday Inn back and they offered me the same rate on another room for an extended stay. But after giving it some more thought, I decided that the Ramada Inn on Lake Shore Drive would be more suitable for me as it's located in Hyde Park near stores, restaurants, and public transportation. So I'm gonna head over there today to look at the room they've reserved for me. I told the desk clerk that I preferred to have a room with a private bathroom, a queen bed, a TV, a mini-fridge, and a microwave.

Check all of the above.

I love the fact that the room has a microwave because knowing me, I'll be eating takeout from Grand Chinese Kitchen every other day. I love that place so much. And it's nice to be on friendly terms with the owners whom I met during my very first visit to their location on 87th street a few months ago. I stopped in to pick up my meals every other day, and that was how we all got to know each other. It reached a point where they already knew what I was going to order and had it ready for me when I called ahead and told them that I was on my way. Ironically, our setup is very similar to the one we had with Terry during our Wendy's days when he would walk in, make his presence known with a joyful conversation, and wait at the counter while our line crew prepared his two singles with everything except onions and mustard.

(Smiling at the memory)

I love the Chang family. And I'm glad to know them.

(Now sighing with relief)

I came home to pursue my lifelong dream of becoming a published songwriter and writer, and that is exactly what I intend to do. I am not going to allow anything — or anyone

— to stand in the way of my dreams. And that would include these faithless people in this dreadful house.

Now her guilty conscience is eating her sloppy ass up because she knows that what she did was wrong. She accused me of stealing twenty dollars from her mother, even though she knew I hadn't done it, and now she feels guilty and regretful. I know this because I can see the outline of her shame extending the width of her chubby ass face. She's been tormented all morning long because of her evil actions. And it serves her bitter, angry ass right.

She called me up to Keke's bedroom to apologize for everything she said the night before. Her tearful words were as follows: "Cat, I'm sorry for everything I said. I kinda have an idea who took the money," blah, blah, blah. And I was looking upside her damn head like Yeah, bitch, I know who took it, too: that ol' alcoholic ass crackhead you call "Auntie."

After she finished breaking down in shame, I accepted her apology and forgave her. Because I don't have to live in her hellish existence, that's all on her. But one day — if she's not careful — her misery and bitterness will both be allowed to consume her like terminal cancer. My life will move on, and the Lord will bless me to get back on my feet and settled; but she, on the other hand, will be stuck here in this contentious house with all of her anger and regrets. These people ain't goin' no damn where. And in due time, I truly believe that the Lord God will avenge my innocence in this entire household because I have not done what is evil to any of them. My only offense is the fact that I exist. They hate what

I represent as a woman because they hate themselves as women.

I taught them how to care for their skin, hair, and nails. *I* shared beauty secrets and makeup tips with them. *I* introduced them to the General Nutrition Center (GNC) on Wabash Avenue where I buy my natural skincare products. *I* explained to them what color palettes were, and so on, and so on. The Lord used *me* to help *them* because they didn't know the first damn thing about femininity, or about how to care for themselves as women. And when they started to believe that they had my shared knowledge mastered (which they don't, and probably never will as it's not their passion) the bitches, from the mother on down, turned on me like snakes.

Speaking of the mother, she "borrowed" my Mary Kay pressed powder and has yet to return it to me. I don't know what the hell made her think that she could wear my pressed powder as I'm three full shades darker than her. Anyway, she can keep it. Because I moonlighted as a Mary Kay representative during my days in retail, and I'm 100% certain that I can get another pressed powder compact in my beloved Chestnut.

Well, it's nearly 4 p.m. and time for me to head over to the Ramada Inn to check out the room and pick up my key. By this time tomorrow, God willing, I'll be looking at Lake Shore Drive from my room's windows. Hallelujah!

I'll do my best to remember the good times we had.

Love,

Cat

Cat's Epilogue:

I cried during my first night's stay in my peaceful and quiet room at the Ramada Inn. I also said a special prayer to the Lord, asking Him to move His hand over what had been an evil situation. I prayed that he caused Poochie and Chub to find Chub's missing panties. I also prayed that he would grant the troubled women understanding that they should come to a knowledge of the truth about what happened with the $20.00. Because I hadn't taken it.

And while I know in my heart that my prayers had been answered, they would not ever admit it to me because the spirit of pride would not allow them to. Therefore, the Lord had chosen to pass judgment on them. And to this day, His wrath penetrates itself through the roof that covers their heads.

The Third Stage

"The Proverb of Like-minded Women"

THE POEM:

See them gathered up?
Hateful women
Come together;
However, they're fair-weather.
They will die soon.

THE ENTRY:

16th October 1991, WEDNESDAY

Dear Diary,

I should be happy, considering that I now have the key to my new room at the Ramada Inn, but I'm not. I'm royally pissed right now as a result of an incident that occurred just this evening on 63rd and Ashland, right in front of Sammie's gyro restaurant. DiDi and I had no sooner picked up her dinner and left the restaurant than this large group of women approached us, led by the neighborhood tramp, Desi. She had a bone to pick with me, and I couldn't understand it, considering that I don't even know her. I've never said two words, much less one, to that woman, but she and hers ran their asses up on me as if they were going to beat me down from my "heights" right there on the sidewalk. Now, a wise woman would have spoken accordingly and held her peace. But a woman of tremendous folly will open her mouth and get fucked up, especially in the event she breaks forth upon a complete stranger to strive without just cause. The woman named Desi constitutes the latter.

Why is it that when certain types of women decide to get into fights with me, they always know they're in error but they still come at me swinging anyway? Is it to test their strength? Are they trying to convince themselves that they have more power in their vaginal cavities than other women do in theirs? Or is it simply the fact that they want to tear other women up because they've already torn themselves up?

It saddens me to say that the answer is all of the above.

When Desi and her gang of ghetto-minded and self-hating women turned onto my path to obstruct my way tonight, they had already been marked out for destruction. Because the Lord, who is my God, is not going to allow even one hand to lay itself upon my person to do it harm lest He should be moved to utterly destroy the human (both body and soul) to whom that hand is attached.

Now, what had been the woman's grievance with me, a stranger whom she doesn't even know? My alleged "attack" on her jealous-hearted and black ass niece, Porsha. As it turns out, Porsha ran and told her whorish ass aunt a lie on me, saying that I'd been "messing with her" or "trying to fight her" or some shit. And her aunt, who'd disliked me at first sight anyway (like so many other bitches of her ilk), chose to believe the lie; hence her confronting me on the street tonight. She could've lost an eye this evening because of a lie that she preferred to believe, just to have an excuse to get in my face and witness my reality up close. For she is a woman traveling along the pitch-black road of self-destruction without headlights. And one day, somebody gon' fuck her shit up.

I have never done anything harmful to Porsha, a friend of Kee's, by the way. Porsh just doesn't like the fact that I love to paint my nails and keep myself up as a young woman. And her ugly ass envy tempted her to run and tell her aunt a bald-faced lie about me. And when that nasty, sperm-breath-havin' bitch approached me, flanked by all her like-minded ass girls tonight, I felt it was my duty to defend myself. And I did. I told Desi the truth, that I had not ever said or done anything inappropriate to her niece. I then asked her if she still desired to contend with me — physically — regardless of my innocence. And while I don't know what triggered it, it was at that moment that she suddenly lost her fake ass courage and started to slowly back away from me. But before fear settled in on her, it made contact with the minds of her sorry ass posse, and they all moved, even with a quickness, to disperse themselves from her.

I just watched her as she backed away saying, "Look, I'on have no problem witchu, Ms. Cat," blah, blah, blah. And my last words to her were, "You better put 'Ms.' in front of my name. Go on your way in peace, Madam."

DiDi just stood her ass there like a coward, not one time opening her damn mouth to defend me. But it's just as well because I didn't need her to speak for me. I'll die (or get my ass whooped) defending my own honor, especially when I know I'm in the right and not the wrong.

I feel like crying right now because I'm angry. I have never taken kindly to a whole lot of women ganging up on me. Because whenever they did so in the past, I saw a hideous shade of red flash before my eyes, and by the time it was all over, I had fucked up a lot of people. The last thing I want to do is hurt anybody, but I will, especially if there should be a whole lot of them to just one of me. I don't bother anybody and I expect to be left alone.

Pappy is on his way over here right now to pick up my two trunks and my travel bags and take them to the hotel. And once I cross the threshold to the opposite side on my way

out, my eyes shall never be strained by the sight of this place
— as it currently stands — again.
I don't harbor any resentment against you, Englewood, but
your community is laid waste to many faithless, hopeless,
angry, bitter, godless, crooked, worthless, and self-hating
men and women. I will now leave you with them so that it
may go well for me.

Hasta la fucking vista.

Love,

Cat

"A Stiff-necked Rebel"

THE POEM:

You're like a donkey:
You bray and kick.
A Rottweiler:
Muscular and shaded black -
And murderous.

Cat's Prologue:

I see them every time I go out, eagerly running to their own deaths, and showing scorn and hatred to anyone attempting to prevent them from running too close to the edge. It's as if they want to die. It's as if they want someone to put them out of their misery. And they're willing to kill to be killed: for them, this has become the most terrifying epidemic.

"Fight Black-on-Black crime with Black-on-Black love."
—The Slogan of Unity Day in Chicago's Washington Park, circa 1982

THE ENTRY:

24th August 1991, SATURDAY
6:45 p.m.

Dear Diary,

I've been home for two months now, and I'm pretty much done with the process of visiting all of my former stomps. And while a lot has changed in the beautiful city of Chicago, much remains the same. I went to my beloved McCormick Place today just to lounge on the grass out back and gaze at Lake Michigan. And sitting there reminded me of the time when Tiny and I got together to have our little picnic on the rocks all those years ago.
Back then, we were girls of only eleven years apiece living on the Low End.

During those old days, we had gang units in our developments that waged war on one another often, shedding rivers of blood in the streets. And it seemed as if every three months or so, funeral notices were being posted over the mailboxes on the first floor bearing the names of either someone we knew or someone else about whom we'd heard. As time progressed, my mother collected close to ten obituaries. And it makes me sad to say that, even now. We lost a lot of people back then, and it's a shame because no one can bring any of those people back. Those who died by way of gang violence believed that they were honorable men (and women) honoring their code standards. But if truth be told, they weren't; they had only been deceived. They were quite easy to deceive, too, because they were already lost souls. Lost and misguided souls. And their ignorance of the truth is what got them destroyed. They died and went to Hell for eternity because they were tempted to believe a bunch of lies. And that is a very terrifying reality.

Hopelessness and faithlessness breed self-destruction. And those who were lost in the days of my childhood were the unfortunate offspring of both. They're gone, and they're not coming back. But I'm sure that if they could, they would give anything for a second chance at life so as not to go back to that petrifying place (in the spiritual realm) from which they were so mercifully delivered.

If only it were that simple.

"We will all die someday, but hope and pray that you don't die in your sins. Because dying in one's sins is extremely dangerous. Baby, please strive to enter into Life and not Death. At least try to do better. Try to believe. And try to make tomorrow a better day than today was. At least try, boo. Do you understand what's being said to you? Don't go the way of the damned. Don't follow the folly of the rebellious and the scoffer. Do you understand me, young brotha? I love you, baby, and I don't want to see you go out like that. Stay in school and complete your education, okay? Don't be out here self-destructing. And stay away from these damn gang units, too, okay? Are you listening to me? black boy? Are you listening to me? You take one step and God'll take two. Put your faith in Him, and He'll deliver you out of it all. And while you're waiting on His deliverance, He'll protect you from all harm and danger. Do you understand me, black boy? Good. Here, here's a few dollars. Give me a hug and a kiss, I gotta go. Be well and stay out of trouble, okay? Stay strong for yourself, and stay strong for me."

Those were a few of the words of wisdom I shared with Tar-Baby when I ran into him on 63rd and Throop this afternoon. I love him with all I've got, and I believe in him. I believe in him because I know he wants to do right, he just needs guidance, particularly spiritual guidance. And whenever the Spirit moves me to speak the words of truth to him, I do so. I also know that he's being tempted to follow in the crooked steps of his daddy and his brother — both gang unit members — but he's fighting against it. And I'm proud of him for that. He's gonna make it, I just know it. I know he's gonna be alright because I pray for him every day. And I know that God is watching over him. Tar-Baby is gonna make it.

But for every Tar-Baby who makes it out, there's another impressionable young brotha being initiated in. And this is where we — as a collective community — need to put our foot down on Satan's neck in the name of Jesus. Because if we don't, vicious and destructive days lie ahead. Because people are falling away into more godlessness, rebelliousness, and lawlessness will have already staked its claim on our future generations.

Stay in faithful prayer, and make love (not war) with your outer reflection.

Love,

Cat

Cat's Epilogue:

Life is worth living, but not dying for; and strength speaks volumes in individualism, not in groups. Hope will carry you to a land flowing with great opportunities, and faith will establish you there.
Live and be free, my beloved people.
Live and be free.

"She Flew In On Her Broom"

THE POEM:

The devil came in:
He wreaked havoc
On the faithful
And on the unsuspecting.
He used his witch.

THE ENTRY:

8th May 1995, MONDAY
3:55 p.m.

Dear Diary,

*H*ow could my grandfather have married such a hateful woman? How could he have taken to wife a woman who had been so hostile towards his mother, and his daughter, and his grandchildren? How is it that he stayed married to her after all these decades? Does he even know what she (allegedly) did? Because if he does, he's a damn idiot for staying married to her.

Since the time that I was old enough to remember, my grandfather's wife has hated my family, especially my mother who was born of another woman, namely my grandmother. She worked her ass off to drive a wedge between father and daughter: for my grandfather and my mother were never as close as they should have been. And even after all the heinous stories that I've heard from my mother about that witch over the years, the one mama shared with me today really set me off, causing me to hate that immoral woman even more.

My mother was raised by my great-grandmother who, despite being older, was still sharply alert. And according to my mother, my grandfather's godless wife purposely pushed my great Nana down a flight of stairs many years ago, hoping that the fall would prove fatal for the older woman. But it didn't. The Lord didn't allow death to sting her. And when my great Nana finally got a chance to speak to my mother, she immediately told her granddaughter about what had happened.

According to my great-grandmother's account, my grandfather had been out that day, leaving both his wife and my great Nana home alone. And as the older woman's witness to my mother also stated, the two women got into a heated argument about something or other, and then in a fit of rage, the younger woman attacked the elder woman by pushing her down a flight of stairs in my grandfather's home. After my great Nana got her wits about her, she testified to my grandfather, my mother, and my godmother about what that bitch had done to her. And while everyone initially believed my great Nana, that witch my grandfather married managed to coerce her husband into taking her side by lying to him that it was just an accident. But my mother and my godmother didn't buy her story or believe her bullshit at all, not even one bit. And needless to say, they wanted to murder that hateful ass bitch. And they would have, had my grandfather not talked them out of it.

My handsome grandfather was a serviceman, respectively. And according to my mother, he met that witch in the nation's capital while his company had been stationed there. After he swept her off of her feet, he was later deployed to his nativity in Chicago. And in due course, that bitch of a witch hopped on her broom and flew in to join him there. The rest is wicked history. And to this day, acid flows through the roots of my family tree.

While I love my aunts and uncles who proceeded forth from her womb, I despise her. She did everything she could to make life a living hell for my lineage of women, including my great-grandmother, my grandmother, and my mother. And that is not something I will ever forget.

I love you, mama. And if we have nothing else, we'll always have each other.

Love,

Cat

"The Evolution of Life"

THE POEM:

Let the past stay dead,
Don't dig it up.
Just let it die,
And wipe that tear from your eye.
It's time to live!

THE ENTRY:

10th July 1986, THURSDAY
8:00 p.m.

Dear Diary,

When mama cries, I cry, too. And I know why mama cries. She cries because she's so tired. She's so tired of taking one step forward only to have someone come along and shove her back two steps. It's like she can't win for losing. And I think that's why she drinks more than she should sometimes. What mama needs to do is take a good breather. Because she can't add an extra hour to any day, that's God's job. And God is gonna take care of us. He always has and he always will. This place we're in now, it's not the best place we've ever lived in, but it's clean, it smells good, and it's home.

I know the landlord is a sinister bastard, mama, but we're not going to be here forever. Soon, we'll be going out just as fast as we come in. You'll see. And I'll see you smile again. You'll smile that beautiful smile of yours again. Yes, you will, dear mama. And we'll live happily ever after.

He's mad, our landlord is. He's mad at my Mama because she wouldn't allow him to take me out on a date. But she's right because I'm only 15. I may be tall with boobs and booty, but I'm only 15.

The first time he saw me, he told me that I looked like Whitney Houston. I had my hair pulled back in a bun similar to how Whitney's hair had been styled for her album cover photo, and I think that's where he got the reference. Added, my bone structure, facial features, and skin tone also played a part in his comparison of me to her.

His name is Matthew Simon. He's a Jewish, third-generation chiropractor with a large fancy house in Falcon Heights. I know this because he took my mother and Brett out there for a visit, and she came home and told me all about it. At that time, he and I had yet to meet, but he was crazy about my mother.

That was in the beginning.

The product of a long line of chiropractors, Matthew confided in my mother about nearly everything he did, as though he were her own son. And I don't truly believe that there was anything he would not have done for her. Whatever my mother asked for, Matthew saw to it — time and again — that she was obliged.

He had been so cool in the beginning.

Of all Matthew's tenants, my mother and Brett were the only ones who knew the truth, that Matthew had won this building in a Poker game. And upon learning that little tidbit of information myself, it all became clear: Matthew doesn't have the slightest clue about real estate. And while I can't help but chuckle at that, I also can't believe that this building's original owner wagered it in a Poker game. Hmm… I wonder if there are any liens on it.

Anyway, everything between Dr. Matthew Simon and my mother had been just fine until the day he came over and met me for the very first time. That was the day he commented on me resembling Whitney Houston. He proceeded to go through the entire building repeating the same words to all of our neighbors: "She looks like Whitney Houston. Doesn't she look like Whitney Houston? Cat is a knockout…"

While I kept on a polite smile and appreciated his compliment (because Whitney *is* a lovely gal), I don't think I look like her at all. But Matthew most certainly does. And ironically, he's not the only one.

There have been other people — way before Matthew — whose eyes had also perceived a resemblance between the newly popular songstress and myself. People like Dani Willis, a girl with whom I attended Highland High. I can still hear her confident voice as she queried some of our fellow students during lunch one afternoon: "Hey everybody, doesn't Cat look like Whitney Houston?!" After many either nodded their heads or said yes in agreement, Dani took it upon herself to assign me an additional nickname. From that day forth, I was given the playful moniker, "Whitney," by the beloved Dani Willis.

I had been wearing my hair styled in a "feathered mushroom" that day, so I assumed it had been the source of Dani's comparison. I'm not sure, but whatever the reason, the moniker stuck to me like a sticker bug to clothing. And whenever she saw me in the hallways or anywhere else in school, Dani would flash her beautiful smile and call out to me saying, "Hey, Whitneeey. Whitneeey… My girl!"

(Smiling at the memories)

I liked Dani Willis. She's tall like me and loaded with class.

Now back to Dr. Matthew Simon.

He became fixated on me after that day, and constantly sought excuses to pay us visits. It was his way of getting close to me whenever he could. My mother began to suspect that something was up, especially after Matthew offered to take me go-karting.
Despite his relationship with a woman named Lela, he continued to pursue me feverishly. And when my mother had finally put her foot down and told him straight out that I was too young for him to date, their friendship soured.
Matthew has been like an eel to us ever since.

I swear, it's like he's a sinister villain in a movie stalking and terrorizing a single woman and her child who live all alone: he's been tampering with our lights and raiding our mailbox and tweaking with our water and lurking around outside of our windows at all odd hours of the night and spreading lies about us and filing false claims against us and defaming us to our neighbors, and so on, and so on. And my mother, a woman who doesn't handle stress very well, has just been a nervous wreck.

To make matters worse, he came over here the other night to violate our mailbox — again — and to boldly threaten us with eviction. In turn, we were left with no other choice but to call the police, and that, we did. But it probably would have been better for us had we not. Because upon their arrival, the idiotic officer elected to take the lying word of Matthew over the many complaints of my mother concerning him. And I could not believe what I had been witnessing as it was so utterly disgusting.

Even as I'm sitting here writing my entry, I'm still irked by the ugly memory of that night.

In the aftermath of that madness, my mother and I both concluded that this place is cursed and that we must move on. And we will.

I could see the anguish and defeat masking my mother's face like liquid foundation, a shade too light for her. And I didn't like it because when my mother hurt, *I* hurt. And it's never a good thing when I'm hurt, especially not when that hurt is unwarranted.

After the so-called police officers showed themselves disapproved in our living room, by not rebuking the lawlessness of the hostile man named Dr. Matthew Simon (who opted to use his status as an advantage), we lost all respect for them. The minute their squad car pulled away from the curb and rolled off down the street, the arrogant bastard stood in our doorway and threatened to evict my mother and me from our apartment *that night* for "unpaid rent." But it only went to show how ignorant and unlearned he was (and is) where legalities are concerned.

It was I who'd urged my mother to stop making our rent payments (two months' total) after he embarked on his bitter and petty "reign of terror" against us. And for him to (legally) evict us from the unit of our occupancy, there are several steps he would need to take. First, he must go downtown to eviction court and file an unlawful order to get the eviction process started. From there, the court will dispatch the sheriff to the tenant's unit to serve the unlawful on which the date will appear, summoning the tenant to appear before a judge in eviction court. At that time, both the plaintiff (the landlord) and the defendant (the tenant) will be allowed the opportunity to either work out their grievances or to part ways. Should the latter prevail, the tenant will be given (30) calendar days to vacate the premises.

That, the obsessed, crazy, cocaine-snorting, pathetic, and privileged brat of a man doesn't understand. He may know about unaligned spines and neck cricks, but he has zero knowledge of the law.

I sat my mother down — after the vindictive man left — and filled her ears with the truth to calm her fears. And afterward I wrote a comprehensive letter to the judge (if mama and I ever had to stand before one) detailing every godless action that our embittered landlord had carried out against us. And when my letter was completed, it totaled five pages in length.

(Yawning)

Okay, it's time for bed. I can go on writing until the wee hours, but then I'll have bags under my eyes. And that wouldn't be good. I'm going to sleep next to mama in her bed tonight - that way I can hold her and she can hold me while we laugh and talk to each other. Thank you, God, for life.

Love,

Cat

11th July 1986, FRIDAY
(The Next Day)
3:38 p.m.

Dear Diary,

God is good! He never loads one down with more than he
or she can bear, but he always comes through just when a
person feels as though they're about to give up. Father God
never lets the weary heart down. Never! He always comforts
the contrite in spirit and moves His mighty hand to deliver
them right on time. I love Him!

Miss Montana (a woman who's like a grandmother to me)
saw the light today, literally. Mama had been over to her
place earlier for coffee and an emotional chat concerning all
the crap we're going through here. And according to what
Mama rushed home and told me, they were just sipping their
coffees, talking, and relaxing, with Montana speaking one
inspirational word after another to cheer Mama up. And it
was while she had been talking, that Montana suddenly saw
a flash of light on her ceiling. She said to mama, "Linda, I
just saw a light flash in my ceiling!" And when mama asked
her to repeat what she'd just said, Montana did: "I just saw a
light flash in my ceiling, Linda." Mama told me that after
they both concluded that the flash of light had been a divine
sign, the phone rang five minutes later. When Montana
answered, the caller asked if he or she could leave a message
for my mother due to Montana's phone being our emergency
contact number. When Montana told the caller that Ms.

Linda just so happened to be sitting right there with her, the caller requested to speak to my mother, and Montana passed the phone to her. Ms. McVickers called to inform my mother that our application had been approved for this beautiful apartment in the Central Village on which we have been waiting. We have been approved. Mama can visit Ms. McVickers' office to sign the lease and pick up the keys! And it had been the most beautiful news, considering that both my mama and I really wanted that apartment. We wanted it, and the Lord blessed us to get it. And with the retrieval of our new keys, our joy has been made complete! After Ms. McVickers told Mama that we could move in at any time over the next three days, Mama nearly did a backflip. And I don't blame her.

We just got done packing up all of our personal belongings, and we're leaving TONIGHT! Good Riddance!

While we're waiting for my uncle Deke to come and pick us up, I'm writing this entry. Mama didn't even want to wait until we got our beds in the new place, she just wants to get us the hell away from here as fast as possible. And I don't blame her. We'll sleep on floor pallets tonight and take care of our beds tomorrow or the day after. Because after the hell we've just been through, we're gonna need a few days to relax and heal. I have my Mama and my Mama has me. Together, we both have God. He has always taken care of us and He always will. And that's the truth.
From tonight on, we will laugh again and be happy. And we will not look back at this dead place. We will let it die so that we can live; and peace will be happy to pave the way.

But one day, Dr. Matthew Simon will pay because while my mother and I may move on with our lives, God Almighty didn't forget. He never forgets those who do evil. And one day, Matthew will be made to cry just like he made my mother cry when he went out of his way to harass her after she refused to allow him to date me. And to be honest, even if I were of age, I would not have gone out on a date with someone as malicious and vindictive as him.

I wanted to hate Matthew, I did. But where would that have gotten me? In the same go-kart as him, speeding towards a concrete wall without a seat belt on.

Love,

Cat

"The Muffin Top"

THE POEM:

Her bulk smothered me:
Her rage screamed out -
Wail like Banshee.
She desires to be me,
But she can't be.

THE ENTRY:

18th April 1992, SATURDAY
9:12 p.m.

Dear Diary,

I hate this bitch because she's trying to hurt me. For my protection, I have elected to simply refer to her as "bitch" in this entry, but you know who I'm talking about, my dear journal. She's desperate to know what I have written within you, but the bulky bitch will never know until I'm ready for her to know. And when I am, she'll suspect it's about her, but by then, I'll be so far away from her ass, that she'll never be able to catch up to me.

I cannot have anything without her heart desiring to have the same. She even wants to smell my damn piss every time I release it from my bladder. And that shit is not normal, it's an obsession. And because she thinks that every man out there has a hard-on for me (which is nowhere near the truth), she figured that she'd just deter their interest in me by scratching my face up and pulling my hair out of my head. Her big fat ass figured that she'd just pin me down beneath her blubbery ass stomach and try to choke the life outta me, knowing full well that I'm not a fighter unless it becomes necessary for me to be one. I will only fight someone back if I'm left with no other option. And tonight, I was left with no other option. I had no other choice but to battle back against that self-hating bitch because I am not going to sit here and allow her (or anyone else, for that matter) to destroy me for no reason. I am not theirs to destroy and fuck up. But it seems like everywhere I go, there sits some bitch with an evil desire to hurt me – either physically or emotionally. And I'm tired of these miserable ass bitches, both the black ones and the white ones alike.

The only thing worse than a self-hating heterosexual woman is a self-hating lesbian. And this bitch would account for the latter. I hate her, I swear I do. I hate bitches like her. All she ever did was try to give me a hard fuckin' time. And I don't like self-loathing and jealous-hearted ass women. I swear, if I had a gun on me, I would've shot that bitch tonight and put her sloppy, nasty ass out of her muthafuckin' misery. Honest to God, I would've shot that bitch in her chest for puttin' her fuckin' hands on me.

I love this South Side, and I love hangin' out with my people down here on the Low End, but I don't need these bitches tryin' to deface me for no other reason, save for the fact that some man — a complete stranger whom I've never even seen before — paid me a compliment. Since I didn't have a gun with which to shoot that big bitch in self-defense, I had to use a ketchup bottle on her worthless ass just to get her the hell off of me. And she's lucky to be breathing right now.
Ol' nasty, filthy ass bitch.
I swear, if it had not been for Boose, I would've killed that bitch tonight and gone to jail.

I need to get outta here and go find my girl Yoli so that I can tell her about this shit. I need to get outta here and go find my girl— aw shit, here this bitch comes. I'll pick this up later, dear Diary.

Love,

Cat

The Fourth Stage

"Single Black Female"

THE ENTRY:

To live inside me,
She desires.
To look like me
And possess my attraction,
She desires.

THE ENTRY:

21st August 1992, FRIDAY
8:30 p.m.

Dear Diary,

*R*enny took me to the show today. We went to the Ford City Mall to see *Single White Female*. And while we sat in our seats watching the images on the giant screen, I couldn't help but steal a glance at her while thinking to myself about just how much she reminds me of Jennifer Jason Leigh's "Hedy." Seriously, in our reality, she's the "Hedy" to my "Allie."

To this day, I'm still cursing myself for getting drunk at Gil's party and allowing her to go down on me. Because ever since it happened, she's been acting obsessed and shit, trying to morph into my being. She knows I love dick, but she wants to keep me all for herself. She idolizes my body, my skin, my personality, and my passion. And she wants everything on my plate because she's being tempted to loathe what's on her own plate.

Men are my one true desire, but I can never tell her that because she'll snap and try to kill me. And while she believes the lie that she has me trapped, the truth is the complete opposite. She can't prove I'm fucking Big Shank, but she certainly suspects that I am. And the erotic thoughts about us are troubling her mind daily. Right now, I can still feel the delectable pain in my right nipple that he pinched only half an hour ago. My clitoris is throbbing in response to my thoughts about him. Dare I say it, that I'm falling in lust with him. I love the way he calls me "baby" in that deep, baritone voice of his. I can still hear it right now echoing in the valley of my arousal. I can still smell the dense smoke from his cigar in my Donna Karan sundress.

While here, in her presence, I must play my part to perfection. I don't want her to touch me again, because, in the wake of the first time, I felt dirty, like I needed to wash my flesh off. And I hated that feeling. My only reason for doing it in the first place was to see how it felt. I was raised by debaucherous women who went through life fucking both men and women, and I just had to find out for myself what the appeal had been. But when I woke up the next morning — with a vengeful hangover, but sober — I felt disgusted. Yeah, the orgasm had been five-octave fierce, but still, I felt dirty as hell. And her? Well, she was all smiles and shit, boasting in her great ability to give mind-blowing oral pleasure.

I felt like I had to throw up.

While I was done with the one-night stand, I haven't been able to shake her ass off of me since. She now wants to dress like me, act like me, and even wear the same perfume I wear. And whenever she sees me with something new, she has to have it, too. She even wants to fuck like me, but she can't because she fears the power of the dick too much. She doesn't love men in quite the same way that I do. And honestly, I don't believe she ever will. In her mind, men are the enemy; but as far as I'm concerned, a man is the ultimate bringer of strength and pleasure. And no pussy-licking female will ever be able to substitute for one in either my fantasies or in my reality. Period.

The truth is that I love being a woman, and feeling like a woman, and looking like a woman, and smelling like a woman, and engaging like a woman. And only the loins of the male species can conjure the full invincibility of my womanliness— Oh, I must go now because people are beginning to file into the apartment— Wait, are those *my* shoes she's wearing? What the fuck?! I just know she did not squeeze her wide, fat ass feet into my narrow shoes! We don't even wear the same damn shoe size!
I-I-I-I gotta go.

Love,

Cat

"Slippery"

THE POEM:

There lies a reptile
In his spirit:
Cold and hateful;
Crooked, slimy, and vengeful.
Where is his doom?

Cat's Prologue:

*H*is little head protruded out from beneath the puckered foreskin of Silicon Valley and set its single eye on me.

THE ENTRY:

11th September 2015, FRIDAY
2:28 p.m.

Dear Diary,

I once saw an episode of *Oprah* on which the Queen of Talk had been hosting her guests, Whitney Houston and Mariah Carey. And it had been during the interview that Mariah said the following words: "People think they know you but they don't…"

I have never forgotten those words because they were words of truth. And the truth will always have a leg upon which to stand, which brings me to the subject at hand.

There is a man in Silicon Valley who thinks he knows me, but he doesn't. He doesn't know me at all. But because he can go online, search for my name, and read about certain aspects of my life, he thinks he knows me. He wants to believe that there is some sort of connection between us, when in fact, there is not. And because I don't provide him with the attention he so desperately covets from me, he has decided to make my user experience on a certain social network a miserable and horrible one.

I'm not exactly sure when his fixation on me began, but it did. And after he grew seemingly weary of waiting for me to respond to his indirect advances, he became more aggressive in his pursuits. He had even gone so far as to create an account on his platform bearing my name (last name, first, first name, last) in its username field. And it was from this account that he commenced communicating with me. But I didn't like this particular maneuver because I thought it was shady and cowardly. I believed that he should have reached out directly — if he wanted to get to know me — but he didn't. His actions spoke volumes about him.

I don't need to hide behind fake accounts to indirectly communicate with anyone. If there is someone with whom I am interested in connecting, trust that my approach will be straightforward. Because whoever he or she may be, they have a right to know who it is reaching out to them, especially if they're public figures. Those who are public figures tend to be very careful about that sort of thing, what people appearing outta nowhere and attempting to contact them. Such communications have to be monitored carefully, because the general public may be able to read information about a public figure's life, but the public figures don't know anything about those members of the general public who may attempt to reach out to them. And that's why I like to approach people straightforwardly. Should I seek to reach out to any fellow creative for any reason, I would prefer for him or her to know my true identity. That's just the way I like to operate. And while the man about whom I speak is also a well-known public figure, he came at me crooked, like a snake, instead of just being frank. And his actions revealed a great deal about the contents of his character: untrustworthy.

I sought to show friendliness to this man by communicating with him via the Boutique Domain (my official website) and gracing him with the playful moniker, "Tech Giant," in each one of my blog posts that had been created to address him one on one. But he was so full of confusion — mingled with fear, self-hatred, and low self-esteem — that he couldn't even play the man and respond to me publicly; he had to hide behind a fake account on his popular social network. And when I saw how cowardly he was being tempted to act, I decided that it was best for me to just leave him alone and cut off all communication. But maybe that was the wrong thing for me to have done because, in the wake of me rejecting him, he proceeded to hatch from his scaly shell like an angry snake and lash out at me by way of harassing actions and obsessive behavior on his platform. He even dared to misjudge the contents of my character by accusing me of being arrogant and narcissistic. And *that*, I didn't like either.

I represent something (or someone) to this man, but whatever (or whomever) that something or someone is, I don't know. Because I don't know him, he's a total stranger to me. I have never seen him up close, and I have nothing to do with him professionally; nevertheless, he continues to stalk and harass my account on his social network. And the more I ignore him, the more aggressive he becomes. He refuses to forget about me; he just can't move on. And because he is at liberty to conceal himself behind the digital curtains of his domain, he feels that he can "stab at me," if you please, in the dark where no one can see him. He also operates under the wicked delusion that he can subdue my account on his social network and do with it as he pleases without any interference or consequence. And that, dear diary, is evil. Evil and ungodly.

But for every wicked deed done, there will be a most severe penalty. And because Father God has a brutal way of righting wrongs, I will hold my peace until the day He rights this one. For the blood of the man about whom I speak is not worthy to be on my hands; therefore, I will wait patiently for divine retribution in defense of my honor.

I can say that I hate the spirit of this man — this stranger whom I know not — because I hate evil. And I don't much care for people — regardless of race, creed, color, nationality, or origin — who practice evil. And what this man has done (and is currently doing) to me is nothing minuscule of evil: for I have not done anything warranting his hostility towards me. And if I may say as much, he truly does remind me of Dr. Matthew Simon: a bitter and vindictive man who is angry that he cannot claim me as his own.
But his day will come. And it will be a vicious day.

Love,

Cat

Cat's Epilogue:

While I have spoken about this man's actions by way of public postings before, no one wanted to hear me. And they didn't want to hear me because they, too, were tempted to be hostile and enemy-minded towards me without legitimate cause. But on the day of divine retribution, I will stand up and speak the truth once again. And not one ear will be allowed to go deaf to it.

"Wind Chill Advisory"

THE POEM:

I know you so well.
I just saw you
Glimpse into Hell,
And it gave you a nightmare.
Reap what you've sown.

THE ENTRY:

27th October 1989, FRIDAY
4:45 p.m.

Dear Diary,

I should be crying right now, but I'm not. Because I simply cannot bring myself to tears. I should feel sorry for him, but I don't. Because I simply cannot bring myself to empathize. He's gone. Like that! He pretended to hate my guts, and now he's gone. Dead. No longer here in the land of the living calling me a bunch of bitches to my face. He had worked up too much energy where I was concerned. And his anger towards me was too personal for someone he didn't even know. Every time I saw him, he became highly agitated at the mere sight of me. And many times, I had to ask myself internally, *Who is this boy? Cat, where do you know him from? What is his problem with you?*
But then something clicked in my mind and I remembered him. He was the boy on the school bus who had been trying to get my attention that day back in 1986. He and some of his friends were shouting out catcalls at me from the windows as I stood at the bus stop waiting for the #21 Selby/Lake bus to turn the corner. And he wanted me to acknowledge him, but I didn't. I ignored him and his friends because I thought they were trying to tease me. Once upon a time, I was a little fat girl who had gotten so used to people picking on me, that I was leery of nearly everybody. And I thought that's what he and his friends were doing; therefore, I turned my head and pretended not to hear him shouting at me, "Hey, girl?! Hey, girl?! What's yo name?!"

I ignored him that day. And because I did, his ego exploded into pieces.

For years, he remembered me shunning him, even though I hadn't done it to be nasty and stuck up. And he never wanted to let me forget it. But I *had* forgotten it. I had forgotten all about it. I couldn't even remember his face that well, but he remembered mine. And whenever he saw it, he greeted it with bitch this and bitch that. He was angry because I hadn't recognized and acknowledged him. And of all the girls in our respective schools' peer groups, I was the only one against whom his embittered anger had been kindled.

When I continued to ignore him — this time deliberately — his rage boiled over in questionable proportions, but he was never allowed to lay a vengeful hand upon me. He was angry because I shrugged my shoulders at his uncalled-for insults and kept walking along in my way. He was angry because he wanted a girl that he couldn't have, namely myself. And my rejecting him had been the primary source of his rage. But when the Lord had had enough of him calling me a bunch of bitches on this Earth in His holy sight, He allowed his misery to be brought to an end at the murderous hand of another young man whom he had called his best friend. When the Lord had had enough of his being a heinous troubler of others, He allowed his misery to be brought to an end at the murderous hand of another young man whom he had called his best friend.

His own best friend murdered him in cold blood.

As I'm writing this entry, the beautiful actress, singer, and dancer Cynthia Rhodes — one of my favorite women in the world, by the way — is on the radio singing "Room To

Move" as the frontwoman for the pop band, Animotion. And being the emotional girl that I am, chances are I'll forever associate the song with this moment.

While I didn't appreciate his unwarranted hostility towards me, I would not have ever wished death on Blackie Jakes. Because death is final. And once they're stung by it, no human being can come back to Earth and redo their lives over. No, not even one.

Blackie lost his misguided life over something as frivolous as his petty indignation. His self-hatred drove him into the realm of death. And as I look out of my bedroom's window at the cool rain falling from the sky accompanied by a brisk Autumnal wind, I soon realize that unlike Blackie, the elements are alive and free. They don't love and they don't hate, they just wash away the old to make room for the new.

The wrought-iron hands on my lovely wall clock continue to inch forward. They have no idea that a young man I once knew of — even if only negatively — has died. And they don't care; their only purpose is to remind us, humans, that they will go on moving forward whether we're here or not.

Blackie has been dead for ten hours now. I know this because I've been counting the hours since my best friend Nessa gave me the news about his untimely demise. And as I sit here in my comfortable recliner, I wonder how his soul feels in death. I wonder if he's okay. I wonder if God forgave him and found a place for his spiritual being in His glorious Kingdom. I wonder if he's finally found peace.

I hope that he has because hope is all I can do; nevertheless, I am not entirely convinced.

I won't be attending his funeral as he and I had never been on friendly terms, but I pray that his mother finally has peace in the wake of his bitter departure from the Earth.

Few people loved Blackie Jakes, but many people hated him because he had been kind to only a few, but unkind to many, including me. And while I am certain that the vast majority of people are feeling a sense of quiet relief today, I, on the other hand, am feeling somewhat sorrowful. I feel sorry for the eternal soul of Blackie Jakes. I feel sorry for his death at such a young age. I feel sorry for his mother and his younger brother. And I'm sorry that we never made peace.

I remember the words of a very wise woman who once said to me, "Honey, people will call you everything but a child of God."

True words, indeed. But one thing I will never be called again is a "bitch" from the mouth of Blackie Jakes.

Love,

Cat

"The Orgy"

THE POEM:

The red light bulb shone
On their debauch.
In the orgy,
Their bodies were joined as one,
Coming alive.

THE ENTRY:

3rd June 1993, THURSDAY
2:48 p.m.

Dear Diary,

Now is a very exciting time for me as I am in the middle of decorating my new apartment. I found the perfect spot for my wine cooler next to the refrigerator, and I'm setting up my coffee station in the extra counter space near the window. Thank God for the wall socket over there.

As I'm writing this entry, I can see five gorgeous paintings resting against the east wall just waiting to be hung upon it; and my bedroom, which sits less than fifty feet away, is probably wondering to itself just how grand I plan to lay it out. Large pots of artificial plants litter the floor of my front room, and my bathroom could do with a shower door rather than a standard shower curtain. I'm gonna get around to it all in due time, but for now, I'm just gonna sit here in my comfy easy chair, sip my bergamot tea, and listen to Troop singing "Sweet November" on V103.

I went to Jewels today to buy some extra things that I needed here in the house: laundry detergent, bleach, fabric softener, kitchen cleanser, toilet bowl deodorizer clips, dish liquid, Caress soap, Jean Naté After Bath Splash, another jar of Noxema, douche powder, tampons, incense, and light bulbs. And it was only after I got to the light bulbs aisle that I remembered what I had witnessed on one particular night many, many years ago.
While looking through the selection for 100 watt clear light bulbs, I saw some colored bulbs that included blue, yellow, and red. And seeing one of the red light bulbs is what triggered my memory.

It was 1978 — if I'm not mistaken — and my family and I were still residing in our old Courtway apartment on 53rd and Calumet in Washington Park. On the day in question, some of our "play cousins," including Chub and DiDi, were spending the night at our house. And while I don't remember exactly what day it was, I know that we didn't have to go to school because school was out for summer. I can remember us playing outside that day and going swimming at the Washington Park pool on 55th & Garfield. We were at the pool for hours before the grown folks gathered everything up and took all of us home to settle down for the evening. Once there, everybody went their separate ways, and we went into the house so that mama could cook dinner. After we finished dinner, we washed up and then watched TV until bedtime. And while we the children floated off into the realm of Dreamland, the grownups stayed awake to engage in grownup conversations and other extracurricular activities. I only know this because I had to get up in the middle of the night to go pee. That was when I saw them — *all* of them.

My eyes may have been young, but they perceived well. And my brain understood what my eyes were witnessing. When we were kids, we called it "freaking;" but as adults, we tend to call it what it truly is: *"fucking."*

The grownups — all of them, including my Mama — were sprawled out on the floor of our front room fucking. And I do mean they were *fucking*.

After the initial shock of what I had been looking at wore off, I just stood stock still watching them in complete fascination. And besides their naked, sweaty brown bodies, there was one other thing that I saw vividly: the illumination that came from the red light bulb someone had turned on. It shone on their wild carousing, giving them a warm and passionate allure that I had thought was both eerie and wickedly beautiful. And I suddenly didn't have to pee anymore. Well, I did, but I held it just so that I could continue to watch my men and my women making love to one another. They were exchanging partners, men with women, and women with women. And that was the first time I saw a woman suckling another woman's nipples and eating her out. And the sight of it fascinated me.

The men's loins had been nothing short of blessed, pun intended, and the women's bodies easily accommodated them. When I saw "Uncle Twinks" sink his big dick deep into "auntie Pearl," with her taking every inch of it, I wanted to scream out, but I didn't. When I heard the pleasure-filled moans and hissings of the women as they were being vaginally and anally penetrated by one big dick after another, I wanted to scream out, but I didn't. Because I didn't want them to stop. I wanted them to keep going and enjoying one another. I wanted to learn about how love was made. And I wanted to be like them when I grew up. I wanted to know what it felt like to be fucked like that, and held like that, and touched like that, and kissed like that, and wild and carefree like that.

Chub, who I didn't realize had also gotten up to use the bathroom, accidentally bumped into me as I stood hidden in the doorway, snatching me out of my erotic reverie and causing me to finally scream out, even though it was barely audible. And it was at that moment that she, too, became a witness to the remarkably sensual orgy happening between our men and our women on the floor in our front room.

In fear and fascination, she said, "Ooh, they freakin'!" I had to shush her. Chub was so scared that she ran and jumped back in the bed, but I stayed right where I was. I could hear Chub saying to me in a frightened whisper: "You betta come an' git inna bed, Kimmie. You gon' git in truhbal if auntie an' 'em see you!"

(Laffin' at da memorees)

My feet remained glued to their spot, but I whispered back to Chub: "Sneak inna kitchin an' git dat chitlin' bucket fo' us so we can pee innit." And she whispered in reply, "I'ain't! You go git it! We gon' git a whoopin' if auntie an' 'em see us."

But auntie whatn't gon' see us because auntie was too busy suckin' Big Rabbit's dick, while at the same time gettin' fucked from behind by uncle Corn. Plus, they had the record player on, spinning "Zoom" by the Commodores. But when they started switching partners and changing positions, I used that opportunity to run through the back exit of our bedroom to get the chitlin' bucket. And after Chub finished peeing first, I peed second. Then we crept back to the door to watch the orgy a little while longer. By now, the record player was spinning "Star Love" by Cheryl Lynn. And when I looked at Chub, her eyes bulged and her mouth hung wide open.

(Smiling at the memory)

It had been quite a night back in 1978. And I have never forgotten the images of what I saw, and neither has Chub for that matter. While I was staying with them, she and I reminisced about the old orgy during one of our quiet moments, and we laughed about it.

Chub and DiDi had been sleeping over at our place that night because Poochie was on 55th and King Drive working an all-night shift at her job. But Poochie, an upstanding and moral woman was there ever one, would've keeled over from a coronary had she known what her precious daughter witnessed happening in my Mama's living room on that fateful night.

While she loved my Mama and her sister, Pearlie, Poochie had always done her best to steer clear of their circle because they were — in her words — "too loud, wild, and revelrous." Nevertheless, that didn't stop her from allowing Chub to spend nights with us from time to time.

Sitting here now, I think about my people and just how much I adore them. They made passionate love, not war. And I could never fault them for that. And though Chub and I carry the secret of what we saw to this very day, I learned a lot from our men and our women about the art of lovemaking, fucking, whatever you wanna call it: for their love had been wild, free, raunchy, and unrepressed. I admire the heck out of 'em.

I have never told my mother or my godmother (another partaker in the orgy) about what I saw that night, even though I know all they would do is laugh about it now. Because had they known that I saw them then, they both would've stopped screwin', got up and told me to go pee, whooped my ass afterward, told me to take my ass to bed, and then went right back to fuckin' again. That's just how my women are. But another reason that I never told them is because I wanted to spare them any embarrassment. Let them keep their dignity. I know they wouldn't give a fuck either way, but still.

God, I love my women.

I can still remember the smells emanating from the front room that (orgy) night. There had been a heady potpourri of incense, reefer smoke, Budweiser beer, Seagram's gin, Richard's Wild Irish Rose wine, cigarette smoke, and the sweet and musky scents of male and female genitals.

(Thinking and smiling)

Yep, seeing that red light bulb at the store today just took me back down memory lane. And the orgy I witnessed as a child is a memory I will never forget.

Right now, the Jackson 5 are on V103 singing "Blame It on the Boogie," and it sounds so damn good. That. Is. A. Jam! I swear it is. Them some badass brothas, the Jackson 5. Talented as fuck. I know Miss Katherine gotta be so proud o' her kids.

Damn, my tea got cold. I need to reheat it, and then I need to get my lazy ass started on my decorating.

Thank you, Lord Jesus. Home sweet home.

Love,

Cat

"The Girl on the Red Line"

THE POEM:

I remember when
You kicked my shoe
And then unleashed.
You raged like a wildfire
On the "liar."

THE ENTRY:

7th October 1994, FRIDAY
10:35 p.m.

Dear Diary,

I had a good time at work today. Shay, Bunny, Tammie, and I spent the entire shift just laughing and talking about some of everything as we drank perfectly brewed coffee and watched our beloved Ms. Charles decorating the office in a gorgeous fall and Halloween theme. I love Autumn, it's my favorite time of the year. And because I also love Halloween, I'm jacked up with excitement right now. It's just so beautiful out, with the leaves (already tinted in lovely shades of gold, russet, and orange) beginning to fall from the trees, and the sky covering us with a cool blanket the color of steel wool gray.

While watching "Charly" (that's the nickname I gave our paternal employer) hanging up her Halloween decorations, I thought to myself about how I couldn't wait to get home and start putting up my own: *It's Friday, my favorite day of the week! Joe and I will have the whole weekend free. And why the heck not? It'll be so much fun! Decorating for Halloween always is!*

The exciting thoughts had kept me hyped for the entire duration of my workday. And by the time my shift ended, I was looking forward to a hot bath, a hot cup of tea, and a mellow evening with my Boo. And everything was getting on just dandy until I got on the El at 95th. While I was seated and waiting for the train to pull out of the station, three loud and contentious women got on and sought to stir up strife with anyone foolish enough to bite their bait. They had no sooner hopped aboard than I felt the negative spirits

— which had been trailing them — rise to fumigate the area like a dead funk.

And to make matters worse, they gravitated right to where I had been sitting and plopped their ghetto-minded asses down in the seats next to mine. A train car full of empty seats, and they had to come over and sit by me. Go figure.

Anyway, I could sense discord coming, and it finally arrived. My shoes, a pair of black leather loafers with silver buckle designs, had been the excuse the girl used to start some shit with me. She sneered at my $100.00 Ralph Laurens and proceeded to verbally attack their handcrafted details: "Them some ugly ass shoes she got on," she spat. She had spoken the hateful words (about *my* shoes) to her two relatives, one of whom had been a dark-complected heavyset broad wearing chunky French braids and a self-loathing scowl. The heavyset broad looked at both me and my shoes and then yelled at me, as though I had been seated an entire mile away from her: "Hey! Can I see your shoes?!" She chuckled in her ignorance, but I had nothing to feed the beast. I had my pepper spray, though. And while I didn't wish to do those pitiful women any harm, I was fully prepared to spray paint their asses with it. I didn't have time for their bullshit because unlike them, I had worked a job all week and I was ready to get home.

With one hand on my potential weapon of self-defense, all I could hear in my mind were the wise words of Joseph Strickland:

"*Boo, always walk away from strife. Don't ever get caught up with strangers. Because people wanna die, and they're lookin' for somebody else to kill 'em so that they don't have to kill themselves."*

With that, I removed my hand from the pepper spray canister and then got up to move to another seat. And it had been while I was walking away, that the first bitch — the one who had made the hateful comments about my shoes — kicked my left foot hard enough to loosen the link to one of the buckles on my left shoe. But rather than turning aside to attack her ass like a Samurai, wisdom commanded me to keep walking until I reached another seat in which to sit. I paid heed to the spiritual instruction and took another seat in the aisle facing the three women. Because after what had just happened, I needed to keep a close eye on them. Still, I was angry that I couldn't unleash any rage on them. And I sat there wishing to God that I could've spilled their blood, even if only a little bit.

Of all the women in that El car, they had to rattle my symbolic cage. And because I'm a born again Christian, I couldn't fuck them up.

It took me a long time to count to ten.

They didn't fuck with me again, but their "anger" was still kindled. And when the brotha in need happened along to ask them for only one dollar, Satan rose up and used all three of them to physically attack that one man right in the center of the aisle. The innocent and helpless man just stood there, the unfortunate recipient of their "fiery" words and punches. And because their attack on that man happened so fast, the other passengers had to snap out of their shock before three

333

or four individuals jumped in to intervene and assist the victim. By that time, the train conductor had already called the police, and I was glad. I was still angry that I couldn't do those bitches bodily harm, but I was glad that they would soon be accosted by law enforcement.

I had to count to ten all over again.

When they got their triflin' asses off the El at the 35th Street stop, I knew that their destination had been one of two places: the Stateway Gardens or the Wentworth Gardens.

While the Lord didn't command the spirit of Death to sting them on the Red Line tonight, it is for a certainty that their day will come.

Judging by what I witnessed on the El this evening, I fully understand now why so many people are losing their lives out there on the Dan Ryan. They're out there gettin' killed and fucked up because they're out there fuckin' wit people they don't know, strangers. That's why we keep hearing about one heinous tragedy after another on these El platforms and shit.

That brotha on the El tonight is obviously going through a tough time in his life right now, although some had falsely accused him of being a liar and a cheat. And his only crime had been asking those nasty, self-loathing ass women if they had a dollar they could give him. But his asking them for money is not what set them off. That man asking them for one dry dollar didn't set off their attack on him as they were already looking for trouble. No, what set off the attack was evident to all: his poverty reminded them of their poverty. It's just that simple. His need was a brutal reminder that they didn't have shit themselves. And by attacking him, they were truly attacking themselves. So goes self-hatred.

A stop too late, the police were waiting on the platform when the train pulled into the Cermak/Chinatown station. And while an ambulance had been called to the stop, the man had not been badly injured. And we all thanked God for that. A few of us took up a collection for him, and before the train resumed along its course, the brotha had about $160.00 or so to go on. And if he needs to eat, he can at least do that.

God bless that man and watch over him. Because he had not done anything at all to deserve that. But I'm grateful that he's okay.

Love,

Cat

The Fifth Stage

"It Happened at Buckingham Fountain"

THE POEM:

The water shot up,
Bright and festive.
And with this ring,
He proposed to me on one knee,
Saying "I Do."

THE ENTRY:

9th July 1994, SATURDAY
11:42 p.m.

Dear Diary,

*J*oe asked me to marry him tonight! He asked for my hand
in marriage while we were strolling at Buckingham
Fountain. And I — a woman who swore that she would
never, ever get married — was overcome with honor,
excitement, and bliss! Ooh, Nessa is going to flip when she
hears this! Both she and Nita. I can already hear Nessa's
response: *"My Cat? Gettin' married?! Uh-uh, not the same
Cat that said she whatn't ever gettin' married, OR havin' no
kids! Say it ain't so, chile!"*

(Laughs)

I know my Nessa.

(More laughs)

Anyway, I was overcome with emotion as Joseph Strickland
dropped down on one knee, flashed me with a stunning
1-carat diamond ring, and proposed to me in front of
everybody out there at the great Buckingham Fountain. And
when I accepted his proposal, all of the people who were
surrounding us started cheering, clapping, and hollering out
their congratulations in reply. I caught immediate contact
high from the secondhand vapor of joy.

God was watching over us as the perfect Chicago winds
blew mists of cool, colored water from the beautiful
Fountain on every person standing before it. And we all

enjoyed the beauty of the evening while munching on complementary Elephant Ears and Luigi's Italian Ice. It was by far one of the most gorgeous and happy evenings of my life. And I will remember it forever.

Some will say to me, "You've come a long way, baby." And my response to them would be, "I most certainly have. And God is way too good for bringing me here."

Let's live it up, Strickland! God is with us and for us, baby! Let's live it up!

Love,

Cat

"Snake Eyes"

THE POEM:

You bet your own life
Against the odds
In my favor.
Snake eyes, snake eyes, shoot your craps!
Roll 'em like dice.

THE ENTRY:

16th February 1993, TUESDAY
6:23 p.m.

Dear Diary,

Chara Sims wishes to see me dead. She wants to see my life come to an end so badly that she would pay good money to watch someone else snuff it out if she can't do it herself. Indeed, her twisted mind tells her that if she can't get rid of me herself, then someone else should. The more she considers my life, the more she hates her own. And they have only gotten worse, what her macabre desires.

Because Chara believes the lie that her life on this Earth would be a whole lot better should my own life be brought to an end, she set out to make it happen: she tried to run me over with her car tonight.

I was crossing the street at 33rd and State near IIT, and she pulled up out of nowhere to make a left turn onto the crossway. I had the right of way to which she should have yielded, but the abhorrent bitch sped up on me anyway. My first impulse was to get her license plate number and call the police on her ass, but where would that have gotten me? It would have been her word against mine. And because obsession troubles her about me, it would've also been a perverse excuse for her to get in my life.
Ironically, tonight's incident was not the first time. Chara's tall, mannish ass has accelerated her car on me before as I had been crossing the street, and I bit that back, too.

(Pausing to light my cigarette)

What gets me about it all is that I don't even know her. Honest to God, I don't know that bitch from Adam.

341

(Chuckling)

I don't know that woman and she doesn't know me. We've never spoken to one another, and we don't share the same associates. I only know that her name is Chara Sims because she works as a security officer for the Chicago Housing Authority, and I was able to get the information from Big Shank. I didn't tell him about what she'd done, of course, but I needed a name to pair with her average, somewhat masculine, ass face.

Every time I see her, she gives me the same dirty look that Taya — a girl with whom I attended high school — used to give me daily. It's an ugly, sneering look that says, "This bitch thinks her shit don't stank." Taya had also wished to see me dead. So much so that she pulled a knife on me one day during Social Studies class and threatened to stab me with it. And why? Because of a lie Shanna told her, which she preferred to believe just to have an excuse to inflict upon me bodily harm. But she failed to receive her heart's desire, just like Chara Sims failed to receive hers.

Here we go again.

Many of these self-loathing women, who prefer to be misguided in their lives by Satan, are not familiar with one another, but they share a common outlook on life: for they are of one mind and likeness, even kindred spirits. And when such self-loathing women see women like myself, the devil always eases up alongside them to whisper his evil lies into their minds. Unfortunately, they are all too willing to believe his evil lies; thereby, giving into many of his wicked temptations and bringing on themselves swift destruction.

What such people fail to remember — while they're busy being flesh-minded — is that the devil hates *all* human flesh. He doesn't care about human beings, he only wants their eternal souls. And the reason certain people keep forgetting this very important element is that they're flesh-minded and not *spiritual-minded*. We are not one another's enemies, but we have one common enemy. And his name is Satan.

When women like Chara Sims see women like me, they're always tempted to believe the irksome lie that women like me get more attention than they do, or that women like me have more material things (or money) than they do, or that women like me "get it all in life," etc. And that's a lie courtesy of the devil with his "divide and conquer" tactics.

When people refuse to acknowledge the Lord God and they strut about the Earth void of faith and spiritual understanding, they become wide open, albeit empty, wells for Satan to fill up. And why? Well, because he has already been successful in tricking them to hate themselves, that's why. And when women are tempted to hate themselves, know for a certainty, that they will also be tempted to hate other women, especially other women who are NOT like them. And while I don't hate women in the human sense, I detest the ugliness of many women in the spiritual sense.

The woman named Chara Sims — who has toyed with the idea of running me over with her car, twice — is tempted to believe the lie that her life will suddenly come out from under its rock and see the sun in all its glory for the first time should my life be brought to an end. She believes the lie that she will no longer have to be irked by the reality of my existence, or by my "sucking up all the air from her" or "getting more attention than she does." And while it's really sad that she believes such lies, she has to live with herself in the hellish cage of her own body.

Hateful of the fact that I exist, women like her are too cowardly to end my perceived happiness themselves; therefore, they wager big to see it brought down to sorrowful levels or destruction by someone else. But the House always wins. And because the Lord God is the Chief Maker of the dice, He has turned the odds around, that the same should look upon me favorably. And for good measure, he has crushed those who have desired my hurt to dust, even beneath my heels. Know for a certainty that I will be allowed to read every one of their obituaries before they ever know the wicked pleasure of reading mine.

That said, people should be careful of nothing.

Love,

Cat

"It Can't Be"

THE POEM:

My transparency?
It's a rebuke,
They can't take it:
Their egos won't leave them be
When they see me.

Cat's Prologue:

How dare she not be at the bottom of society beneath my feet!

Those are only a few of the evil, ungodly, and ugly words — whether spoken aloud or privately thought — by many men and women in the world today with regard to yours truly.

THE ENTRY:

19th March 2018, MONDAY
1:34 p.m.

Dear Diary,

Why are those people baffled? Why are those people troubled? Both the Black and the White, and the White and the Black are baffled and troubled. Why? Well, because while the mind of the oppressor believes in stereotypes and the old status quo, the mind of the oppressed is conditioned to believe in the old way of subserviency, that's why. See, I answered the question for you.

(Smiles)

The Spirit of Truth, speaking in the ears of one who is tempted to love a lie, is like a bucket of ice-cold water being thrown on one who sleeps naked.

Heh, funny, not funny.

According to many of them, I should be cast in society as a maid. According to many of them, I should be a so-called "Welfare Queen" struggling to make ends meet. According to many of them, I should be working a back-breaking job making barely enough to survive. According to many of them, I should be a big, fat, loud, and sloppy cow who knows her place — and who stays in it — at the bottom of the "Totem Pole" in society. According to many of them, I should be bleaching my skin, coloring my hair a bright shade of yellow, wearing light-colored contacts, and mimicking the standard valley girl, all to pledge my allegiance to the White Caste System in society. According to many of them, I should be a subservient employee suffering beneath the thumb of a so-called "Gatekeeper" (particularly a *White* so-called "Gatekeeper") in some corporation void of any rights. According to many of them, I should be breaking my neck for an opportunity to kiss the ring of the modern-day Caesar. According to many of them, I should be willing to kowtow to the depraved for a slice of bread at their tables of godless feastings. According to many of them, I should be some common and unknown urchin without any honor. According to many of them, I shouldn't have any honor at all unless they're the ones bestowing it upon me. According to many of them, I should be satisfied with scraps and not deeming myself worthy of the T-bone.

For that is the nature of the evil world system. And I hate its ugly and ungodly stereotypes and biases, even with everything in my inner being.

I could play the bitch and tell 'em to get the fuck over it, but that wouldn't help them, they'll still be troubled. Because the troubler will go on troubling them in their minds until they go to the Lord.

I could play the bitch and tell them to kiss my (entire) ass, but that wouldn't help them either, it would only give them another reason to hate me.

For far too long, many people in the world — both the Jew and Gentile alike — have been conditioned in their minds to adhere to negative stereotypes concerning others in society, especially African Americans, but particularly African-American women: for such people *need* to believe the worst about women of color because it makes them feel better about themselves, even though they know their beliefs are all rooted in lies.

Who says that black women should not have any honor in society? Who says that black women shouldn't be happy and enjoying their lives on this Earth of the Lord's? Black women shouldn't have the finest that life has to offer? Says who? Who says a black woman is not supposed to be the First Lady of these so-called "United" States? Says who? So says over 400 years of spiritual brainwashing courtesy of Satan, that's who.

When many people in the world see a black woman like myself, it confuses them. Because they have been spiritually hoodwinked by the devil — for over four centuries — to believe that such a thing ought not to exist. But it does. And I'm living proof that it does. I contradict every stereotypical bias that many of these people are being tempted to foster in their hearts and minds where it pertains to black women in not only American society but around the world. And for this very reason, they're baffled and *purposely* speechless. They shut their mouths on purpose because they know the truth, that should they slip up and mention my name publicly, they'll bring me to life. Therefore, they remain careful — *at least for now* — not to mention me (or my name) publicly. However, still, they know that I'm real. And it would be good for them to also know that I'm not going anywhere until my Lord and my God command it: for this is *His* Earth and not Man's.

Love,

Cat

Cat's Epilogue:

The one whom they cannot control they pretend to ignore, but they're liars. Because while they know the truth, they're being tempted to hate the truth; hence the preceding Gogyohka, *It Can't Be.*

"Misery Loves Company"

THE POEM:

I was freed from need -
Plucked from the muck -
And you're troubled?
You hated to see my flight;
You loved my plight.

THE ENTRY:

16th July 1996, TUESDAY
(Five Years Later)
12:38 p.m.

Dear Diary,

"**Y**ou may be doin' fine now, but what comes around goes around!"

Those were the bitter, ill-wishing words that Chub's angry ass said to me over the phone – right before I hung up on her not even half an hour ago.

Ain't that a bitch?! Right before I hung up on her stupid ass, I retorted, "Oh, you're absolutely right about that, bitch! And it already has – on you and yours!"

Lying ass muthafuckas. They make me sick, I swear they do. Have those bitches forgotten how they treated me during my short stay in their house? Have they forgotten that?! No, of course, they haven't forgotten it. They haven't forgotten shit. And neither have I.

I will *never* forget it.

It's been five years since I last saw that miserable ass family of women. And much has changed in my life since then. I am now a brand new mother to my beautiful newborn son, Nathaniel, who, by the way, was named for Jordan Knight. I once told my best friend Nessa—during the fun-loving era of our late teens, in the 1980s—that if I ever gave birth to a baby boy, he would be named Nathaniel in honor of Jordan Knight, whose full name is Jordan Nathaniel Marcel Knight. I thought that was a sharp ass name, and I loved it. I loved the beauty and syllabic flow of it, and I admired the young man to whom it had been given.

A woman of my word, we're here in this present day; and baby Nathaniel is sound asleep in his lovely crib. Peace dwells, but some just can't stand the fact that it dwells with me.

Five years later, and they're *still* searching me out all over the greater Chicagoland area. And while that's saying something, I am not at all shocked by their actions. I knew all along that these days would come.
When I told them back then that these days would come, they were full of pride and tempted to disbelieve me. But now, the days are here.

On the night that I walked out of their house to head to my new residence at the Ramada Inn, Lakeshore, I had informed them that it would be a very long time before they saw me again, if ever. Poochie was full of remorse and regret about the way that she and her two daughters had allowed themselves to treat me while I was staying under their roof. Even after all these years, I can still remember the words she spoke to me on the last night of my stay there: "Cat, please don't be like that. We shouldn't be on bad terms with each other, we should be at peace," blah, blah, blah.
I swear, it took *every* molecule of my strength not to burst out laughing as I looked at her puffy ass face. And it took *every* molecule of my strength not to spit in her puffy ass face. Instead, I spared us both any further animosity by simply smiling as I looked at her puffy ass face.

I'm the last woman in the world that they should want as an enemy, but they foolishly went ahead and turned me into one anyway.

Poochie has known me nearly my entire life, but Poochie doesn't know me at all. She doesn't understand the code that I live by, which is this: I'll give you my last dollar if you need it, but once you fuck over me, especially if for no legitimate reason, I'm done with you forever. That's the code I have always lived by, and only the Lord thy God himself has the power to sway me to breach that code. And if the Spirit doesn't move me to relent, I will by no means relent.

Now am I an unforgiving person? No, not at all; I'm just not going to allow anyone to kick me twice after they've already enjoyed the pleasure of kicking me once lest my hand should be forced to inflict upon them severe harm.

When the Lord humbled me to the point of nearly being cash broke five years ago, I agreed to live in their house (after KeKe kept begging me to) for pennies on the dollar while I awaited a rent-controlled place of my own. And in due time, they gave themselves over to hardened hearts and dogged me out. And they still haven't taken responsibility for their evil actions, because they are still full of pride. They are refusing to admit their wrongs.

On the day that my son was born, Kee called *every* hospital in the city of Chicago in a desperate attempt to try and find me. I know this because she told me. And when I inquired of her as to how she came in possession of my phone number, she quickly told me that she'd gotten it from Bam, blah, blah, blah. Then I understood it. I didn't like it, but I understood it.

Bam wants to see us all make peace, I get that, but they have yet to apologize to me for their evil actions against me. Not once — in the last two weeks — have they confessed remorse for all the evil and hateful things they subjected me to during my stay as a temporary guest in their house. And I can only assume that it's because they want to believe that I have forgotten about it. But nothing could be further from the truth. I haven't forgotten about anything they did and said to me, and I never will. I wouldn't give a fuck if it's been ten years, I haven't forgotten shit.

I had left those people alone and moved on in my life. But they searched and searched until they finally found me via Bam. And now that their asses are sittin' over there in Englewood in that tired ass house contemplating their poverty and struggles, they're forced to acknowledge their reality. Now that they're in dire straits, financially, they desperately need me to assist them economically. And while they're too proud to come right out and ask, I know it's the case.

That's the *real* reason why Keeks has been seeking me out all over the city of Chicago: the Lord's wrath has hit their household hard, and the devourer is now consuming what little they had in the first place.

KeKe, the good beggar that she is, "convinced" Bam to give her my phone number, and the bitch hasn't stopped calling me since. Every day, all day, she rings my phone off the hook, not because she wants to hear the sweet and feminine husk of my voice, but because the dumb bitch is obsessed with me (as she always has been) and can't believe that I survived their asses. She can't believe I made it out, despite their many hopes that I wouldn't. But if the idiotic bitch had asked her mother, her mother would have told her that I made it because I spewed forth from a long line of hustlers and survivors, and I would have been quick to concur.

In all of my years, even since the time that I was old enough to understand, I ain't ever seen a failed hustler, or a survivor begging bread. And every man and woman on this Earth with a success story to tell can be counted among such.

While Chub and KeKe will no doubt need their mother until death — God forbid — does them part, I have been out of my mother's house since I was 20 years old, and by the grace of God, I have not had to return to it. And they know it. But that's beside the point. What they truly want to know is how I did it, what survived the cold and hard ass streets of Chicago with very little (in monetary assets) to go on. And given the opportunity, I would tell those triflin' ass bitches that I survived the toughness of our city by the grace of God. And while they struggle to buy toilet paper today, I can sit on my ass in this fancy lakefront condo and eat Maine lobster sauteed in melted butter whenever my taste buds may desire it.

Now *that's* true Karma.

I tried to be nice, even though I knew the truth, that Poochie and Chub encouraged KeKe to keep in touch with me so that they could stay abreast of what's going on in my life. Guilt is all over them like a cheap suit because they know that what they did to me all those years ago was evil. And even to this day, they're still refusing to deal with it because of the spirit called pride. But when KeKe forgot her place and spoke amiss — out of jealousy — concerning my baby, I told her not to ever call me again and hung up on that bitch. And when Chub called me back — only seconds later — to defend her shitty ass sister's honor, I eventually hung up on her bitter ass, too. But no sooner had I done so than she called back and left a nasty ass message on my voicemail when I didn't answer: "You may be doing fine now, but what comes around goes around!"

Joe howled with laughter after he listened to it. And once his laughter subsided, he put his foot down on those people from my past for good, saying that they were to never call our home again.

For what it's worth, Ol' Chub was right about two things: (1) I *am* doing fine now (thank God), and (2) what goes around does come around as is the case with their entire household.

They did what was evil to me, I didn't do what was evil to them; therefore, I can sleep peacefully at night. Because unlike them, my conscience is not seared as with a branding iron.

Love,

Cat

"Blessed Are You"

THE POEM:

They run in the sun,
Basking for fun;
But no one endears
The girl who cries from her eyes
Sorrowful tears.

Cat's Prologue:

"Blessed are you when men hate you, and when they
exclude you, and revile *you*, and cast out your name as evil,
for the Son of Man's sake."

Precious Lord? My eleven-year-old self could relate to that.

THE ENTRY:

22nd April 1982, THURSDAY
4:14 p.m.

Dear Diary,

*T*here was this pretty song on the radio today that I liked. In the song, the lady singing was saying something about choosing sides for basketball and ugly duckling girls. I didn't know the name of the song, but I liked the way it sounded and the words.

The song was so pretty that it made me wanna call the radio station to ask what it was. And I did. I called the radio station. And when the phone started ringing, I couldn't believe it, because every time I called The Loop, the phone was always busy. But when I called WLAK, the phone rang and the DJ answered after the fourth ring. At first, I was scared and thought about hanging up, but then I said "Hi" and asked him what the name of the song was that he just played. He told me that it was called "At Seventeen," and he spelled it for me. Then he told me the lady's name. And at first, it sounded like he had said the song was by Janet Eyon, but when I asked him her name again (because I was writing it down) he spelled out her name: J-a-n-i-s I-a-n. Janis Ian, pronounced "ee-in."

I thanked him and then I asked him if he could play the song again, just for me. And he said yes. He asked me what my name is, and I told him my name is Cat. And then he asked me how old I am, and I told him that I'm eleven. He was so nice. He told me that the song was coming right up and that I should wait for it. And I said okay. We said goodbye and hung up. And then I waited for the song to play again.

Before the DJ played the song, he played a recording of us talking on the phone. And I heard my voice on the radio for the first time. When the song started playing again, I started crying because it reminded me of myself. And it is my favorite song now because it's about girls like me.

In gym class today, Mr. Duschene split up our entire class into teams. All of the captains that Mr. D picked had to choose their teammates. And I hated the game because I already knew that Anna Moraine and I would end up being the last ones picked for any team. And sure enough, Anna and I were the last ones picked. Nobody likes us because we're fat. My brother always gets picked first and treated better than me because he's skinny and wears nicer clothes.

But I'm overweight. And my clothes are not the best because it's hard for mama to find nice clothes in my size.

They make fun of me every day and talk about my teeth. They said my teeth are crooked. Sometimes I cry, but I don't let anybody see me cry. I write words that rhyme with each other when people don't treat me right. I went to my room and cried. And I write when I cry. They called me fat, black and ugly, but Ms. Gerry said I'm beautiful. And Dottie said I'm pretty and the most special girl alive. Ms. Bell said I'm her pretty black girl. And I like old ladies like Ms. Bell because they take care of me.

A lotta people don't wanna fight for me, so I always fight for myself. And I always win, too. All I have to do is sit on them.

Love,

Cat

Cat's Epilogue:

Dottie once told me that I was going to be a star someday. She said, "Baby Cat, today they call you fat and ugly, but tomorrow those same folks, and then some, will call you beautiful and say that you're one of the greatest people that ever lived. Because God would have proved them wrong and shut their mouths. The Lord loves you, baby girl, and don't you ever forget it. Soar with the great abilities that He alone has given you."

I believed my Dottie. Her words would carry me over the threshold of much opposition and resistance to my own life on this Earth. For the Lord God was with me and for me then, and the Lord God is with me and for me now. Indeed, I am His very own special work. And through me, He will rebuke the proud and the ungodly in their way, that these people will know that He, and He alone, has brought me forth in honor of His earthly work, that I should glorify His holy name. Out of them all, I am Cat Ellington.

For the Lord takes the one who amounts to nothing and brings him up to something; and the one who amounts to something, the Lord brings the same down to nothing, that every tongue made by His hand shall speak in acknowledgment of His glorious dominion.

Blessed Are You.

The Sixth Stage

"The Whisperer"

THE POEM:

You needed me first,
But her tongue wagged
To divide us.
It dribbled cutting words
That left deep scars.

Cat's Prologue:

"…And a whisperer separates the best of friends."
—Proverbs 16:28

Very much like the whispering tongue of Nellie Portage, which drove a wedge between LaTisha and me.

When our close and happy friendship jeered at her lonely misery, she plotted ways to get even until she finally succeeded and won: for she couldn't wait to flaunt her "victory" before me.

THE ENTRY:

24th September 1985, TUESDAY
4:35 p.m.

Dear Diary,

What is it about me? Why do so many girls act as though they're threatened by my mere existence? Why do they pretend to hate me, when at the same time, they want everything I have, including my clothes, my shoes, my jewelry, my coats ... and my dearest friends? Why do they always want to fight me? Why do they need to use me as a barometer to prove their self-worth?

Why am I always the one to "beat"?

My mother said it's because the bitches are jealous. My godmother said it's because the bitches are jealous. My teachers at school said it's because the girls are jealous. Other people with whom I get along — like Dani Willis — said it's because they're jealous of my magnificence.

LaTisha said it's because one of the cutest boys at school told the entire student body that I look like a black Barbie doll.

"No, I don't," I told her. "I don't know why he keeps saying that," I added.

LaTisha Wallace. She was my best friend.

Tish and I live right down the street from one another. And there was a time when we were inseparable. We did nearly everything together: shopping (every weekend) at the Midway shopping center or at the Har-Mar Mall, manicures and pedicures at home (I taught Tish how to apply acrylic nails), cooking, baking, reading, hairstyling, etc. We even bought matching shoes (the red leather ones) and Safari vests, and went to school as "twins." But our bond started to come apart at the seams after Nellie Portage (the girl who lives with her parents in the little old house next door to my mother's and my place) entered the picture. Well, she didn't *enter* our lives on an invite, she *imposed* herself on us, particularly on Tish. And before long, Tish started spending more time with Nellie, time that Nellie used to backbite me in the hope of turning Tish completely against me. And she succeeded. Tish and I soon drifted apart like two lost ships at sea. Our beloved routines slowly passed away. There were no more weekend shopping sprees, or spur of the moment sleepovers, or cooking experiments that we made up as we went along (Tish's "upside-down pizza" was by far the best one of them all), or hours-long phone chats, or weekend egg facials at home, or anything else that we had always done together for that matter. The wedge that had been driven between us was the ultimate wound that, to this very day, still has not healed. And I miss her just as much as I know she misses me.

When I saw her in the hallway at school today, we were able to say a solemn hello to one another before Nellie suddenly appeared out of nowhere to whisk her away.
She loved my taupe bell-bottom pants with the back zipper at first sight, and I loved her lavender cowl neck sweater at first sight, but neither one of us said anything. Our admiration of one another kept silent, and I could feel her pain just as I knew she could feel mine. We live less than a block away from each other, yet we're worlds apart now.

It's been nearly 7 months since the last time Tish and I were close. She was destined to be my "blood sister" for life after we pricked our fingers with sewing needles and mingled our blood in her pretty bedroom one afternoon. She was also there with me on the day that I got my braces. And when my teeth and gums were so sore that I couldn't eat the day after, it was Tish who'd made warm tomato soup for me to slurp while she and my mother pigged out on Kentucky Fried Chicken. She was at the pet store with me when I bought TC, my pet guinea pig named for our first initials. And whenever I needed a good cry, it was Tish's shoulder that I cried on, and vice versa. Now she's not around to finish my sentences, and I'm not around to finish hers. Her special duckie sheets are still here at mama's and my place, and I keep them clean for her in case she ever comes back. I call her "Duckie" and she calls me "Cat Scratch."

(Tearing up)

Watching her at school today, she looked out of place sitting with Nellie and her shafted friends in the lunchroom. And when she kept stealing glances at me, I could sense that she was regretful and unhappy. Her classy finesse just didn't look right in the same space as the pathetic girl as the two of them clashed like Le Jardin and scented fabric softener sheets. And I knew that she knew she deserved better. I could feel her kicking herself internally as she was trying to figure out where she went wrong. And when I caught her eye again, I could see it watering over.

I've been wanting to call her at home, but every time I reach for the phone, I end up dropping my hand and deciding against it. Why should I call her first? She was the one who listened to Nellie Portage and her lies. She was the one who let Nellie and the rest of those jealous-hearted and angry girls tear our bond of friendship apart. She knew me better than anyone else but she still took the words of the girls who hated us over my own, because she couldn't take the peer pressure, or envy, or snide remarks. She was the one who allowed Nellie to wear her Safari vest, the one just like mine. And when I saw Nellie wearing it at school, I almost puked because it looked so ugly on her. The vest looked so miserable on her body that I wanted to rip it off of her as I hated to see her wearing it. But that was what Nellie had wanted all along. She wanted what Tish and I had. And when she couldn't get it from me, she targeted Tish. But it won't make her feel any better, she'll still be the same hopeless and unattractive girl that she is – just like all of those other hateful girls. And she'll still dislike herself intensely – just like all of those other hateful girls. She can wear Tish's entire wardrobe and it still won't do her any good. Because she will never have the same confidence, finesse, or sense of style that Tish has. She and those other girls will never be Tish. She and they will never be me either.

The phone in the living room just rang twice. And it's Tish calling, I can *feel* it. My mother's voice: "Cat, it's Duckie on the phone!"
See, what did I tell you? "Okay, mama. Tell her to hold on a minute," I say back.

In the good ol' days, Tish and I will be boiling water for our instant Sanka around this time. We would always come home after school to make our instant coffee and watch *Magnum, P.I.* I think she wants to make up now, but we're so broken I don't know if we can ever be fixed. Maybe our Mamas can glue us back together again piece by piece.

I need to go and see what she wants. Signing off.

Love,

Cat

Cat's Epilogue:

Tish and I talked for close to an hour that day, but our conversation bordered on awkward the whole way through. We tried to catch up on everything that we'd missed during our separation, but we seemed to be running in place. As we chuckled through our words, things just didn't feel the same anymore, and we only made enough peace to chip away a little bit of ice that was wedged between us. Whenever I saw her at school, we'd say a few words but nothing ever progressed. And while we both wondered where our former bond of friendship could've gone, neither one of us knew for sure. We did know that it had been stolen from us, but we were never able to find it again; therefore, we drifted apart for good, with her going west and me going east. And over time, we both forgave but never forgot.

LaTisha Wallace has always been one of my nearest and dearest friends, and I will always love her; but I will never forget how our close-knit bond was laid waste by those who hated us. I say that because not long after Tish and I parted ways, Nellie's and her association also came to an end. And it pained me that Tish didn't listen when I tried to tell her about the true intentions of Nellie Portage. I had not been "jealous" as some of those girls accused me of being (because I'm not the jealous type), I had only been suspicious of those who meant to do us harm.

I learned a lot from what happened between Tish and me. And I will fight tooth and nail to never allow the same thing to happen again. True friendship is all I've ever had to offer, and I will never allow anything or anyone to undermine my loyalty again.

To cherish every day of life is wisdom, and to nurture that life is understanding. Because the next second, minute, hour, day, week, month, or year is not promised to any of us;

therefore, I've learned not to take anyone in my life for granted ever again, and to love them just a little bit more.

"The Bitch Called Karma"

THE POEM:

The hand that guides me?
It's the same hand
That has crushed you.
Now you cry and wish to die,
But death eludes.

Cat's Prologue:

"Do not rejoice when your enemy falls, and do not let your
heart be glad when he stumbles;
Lest the Lord see *it*, and it displeases Him, and He turn away
His wrath from him."

—Proverbs 24:17-18

I was tempted to gloat over the downfall of Dr. Matthew
Simon, but I was wisely advised to refrain myself lest I
should have become as wicked as he had been, and the Lord
punished me instead.

I'm one of those types of people who love to see the wicked
get back what they put out. And there is absolutely nothing
wrong with that. The Lord doesn't hold a passion for truth
and justice against anyone. Even the angel of the Lord said:
"They deserve it." And that's the truth.
But what the Lord doesn't want us doing is laughing and
cackling at the misfortunes and punishments of those who
had allowed themselves to do evil to us. Because they were
tempted to sin against their own souls. And once His terrible
wrath befalls them, He will never take it off of them unless
they repent. And once they do, He will still repay them, that
the people should know that God is not a respecter of
persons and that He shows favoritism to no one.
He will right the wrong by allowing another person —
who's just as evil and hateful as themselves — to do the
same to them as they had been tempted to do to someone
else, but worse.
Trust that it's always worse when it comes back around
because that's the nature of a boomerang. And while some
people learn from their mistakes, others don't, unfortunately.

THE ENTRY:

6th May 2015, WEDNESDAY

Dear Diary,

My eyes weren't failing me, it was him. Dr. Matthew Simon, my mother's and my former landlord from 30 years ago. A thought entered my mind earlier today to search for his name on the Internet. And when I did, bam! His face, age-progressed, yes, but still his nonetheless; and his unforgettable eyes, still as sinister-looking as ever. But most importantly, there was his name, linked with his former profession. He was spot on. No further proof was required to know that it was him. And when I commenced reading the detailed article about him that had been plastered on the pages of a major Twin Cities media publication, I soon came to realize that the Lord God didn't forget about Matthew Simon. The Lord had moved to strike the depraved and perverse man down while the human still had the vegan kibble in his throat.

Not only did he serve a long jail sentence — after having been found guilty of countless crimes against both man and beast — but he also had his medical license revoked permanently.
While that's only half of it, the article was enough to satisfy my insatiable desire for justice: for what the terrible man named Matthew Simon had sowed, that he also reaped.

Love,

Cat

Cat's Epilogue

After reading the shocking news about the great downfall of the former doctor Matthew Simon, it took me a few minutes to gather myself before I called my mother to share it with her. And after close to ten seconds of silence, she finally spoke, saying, "He was the landlord from Hell. And I was so glad when we got away from him."
I replied, "I was too, mama. I was too."

For mama had long forgotten about Matthew Simon; but then again, she had never forgotten about Matthew Simon. And neither had I.

"Looks Can Be Deceiving"

THE POEM:

A destitute man
Who is in need
Received the scorn
From those in society.
So they treat God.

Cat's Prologue:

Since the time that I was old enough to remember, my
mother had never ceased to share with me the following
wisdom: "Always watch how you treat people because you
never know how God is coming. He can come in the form

of a baby, or a homeless person, or an elderly person, or a small child, or a handicapped person, or a person of a different race, or even as a perfectly healthy person. He can come in any form just to test people, to see how they treat others. And they'll have a lot to answer to Him for if they're on His Earth doing evil and lowdown things to other people."

And I always said "Amen."

THE ENTRY:

17th June 1989, SATURDAY
2:18 p.m.

Dear Diary,

On my way home from work today, I saw an old black man going through the big dumpster outside in the parking lot. He had been looking for cans to collect so that he could cash them in for money. And when I looked at the old man, I loved him on sight because he was worthy of love and not of scorn. Despite his being at a disadvantage in society, he was still worthy of love.

I changed course to go over to where he was at the dumpster, intending to help him in any way I could. And once I got close enough to him, the first thing I noticed was the smell of his clothes, which smelled as though he'd slept in a puddle of sewer water the night before and they had yet to dry completely. But it didn't bother me one iota, I just wanted to be a blessing to him.

He was preoccupied with his search for empty cans when I said "Hello." The older man looked up from what he was doing and just gazed at me for a few seconds with wandering eyes. His hair was steel gray, and his skin was a hue of buttery caramel. And when I looked into his eyes, I could see a sharp awareness in them; nevertheless, he remained silent. I handed him all the cash I had on me at that moment, $5.00, and told him to take it. At first, he looked at me skeptically, as though I were trying to trick him or something. But I assured him that I had not been playing any game, I just wanted him to have the money because he needed it more. And he took it with gratitude. Then he smiled at me and said "Thank you," to which I replied, "You're welcome."
As I turned to walk away, I said to him, "God bless you, and be careful." And he just glanced at me and continued on in his search for cans.

I came inside to get some more money for him, but by the time I went back outside to where he had been at the dumpster, he was gone. And I was disappointed because I wanted to give him another $100.00. Damn. I wanted to give him more than $5.00, but that was all the cash I had on me when I saw him. Shit. Damn.

I came back inside, took off my outside clothes, put on my house clothes, got a pot of coffee goin', and sat down to relax while it brewed. I kept looking out of my bedroom window to see if he came back, but he never did. And that sucks because I would have loved to give him this hundred dollar bill on my nightstand.

As I sit here writing and listening to "Wild, Wild West" by Escape Club on WLOL, I wonder to myself if he was the Lord in disguise. Because he disappeared too fast. I looked up and asked the Lord, "Lord, was that you? Was that old man your Angel in disguise? Because if so, it was nice to meet you, my Lord. And I love you."

Great things have been happening for me (and to me) all day. So I'll say the Lord is pleased.

Love,

Cat

Cat's Epilogue

While I entertained myself with the thought, I can't say that the old man to whom I had given the money was the Lord in disguise or not. But what I do know is that God is good and that it pays to do unto others as you would have them do unto you.
Because after all, you never know.

"Talkin' 'Bout My Generation X"

THE POEM:

Nineteen-seventy,
My first year here.
We'd so much fun
In the Park named Washington;
But now it's gone.

THE ENTRY:

16th April 1993, FRIDAY

5:38 p.m.

Dear Diary,

*N*ostalgia. I'm overcome with it right now, thanks to First Choice. The all-girl trio is on V103 right now singing "Dr. Love" as I write this entry. And man, does it still sound good, even after all these years. One of my favorite songs of all time, "Dr. Love" is a classic of which I will never, ever get tired. I swear, I could listen to this recording all day.

Rochelle Fleming is passionate about her conviction that the subject of her desire can kill her every pain and make her well again. And every time I hear her recorded witness set to such a beautiful melody, it takes me way back to when I first heard it: 1977.

I can remember it as if it were only yesterday…

My entire family and I were all living on 53rd and Calumet on Chicago's South Side. Well, my Mama, my big brother Ray, and I all lived on 53rd and Calumet in a Courtway; but my other relatives (my aunties and my cousins and 'em) lived right around the corner (or as Pappy likes to say, "da kawna") from us on 53rd and Prairie. They lived in a white brownstone right next to the Green Line El tracks. We loved it because we were all together, living near one another. Back then, all the kids went to Burke Elementary on 53rd and King Drive. And I loved attending Burke because they used to let us go home for lunch and then return to resume class once lunch was over. And honestly, I never wanted that time in my life to end. I wanted it to stay the way it was forever and ever, because we were having so much fun. We stuck together because we were all we had.

One of our friends, Drew Baby, had a little dog named Smokey whom we all loved. And whenever any of us had Oscar Mayer Smokie Links for dinner, we would playfully tease Drew that we were having Smokey for dinner, and she would just smile or cackle with laughter. And because all of our parents hung out on "the Lot," which was basically a huge parking lot paved with dirt in front of the East Courtway (we lived in the West Courtway), we kids were able to stay out as late as we wanted on weekends, or until we got sleepy. And during the summer months, when school was out, we really had a ball.

Every year, my Mama and her remarkably enterprising boyfriend Big Jimmie would go to Moo & Oink and buy tons of ribs, hot links, polish sausages, chicken, beef patties, and hot dogs to sell at the Bud Billiken Parade. And every year, they were highly successful in their ventures. They spent money to make money. And I admired them to the furthest extent. I used to just sit at the kitchen table and watch my Mama as she seasoned all of her meat up real good and packed it in protective plastic to marinate in the refrigerator overnight, the night before the Bud. Then she would pull out our huge cooler and fill it up with ice cubes and cans of pop so that the drinks would be icy cold in the morning and ready for the beloved parade. She was the queen of organization, my Mama, and she had a keen mind for business. She knew exactly what she was doing and I admired her, as did many others who knew her. She was pretty, witty, smart, and fun-loving; and she took care of business and had everything prepped: the Jay's Potato Chips and stuff were ready, the "tayta salad" was ready and in the fridge chillin', the coleslaw was ready and in the fridge chillin', the condiments were neatly organized in their containers and ready, the hot dog buns and hamburger buns were ready, the kitchen was cleaned up, my Mama's cigarette was lit and ready to be smoked by her, her cold beer was ready for her to drink, and she was done until Parade day.

I knew that she and Big Jimmie would be up bright and early the next morning waking my brother and I up to get ready. Because they had this system where they wanted to be among the first to get out there on King Drive (which was only one street over from us) and find "a good spot." They were ALWAYS blessed to find one. Things always worked out perfectly, every year. By the time the last float cruised by, we had made hundreds of dollars in profits.

(Laughing in a spirit of indescribable love)

Free enterprise, baby! Free enterprise.

(Still laughing)

God, I love my people. I truly do, I love my people.

We had a friend named Gloria to whom we all used to sing the old Enchantment song of the same name. Every time the song came on, we would all gather around Glo and start singing it to her just to make her blush, because she was so shy. We would all sing along calling her "Our Gloria," and

telling her how things ain't been the same since she went
away...

(Smiling and teary-eyed)

Good times. Good times.

Back then, we took care of each other. All of the adults
looked out for one another's children. And if any adult got
too tipsy to take care of business at home, their kids would
spend the night at a friend's house. That was how it had
been all those years ago. We had a sense of community,
despite what had been going on in the world around us. And
we had hope. We had great music and we had great times
full of joy and laughter. We had self-love and we had true
love from our neighbors. We had black love in and of itself,
and we had a sense of security in that strong, cultural bond.

On some days, we ate Bologna and cheese sandwiches like
they were surf 'n' turf because they were made with love ...
and just the right amount of Miracle Whip. There were days
when we ate as much steak as we wanted, and then there
were other days when mama would make a big pot of Lima
Beans and ham hocks with a cast iron skillet of perfectly
baked cornbread that had been just as good. And we were at
peace because the Lord's peace was there with us.
We would have fights and arguments one day, and be right
back to our rightful places as friends and lovers the next day,
living and loving in harmony, cherishing every day. Now
was there evil in existence? Yes, there was, but it didn't
hinder us because we had too much faith. The older folks
had passed it on down to the younger folks, and our hope in

our Lord and our God sustained us. But despite it all, none of us could foresee the lost generation that would one day succeed our own: for it would be a faithless, demonic, and perverse generation.

To this day, they spit on the legacy of those who came before them. And theirs is a hardened heart loaded down with bitterness. They're a proud and rebellious lot that scoff at the builders and speak well of the self-destructive. And they make me sick.

One day we'll find that old peace that we lost as a people of one heart, one mind, and one body. One day our children will again be free to stay out late and play for as long as they like without having to fear stray bullets ("with no names"), or the destroyer that does not come except to stir up strife and chaos in our communities. One day, by the grace of God, we, as a people, will be made whole again.

Love,

Cat

"Amazon Women on the Earth"

THE POEM:

The "trees" stand up tall:
They look far down
From their great heights
Into the valleys below,
To eclipse them.

THE ENTRY:

14th August 1991, WEDNESDAY
9:29 p.m.

Dear Diary,

*T*he son of one of Chicago's most notorious gang chieftains
fosters a hapless infatuation with me. I know he's the
chieftain's son because Chub told me so. She said, "Girl,
you didn't know? Girl, shiiid, errbody know."
And I was like, "Hmph. No wonder he gets treated like
royalty around these parts."

The young man in question is a light-complected dude with
large eyes. And every time he sees me, even if I'm across the
street from him, he yells out in my direction,
"Am-a-zonnnnn!" I swear, he says it every time he sees me:
"Am-a-zonnnnn!"

This dude is much shorter than me (5'7", if that), and has a
strong craving for my attention. And I tend to satisfy him
with a spoonful of it by way of a friendly smile from time to
time.
Now, while I'll admit that his playful teasing about my
height (5'11") initially got on my nerves — because I
thought it was childish — as time passed, I got used to it.
And when I continued to only smile at him in response (for I
didn't find him worthy of my verbal communication), it only
worsened his silly ass aggression. He now ventures into my
personal space to get his desperate fix: "Am-a-zonnnnn!"
That's right, he says it straight to my face now. And because
I find him to be rather silly and childish, my simple smiles
have now advanced to full-blown outbursts of laughter. I can
tell that it throws him off, and it should. My laughter has him
puzzled and he can't figure out why. He doesn't understand

that I'm laughing because I can now see him for who he truly is up close, whereas when he had been at a distance, all I could see were his big ass eyes.

While he's indeed hilarious, he has also been exposed for what he truly is: a young man with an infatuation hiding behind a thugged-out pedigree.

God bless him.

(Pausing to take a drag on my cigarette)

I will say this though, that he looks exactly like his daddy. I saw his daddy's picture in the *Sun-Times*, and that negro looks just like him. Seriously, he is the spit of his old man.

(Chuckling)

Just the other day, I had to tell his silly ass that I was too tall to be his "Queen."

(Smiling now)

When I saw him in Tiger's Food & Liquors earlier today (I walked down there to get my cigarettes, some oat bran muffins, and a pack of Dentyne), he rushed up in my face with that Amazon shit. And when I didn't acknowledge his shawty ass, he started talkin' a whole lotta shit, sayin', "Aye girl, if somebody down here fuckin' witchu don't run tell me, 'cause I ain't gon' do shit about it," blah, blah, blah. And that was when I came out of my so-called "prim-and-proper" shell on his ass and decided to speak his language, replying, "Yes, you will, nigga. If I'm down here being fucked wit' and you hear about it, you gon' make sho you and yours get their ass off me. 'Cause you know I don't fuck wit' nobody. If I can't help 'em, I ain't gon' do nothin' to hurt 'em. You know dat. Plus, you luh dis Amazon woman, don'tcha?" And all lil' his ass could do was smile because he knew I was telling the truth. After that, he threw the term *sidity* in my face again, saying, "Hell yeah, Amazon. You know you kyna sidity an' shit, but chu mah girl, tho." Now serious in tone, he asked me, "Aye, somebody down here fuckin' witchu?" I smiled and told him "No" just to keep the peace around here.

We shit-talked one another a few minutes more, and then he offered to pay for my Virginia Slim's, muffins, and Dentyne, which I accepted. After that, I went my way and he went his. But as I was walking away, he called out to me and said, "Aye, Amazon? Aye, if muhfuckas down here fuckin' witchu, come tell a nigga, aight?" And I nodded my head and said "Okay."
Looking at Prince Shawty (Yeah, I gotta moniker for his ass, too), my heart fluttered with love for him, not in an intimate sense but a platonic sense. And I said a silent prayer to the Lord to always watch over him.
If we both shall be allowed to live until our heads are snow-covered in gray, I bet Prince Shawty will still be calling me "Amazon." And you wanna know somethin', dear Diary? I'm aight wit' dat.

(Smiles)

Yes, I'm statuesque, but so are all of my girls. All of my girls are tall like me: Yoli, Bam, LayLay, Rizz, and Pumpkin. Prince Shawty just hasn't met any of them yet. But if he ever does, his ass may just start doing cartwheels because Bam is 6'1 alone.

(Laughs)

You're damn right, we're Amazons. We stand out. Everywhere we go, we get noticed, baby. And them lil' short ass negroes are always tryna fuck wit' us when they see us together on the Low End, 49th, and 63rd - calling us all kinds o' "Amazons" and "trees" an' shit.

(Laughs)

But you wanna know something, dear Diary? We know they love us, and we know that they would defend our honor in a heartbeat. So it's all groovy. We love them, too.

Once upon a time, I used to feel so self-conscious about my height, especially when I was a younger girl because I was tall for my age. But that all changed in junior high when my violin instructor (Mrs. Magowski, God bless her heart) told me that "All models are tall," after I initially refused to stand before the class out of fear that the other kids would tease me about my height.
Encouraged by her words, I stood up and I stood tall. And the kids didn't tease me at all. In fact, their reactions were the complete opposite of what my fears had told me they would be. Surprisingly, Jermaine wanted to take me out on a date.

(Smiling)

Tish told me that after I stood up to play, she heard him say,
"Ooh, look at that body."

(Still Smiling)

I had lost all of the old weight and was left with a cute lil'
figure eight.

(Still smiling)

From that day forth, many beautiful men and women entered
my life speaking a variety of encouraging words to me about
the blessedness of statuesqueness. And I was inclined to
both believe and rejoice in every word they spoke, including
those of my beloved Greg (6'3" himself) when he told me
that "All of God's angels are tall like us."

(Chuckling)

It doesn't get any better than that, baby!

All you tall girls? Stand up straight!

(Laughs)

Amazon women are a beautiful race.

Love,

Cat

"For Old Times' Sake"

THE POEM:

The Night Rider yelled,
"Baby Golden!"
His car went deaf
As Sabastian Bach screamed out
Into the night.

THE ENTRY:

19th August 1989, SATURDAY
9:56 a.m.

Dear Diary,

*N*o sooner had I left Target on University Avenue and proceeded to walk home last night than I heard Sabastian Bach singing the first verse of Skid Row's "18 And Life." The heavy metal hit had initially sounded muffled as it blasted from the interior of some vehicle that had its windows rolled up. But as the car in question slowed down alongside me, the driver rolled down his or her passenger side window and the music suddenly sounded crystal clear. I didn't turn to my left to acknowledge the car traveling East on University Avenue, I just kept on walking. But then the music's volume lowered and I heard his unforgettable voice as it spoke to me: "Hey, Baby Golden! Where you goin'?!" Instinctively, I smiled and then turned to my left to take him in. He was the great Terry Salerno sitting behind the wheel of his legendary Batmobile.

His eyes darted back and forth from me to the road, from the road to me. When I said that I was headed home, he told me to get in, automatically unlocking the passenger side door. I hurried over to hop into the passenger seat, closing and locking the door behind me, placing my Target purchases (four jars of Revlon's New Age Naturals Buttermilk and Honey rinsable cold cream, one bag of Brach's Butterscotch, a pair of fluffy house slippers, a canister of Hills Bros. Coffee, and a new sleep mask) on the back seat, and putting on my seat belt to settle in. Returning the volume on the stereo system to its original level and giving me a quick kiss hello, Terry checked his mirrors and eased us away from the curb and onto the road.

Sabastian Bach was now repeating the chorus after the second verse, telling Ricky, the hard-hearted 18-year-old subject of the tune, that his committed crime had brought upon him a life sentence.

Terry got us situated in the Friday night traffic, then asked me over the music, "So what's up, baby?"
"Nothing," I answered. "Just left Target and was on my way home when you pulled up," I added.
"Come on, baby, it's a Friday night, too early for you to go home," he decided.
"So where to then?" I asked.
"Anywhere but home, Goldy. Wanna just cruise around the city with me for a little while?" He asked playfully.
"Sure, why not, Night Rider," I quipped back.
He smiled and tapped the tip of my nose with his right index finger, saying, "That's my Baby Golden." And the next thing I knew, we were cruising towards Wayzata.

He played "18 And Life" again and then put on Motley Crue's "Live Wire," one of my favorite heavy metal tunes of all time. I sat back in my seat fully relaxed.
He turned down the volume just a touch and we broke into a conversation about some of everything and everybody. And when I told him that I'd seen Jakie Goss yesterday in the Midway Center while I was there at Big Top Liquors buying cheese and Riesling, he exploded: "That oily sonofabitch! I hate that motherfucker, Goldy! What the fuck was he doing there?"

I told him that Jakie was in Big Top with Scott Mankowski buying six-packs and vodka for some get-together they were having at Ted Overacker's house.

"Hmph," Terry mumbled. I laughed in response.

I asked Ter if he had "For Those About to Rock" in the car. And when he answered and said, "Hell yeah! I got it right here just for you, Baby Goldy," I asked him to put on "Breaking the Rules" for me.

While yet another one of my all-time favorite recordings in the Heavy Metal genre began to play on the Batmobile's dynamic stereo system, I gazed out of my window at the beautiful lights of the city at night, bobbing my head in sync with the rhythm of the metal masterpiece and mouthing the lyrics. I was caught up in the exceptional music coming out of the speakers when I heard Terry's voice say, "What's on that mind of yours, good lookin'?"

"Nothin', baby Rider," I answered. "Just enjoyin' this moment," I added.

The night was so beautiful, dear Diary, as were this row of townhomes that I scoped while we cruised the road of an overpass. I said to Terry, "Ooh, look at those townhouses over there. They are so beautiful."

"Yep, they sure are, cutie," he replied. Then added, "You want one of those?" Laughing, I asked, "Why, you gonna buy us one?" He then looked over his right shoulder while putting on his right signal and said, "Hell yeah, if you want one. We can shack up, settle down, have a whole bunch of beautiful ass mulatto kids, and fuck the rest of our lives away." I exploded in laughter and then said, "Nah, no house.

A house will be too much work. I'll take a loft, though."
And he replied, "Okay, sexy lady, you got it." We both
laughed in unison.

My head continued to bob to the magnificent melody of
"Breaking The Rules" as the song started to wind down. I
swear, I could listen to "Breaking The Rules" for the rest of
my life and never, ever tire of it. Beautiful ass song. Perfectly
composed!

After Ter played "Electric Eye" by Judas Priest for me, we
jumped right back into our conversation about some of
everything as the Batmobile cruised around Lake
Minnetonka. And by the time we hit the highway to head
back home, my stomach was in knots from all the laughter
Terry had me in during our makeshift road trip. By now, we
had KQ-92 on the FM dial spittin' out Thin Lizzy's
"Jailbreak," which sounded so good in the late-night hours. I
wanted to call KQ to request that it be played again, but I
didn't. I just fell right into Deep Purple's "Smoke On The
Water" after it went off.

When I got in, it was exactly 1:27 a.m. That was according
to my digital bedside clock. And nowhere near sleepy yet, I
prepared to run a bubble bath and just kick back with some
more music until my body told me to wrap it up. With my
radio tuned into KDWB-FM, the last song I can remember
hearing before my eyelids closed and I headed off to
dreamland was "The Living Years" by Mike + The
Mechanics. And when I woke up this morning, I awoke to
the jumpin' rhythm of Bobby Brown's "My Prerogative."

Though we're not too much of an item anymore, Terry and I spent over four hours cruising in the Batmobile and talkin' shit for old times' sake. And I enjoyed myself with him as always. We stopped at this restaurant called Gram's Kitchen for a quick bite to eat, then we got back on the road for more nighttime sightseeing, sealing another great moment in time.

I turned my phone's ringer back on this morning, and already it's Grand Central Station. Ooh, it's Nessa. Hang on, dear Diary.

(Pausing to answer the phone)

One minute later.

(Resuming in laughter)

It's my girl, dear Diary. She went out with that idiotic ass Daryl Banks last night and wants to give me the scoop on what happened.

(Laughs)

And if you know me, then you know I have to hear this shit.

(Still laughing)

Ol' Nessa, about to give me another reason to detest that triflin' bastard.

(More laughs)

Oh well, it's the least she could do on this groovy Saturday mawnin'.

(Smiling)

I can't stand Daryl's ass and he can't stand mine. That makes us about even-steven. Still, I'll hear my girl out. And then I'll eat whatever it is my lovely mother is cooking downstairs. Mmm... It smells so delicious. Until next time, dear Diary?

Cat ciao!

Love,

Cat

The Seventh Stage

"The Artist and His Subject (My First Lover)"

THE POEM:

The Wiz sketched my face,
Etched is my body.
In the warmth of his embrace,
I floated up,
High above life.

THE ENTRY:

Dear Diary,

*T*hree months ago, Corey Weatherspoon (a.k.a. the Wiz) asked me to be his girlfriend. And at first I thought he was playing, but he wasn't. He asked me right in front of Bo and Juicy and I felt kind of embarrassed. I'm shy for a lot of reasons, but especially because of my weight. Mama put me on this special diet where all I eat for breakfast and lunch are salads and grapefruits. And I hate both of them, but my Mama says I have to eat them because they're healthy and good for me.

They're not that bad (because mama dresses them up real nice), they're just not my favorites. I haven't been able to eat Moo & Oink sausage pizza, or Steak on the Buns from Jits, or Lorna Doones, or Nutter Butters, or nothin'. I've just been eating walnuts, salads, and grapefruits mostly – oh, and salted popcorn with no butter. And I've been walking a lot. Mama took me to my doctor's appointment on Wednesday, and when I got on the scale they told mama that I had lost 22 pounds. They checked my height, too, and told mama that I'm five feet eight. People always say I'm tall for my age, but I'm not the only one. Some of my girlfriends are tall for their ages, too. Yoli is tall like me, and so are Anna Moraine, Gigi, Niecy, and LayLay. We're all tall. And we like each other.

I can hear the music coming from the stereo in the front room. And right now Luther is on WGCI singing "You Stopped Loving Me." I love that song. It's gon' still be playin' in my head when it goes off. Watch. I'm gonna still be hearin' it. I should go in there and ask mama if she can play the whole *Never Too Much* album, but I don't feel like getting up. I just want to keep writing. I love writing so much, that when I start, it's hard for me to stop.

Anyway, Wiz and I are going together now. And when my best friend Bo (Bo is a boy) told me not to tell my Mama about it, I asked him why. He said it's because Wiz is 18 and mama wouldn't like it. So I haven't told her. I hope she doesn't find out. I like the Wiz because he likes me for who I am. He doesn't care about my weight, he just thinks I'm pretty regardless of it. And I think he's cute, too. Tammy and 'em be callin' Wiz four-eyed and stuff because he wears glasses like "Raj" on *What's Happening!!* But that only makes me like him more.

We call him Wiz (and he calls me "Piggy") because he's smart and he can draw. Wiz can draw his butt off. And he drew me today. He's the first person who has ever sketched me on paper. And I got to see how I look in a drawing. He drew my body, too, and told me that I looked good. And I couldn't stop looking at the drawing because it fascinated me. I have always liked people who can draw because I can't. I like the way Wiz draws.
We're gonna last forever, me and the Wiz. We're gonna make history as the "King and Queen of the Ickes." And he'll draw me forever. He called me his subject, then he told me what that meant after I asked him. He told me that he's

gonna paint me all over the lonely walls, and I'll be the Mona Lisa to his Leonardo. After I asked him who he was talking about, he pulled out his book and showed me the man. And I wrote down his name: Leonardo Di Vinci. And then he showed me the woman he had been talking about and I wrote her name, too: Mona Lisa. At first, I thought the man's name was pronounced *Die Vincy* and her name, *Manalease*. But after Wiz told me how to pronounce them, I caught on and will never forget it. Wiz said the painting of the lady is famous. And he spent the afternoon teaching me about art.

After that, I sat in his lap and we started kissing. I'm a good kisser because I taught myself how to kiss using my arm. And I shocked him. He's older than me, but he was shocked by how good of a kisser I am. We kept kissing, and then the next thing I knew, he was asking me if I wanted to do it. And when I told him yeah, he took me to another dimension.

The Wiz popped my cherry today. I felt a lot of pain at first, but then it went away and I started floating through the universe on my way to Heaven. It was a feeling that I've never felt before, and I liked it. I wanted to keep floating forever and ever. I floated way up to the clouds and the clouds formed like smiling faces to greet me. The stars twinkled and winked at me, and then I saw galaxies exploding, bursting out particles of glitter that blew into my eyes. It was like I was doing flips in the air, turning over and over like the Zipper at the carnival. And after I stopped doing flips, I started falling real slow back down to the soft ground below. I was like a feather, light as air and delicate, landing on a mattress. And then I was back in the real world.

I laid in Wiz's arms wrapped around him like a shawl. And he held me like a baby, *his* baby, asking me (in a breathy voice) how it felt and if I was alright. I told him that it was good and that I was alright. But when I said the word *alright*, I sounded like my Mama when she's drunk. Wiz kissed my face then. And his kisses felt like warm, wet feathers being blown against my cheeks by a gentle wind. We were quiet, just breathing. And when Wiz spoke again, he told me that my pussy is good and that I'm his Piggybaby and shawty fo' life.

I nodded my head in agreement and our bond was sealed. He also told me that I was loud and that I made a lot of noise. But while I was floating, I couldn't hear myself.

We have a date tomorrow, me and the Wiz. He wants to paint Big-Head Ced on the wall under the viaduct. He asked me to go with him so that I could watch. We saw Big-Head Ced smokin' a joint on the first floor today, and Wiz wants to paint Big Head's image with the joint in his mouth from memory.

My Mama always says that niggas like Ced look like the projects, meaning you can tell they live in the projects. But I don't blame Wiz for wanting to paint him, because Ced did look too cold with the joint.

Ooh, mama's calling me because dinner is ready. Mama made beef stew, a big pot of white rice, and corn muffins. And it smells so good.

I still feel sore, but I'll try to walk normally.

403

I would tell Pumpkin and 'em about me and Wiz, but they might end up runnin' their mouths. Pumpkin is always talking about boys and men with big dicks, and I know she would trip if I told her how big Wiz's dick is. It's *big*.

Oh, I gotta go. Time to eat.

Love,

Cat

"The Low-End Legends"

THE POEM

At twenty-second
And Cermak road —
Where State Street meets —
Once upon a grand ol' time,
We wore our silk.

Cat's Prologue:

I remember us and I'll always remember us. Time has passed, but our history remains. We had it all in terms of each other and we made it. Through many seasons, we made

it. Through many struggles, we made it. Through many battles, we made it. And through strength and unification, we made it.
We stood strong through much opposition, and by the grace of God, many of us are still here.

Countless numbers of people in Chicago were tempted to glance upon us with contempt, calling us a bunch of "broke and worthless niggers living on top of each other." But despite their hatred toward us, the Lord put praise for His holy name on our lips, jokes and laughter in our mouths, love and self-love in our spirits, pride in our culture, desire in our loins for one another, understanding and empathy for the trial we all shared, unmatchable talents in our physical beings, and survival in our souls. For He did not allow our spirits to be broken in the cesspools of segregation, racism, malice, bitterness, anger, corruption, spite, and injustice; but His hand showed mercy upon us and blessed us to retain hope, even when we were under assault by both physical and spiritual forces in the evil world system.

We're still here. And we're still here because of Him.

When they brought in their bulldozers to destroy our weakest by way of displacement, they failed to destroy everyone: for those who had fallen by the edge of their dull sword had given up anyway, but the Lord didn't allow everybody to perish.
He used their wicked deeds as a tool to strengthen our faith in Him lest we lose our way and forget about our Lord and our God. And though we were targeted to be scattered

abroad, we remained whole as one solid fabric. And we're still here.

Those who dish out evil can never take it in return. And the world will be allowed to look upon their misery when the time comes for His hand to scatter their bones and destroy their places of dwelling.

Someone once said to me, "The weak hate the strong; Hyenas hate lions." And to that, I said "Amen!"

I've heard some spectacular quotes in my time, but that particular quote was by far one of the greatest of them all.

Truth. I love it.

THE ENTRY:

22nd October 2009, THURSDAY
8:05 p.m.

Dear Diary,

On Chicago's South Side, where the Raymond Hilliard Homes met Harold L. Ickes Homes, that was the Low End, baby. Right there on 22nd and South State Street at Cermak Road? That was the Low End, baby. And it was where we dwelled. Indeed, it was where we partied and raised hell.

It was where we played softball in the big field in front of 2233 S. Federal every summer. It was where we stayed out late in the same season, playing Hide & Seek and Four Corners. It was where we made war and amends.

It was an area we all called the Low End.

It was where we barbecued and screwed in the nude. That's where we blasted the sprinklers outside of 2320 and lit up the twinklers behind 2240. It was where we skated every Friday night at the Henry Booth House behind 2330. It was where we bought ice cups and penny candy in every building that had a Candy Lady. It was where we made war and amends.

It was an area we all called the Low End.

It was where we bought snowballs on every corner during the summer months. It was where we bought our Chick-O-Sticks, Jungle Jollies, and Big Bols on the rolls. It was where we put skinny peppermint sticks in our large sour pickles and tried to make 'em last all day. It was where we bought all our drinks and snacks at ChaSues Liquors around the way. It was where we made war and amends.

It was an area we all called the Low End.

It was where we jumped Double Dutch like champions and played Backgammon like masters. It was where we sat out on the front porch of 2233 and played Jacks provided by the "pastors." It was where my girlfriends and I took all of the rubber bands that had been intended for use on our hair and connected them to make Chinese Jump Ropes. It was where we frequently happened upon the lawless in-crowds drinkin' Colt 45 and smokin' all manner of dope. It was where we made war and amends.

It was an area we all called the Low End.

It was where we cleaned out the 23rd street viaduct real good before turning on the fire hydrant at full blast to play in the water and make our swimming pools every hot summer.

It was where we referred to every building in the development by only its number. It was where we lit up firecrackers, sparklers, snakes, smoke bombs, and M-80s right out in the big field every fourth of July. It was where we would sometimes sneak in and out of one another's apartments on the sly. It was where we made war and amends.

It was an area we all called the Low End.

It was where we heard the Ickes Angels shouting out "Right on, right on, Ickes Angels! Right on, right on, let's go!" This is where we lost a few folks but gained a few mo'. It was where all the kids could hear their daddies or their mamas calling out from the windows and telling them to come in the house when it got too dark outside. It was where we played hopscotch and rode our bikes from one end of the big field down to the other side. It was where we made war and amends.

It was an area we all called the Low End.

It was where we took modern dance classes in the Henry Booth House, or just lounged around in the rec room on the couch. It was where we came together in the offices of Ickes Cadre in search of a more productive and brighter day. It was where we made war and amends.

It was an area we all called the Low End.

It was where many strangers became friends.

It was an area we all called the Low End.

Love,

Cat

P.S. We had Jits, Leon's, Catfish Digby's, and Soul Queen.
We also had BC's on South Michigan Avenue, and the ice
cream parlor on the SE corner of Cermak Road at Wabash
where we bought our hoagies. Sometimes we would watch
the Dan Ryan El trains speeding North and South along the
tracks until we got tired of countin' 'em. And we would sit
in the Pavilion in the Hilliards crackin' jokes and eatin' our
zesty Cheetos while we planned our futures. We had music
— fun, loud, and dominant, like the people it served —
traveling through the Ickes development every weekend.
And we enjoyed every single soundtrack. Every Friday or
Saturday night, somebody in either the Hilliards or the Ickes
(or both) threw a set, and my brother was always in
attendance at every one of them. And if the sets weren't
happening in one of the developments, they were happening
at The Playground, a popular nightclub for young folks on
South Michigan Avenue. My big brother attended every one
of those, too. In Chicago, we don't call 'em "house parties,"
we call 'em "sets;" nevertheless, they are all the same. And
of our dwelling places and various forms of entertainment,
we had never been ashamed.

Remember who we are.
We are the Low-End Legends. And to this day, we are
without equals.

Get it, Jossie!

Love,

Cat

Cat's Prologue

I love(d) my people. And I'll always remember the good times we had. And while I'm sitting here sipping this chilled Chardonnay and listening to the mellowest V103, I think about Wiz as "All This Love" by DeBarge plays in the background. This was our jam back in the day, *our* song. And it's still our jam now, even after all these years. We may not be lovers anymore, but I'm still his "Piggybaby" and his "shawty," and he's still my "Wizzy." The last time I saw him (which was about 5 years ago), he was on the Low End in front of 2310 with Stony and 'em smokin' a blunt cigar and sipping Hennessy on ice out of a clear Solo cup. We hugged and shot the breeze for a minute or two before I had to leave. But he gave me his number and I gave him mine. We parted ways with a fist pump symbolizing our platonic unity.

He was my first love and he'll always be very special to me. He will always have a special place in my heart, and nothing will ever change that. I will always love him and he will always love me. And we will forever share that special bond between us. But we had been separated for a long time. And somewhere along the line, our lives went in different directions. And that happens, ya know? It happens. But thank God we're both alive and well. Thank God for that. He knows where I am, and I know where to find him. And it's all groovy.

I had been angry at my mother for a long time for ruining both my relationship with him (which she never knew anything about) and my chance to attend Dunbar High School (which had been my dream, and about which she did know) for moving us out of Chicago to Minnesota. But she said it was for the best. And maybe she was right because I emerged from my shell and came into my own in Minnesota. And that Science and Technology degree that my mother had worked so hard to earn came in handy, too.

All in all, I decided that life was too short to waste with regret. So I did away with grudges and went in search of gratitude and happiness.

Whenever I'm on the #29 State Street bus traveling past that area, my head always turns (instinctively) to look at the badass mural Wiz spray-painted along the wall under the Green Line El tracks. And I always think to myself, *Damn, he should have put it on the Metra Line wall across the street from 2233.*

(Smiling at the thought)

Frankie Beverly and Maze are on V103 performing "Southern Girl," and I'm laying low waiting for the weekend to ease in.

God is still good. And I'm grateful for the womb out of which I came because people can't choose the wombs they come out of. And that's the truth. But I'm glad that my mother's womb had been my pathway into this world because I got to live my entire life (save for the few years I lived in Minnesota) on the South Side of Chicago with some of the most beautiful people in some of the most beautiful neighborhoods in the world. And I love them both, even with every blood vessel in my being. The South Side of Chicago is my oyster. It always has been and it always will be: for I am profoundly proud of both it and its people.

Father God, continue to bless us. And bless us to continuously glorify you.

"The Private Investigator"

THE POEM:

He was a smooth sleuth,
Piercing me through
His private eye.
He dialed not the wrong number,
I'm his "Angel."

THE ENTRY:

17th November 1990, SATURDAY
11:40 a.m.

Dear Diary,

*T*he strangest thing happened last night. Mama and I were
just sitting downstairs in the living room laughing, talking
about life, listening to KDWB on the FM dial, and enjoying
our time together on a Friday night, when the phone
suddenly rang, interrupting Jane Child as she got ready to
belt out the first verse to "Don't Wanna Fall In Love." When
mama answered the phone and said hello, I couldn't hear the
caller's response, all I could hear was mama apologizing and
telling him or her that they had the wrong number. She hung
up and our fun-filled conversation resumed. Then the phone
rang again. It was obviously the same person who had just
called before asking my mother the same question to which
she replied, "Sorry, honey, but you have the wrong number.
There is no Angel here." I sat and watched my smiling
mother as she listened to what the caller was saying on his or
her end. And then she (my mother) spoke to the caller again,
saying, "Well, baby, she must've given you the wrong
number on purpose, because nobody by that name lives
here. The only angel I have here with me is my daughter."
The persistent caller must've had a sense of humor, because
my mother soon started laughing at whatever it was that he
or she said in response. It was then that Technotronic's "Get
Up! (Before The Night Is Over)" started coming out of the
speakers of our primary stereo system.

Mama to the caller: "…Here, I'll let you speak to her, to my
daughter, because she may know who Angel is…"

As I listened to my mother's words, I was thinking to
myself, *I hope Angel's tramp ass didn't give my phone*

415

*number to any of her conquests as a joke to throw them off
her trail.*

Still laughing, my mother handed me the phone. And when I
addressed the caller (whom I now knew was a man), he
spoke to me in a friendly voice and introduced himself as
Behr Rossi. He asked me what my name is and I told him
that it's Kimberly, but people call me by my nickname, Cat.
And after the formal introductions were over, he started
asking me about "Angel," telling me that he'd met her and
she'd given him this number, blah, blah, blah. I told him that
as a matter of fact, I do know an Angel, a girl with whom I
had worked for a little while. And then I asked him to
describe her to me, so that I would know whether or not we
were talking about the same Angel. When he did, I
immediately knew that we weren't. Because whereas his
"Angel" had dark hair and classic features, my Angel is a
blonde who looks a lot like Madonna.

Behr Rossi suddenly forgot about the mysterious "Angel"
and wanted to talk about me instead.
Agreeing to continue the conversation with him, I gave him
my private phone number (to free up the mainline) and asked
him to call me back on it, which he immediately did. And
once I got settled in the comforts of my bedroom, our
conversation resumed, lasting well over two hours.

I had hoped that I wasn't abandoning my mother as we were
having such a lovely Friday evening with just the two of us.
But she kept drinking her beer and told me, "Naw, you ain't
botherin' me, baby, go on and talk to him." And I did,
promising my mother that I would be right back.

I laughed internally thinking to myself, *How in the world did this happen? How did I end up talking to a complete stranger who called the wrong number, looking for someone named "Angel?"*

I couldn't figure it out, but I was enjoying our conversation and so was he.
We talked a lot about me, and then we talked a lot about him. And I often found myself thinking about just how interested he seemed to be in me. Something about the tone of his voice lingered in excitement. And I got the distinct feeling that if it were up to him, our phone conversation would have never ended.

He asked me to describe myself to him and I did so truthfully: "I'm tall, dark-skinned like the color of milk chocolate, large bust, concave mid-section, round hips and buttocks, curvy thighs, Cupid's bow lips, oval face, dark brown eyes, short pixie haircut with a lot of length up front, blah, blah, blah." And he was like, "Oh wow, okay, wow, that sounds good… Sounds good."

I then asked him to describe himself to me, and he did: "Well, I'm a tad bit shorter than you, I have dark hair with a bald spot on top, mustache, dark eyes, hairy chest, typical Italian, blah, blah, blah."

We both laughed at his nonchalance before falling back into our conversation. I soon learned that he's 40, and he soon learned that I'm 19 going on 35. We both laughed again, this time at *my* nonchalance, and our conversation continued.

At some point, I asked him to hold the line while I went to check on something. And when I returned to the phone (after finding that my mother had already hit the sack) I soon realized just how late it had gotten as it was well after midnight. I lost track of time, but Behr Rossi? He wanted to keep talking to me. We went on to share more information about ourselves:

Me: Born and raised in Chicago.

Him: Born and raised in the city of Rogers, now living in Edina.

Me: Hopeless Shopaholic and passionate beauty buff.

Him: Frequenter of Saks Fifth Avenue, lover of wine and Smirnoff vodka, enthusiast of Aramis cologne.

Stop. He had me at Saks.

(Laughs)

We talked on and on. And the next thing I knew, I was waking up this morning with the phone receiver laying at a lopsided angle beside my pillow. When I picked it up to give it a listen, I heard no dial tone, no static, no breathing, no nothing. It was just dead air.

(Laughs)

Oh my God! I fell asleep on the man!

(More laughs)

Oh my God, I am so terrible.

(Embarrassed chuckling)

Oh nooo. Wow. I must've been tired after such a long week at work. Plus, I had two glasses of Pinot Gris, and chances are they added to my bodily fatigue causing me to fall out no sooner than I laid down to talk to him. I swear I love my job in luxury retail, but all that running around from here to there will getcha. Thank God I have this weekend off to recoup.

Still, I fell asleep on Behr Rossi. And I'm trying to remember just when I did.
I can remember telling him that I work as a junior buyer in retail, and him telling me that he's a private investigator… But I pretty much drew a blank after that. I can remember him being reluctant to tell me about his work as a private eye because he "didn't want to scare me off," he had said. And I can remember asking him if he was serious before telling him that it was okay, his line of work didn't repel me at all. I may have either said or thought something about *Magnum P.I.* after he told me that he's a private investigator, but I don't remember. Oh wow, I must've been famished. I can remember him telling me that he likes to stay at the Drake Hotel on the Gold Coast whenever he's in Chicago on business, but I drew a blank after that.

(Slightly smiling)

419

Glen Medeiros and Bobby Brown are on KDWB right now performing "She Ain't Worth It," and it is such a pick-me-up. Damn, I think I might be a little bit hungover. I need a Sprite. Hold on, dear Diary.

(Pausing to grab a can of Sprite from the mini-fridge)

(I'm back)

After I hook up with Glen Madeiros, we're gonna live happily ever after on one of those stunning Islands in Hawaii…

(Pausing to take a *big gulp* of ice-cold Sprite)

(I'm back)

…Just watch me.

(Quietly burps)

He's a bit young for my taste, but he's cute. Jordan Knight, eatcha heart out.

(Suddenly thinking)

I wonder if Behr Rossi knew who he was calling last night. I wonder if he called our number on purpose. Seriously, now that I think about it, I wonder if this Behr Rossi called us on purpose under the pretense of having dialed a wrong number.

(Suspicions arising)

Because right after he called me back on my private line, he suddenly forgot all about "Angel." He never mentioned any such person again, his only point of interest seemed to be me. He couldn't care less about anything or anyone else. Oh, and there was one other thing that struck me as odd: his familiarity. My antennae really went up when he spoke the following words to me: "Women hate you because they think their men are looking at you."

Now how would he, a complete stranger, know that?

(Bobby Brown is now in the midst of his rap solo, telling Glen that despite her jazziness, the girl ain't nothin' but trouble)

Oh my God.

(Laughing in spite of myself)

Oh my God, dear Diary. Oh, that was good. I'll give it to him, that was good – and slick. *I'm* the "Angel" he was calling to speak to.

(Laughing in awe)

Oh my God. Oh, that was slick.

(Laughing again)

He purposely called to speak to me, and I fell asleep on him. Imagine that.

When he calls me back (and I know he will), I'm not going to say anything to him about my suspicions, I'm gonna just play along with him and see how far it goes. What gave him away? His profession and his familiarity. Now that it's dawned on me, I realize that he didn't call us by coincidence. He called us deliberately— Oh hang on, dear Diary.

(Pausing to answer my ringing phone)

(Resuming 30 seconds later)

Well, speak of the ~~devil~~ angel, dear Diary – it's him. His first words to me? "Hey, beautiful. You fell asleep on me earlier this morning."

Uhhh-huh.

My dear Diary? I will be back later.

Love,

Cat

"Motivated by Hate"

THE POEM:

The girl won hands down,
And they loathe it.
They loathe her too,
Because she contradicts lies.
Let them eat cake!

THE ENTRY:

7th February 1989, TUESDAY

Dear Diary,

God, I despise those self-loathing and enemy-minded ass women that I attend beauty school with. They can't stand to see anything positive happen to me. They act like they can't stand my guts, but as Ms. Mannequin Day approaches, they're all in my face trying to borrow my hats and my scarves and my jewelry to "doll" their mannequins up for the contest. Ain't that a bitch?! Those bitches gather themselves together to show hatred towards me as one solid body, and then think that I'm going to allow them to use *my* accessories to make *their* fuckin' mannequins look good? Are they outta their fuckin' minds?! Fuck those bitches! I'm gonna stomp their asses on Miss Mannequin Day! My mannequin will look so good, it's gonna kill their asses! I have copies of *Vogue* and *Essence* in bed right now channeling ideas as to how I want to dress my mannequin for the big day. Should God be with me, I'm gonna tear their asses up and get that trophy just for the fun of it.

Ain't that a bitch? How dare those nasty, faithless ass bitches! They gotta lotta muthafuckin' nerve. How the fuck are you gonna act as though you hate me for being me, but then ask me if you could use my possessions to make your shit look good? Damn, have they no shame? Good God. That must mean that I have something that those average ass bitches — from the air-headed instructors on down to my fellow students — don't have. And they're tempted to hate me because of it. Damn those bitches!

A school full of women, save for a few men, and *I* have to
be the primary target of their fuckin' animosity?
Honest to God, it's just crazy how much shit I have to put up
with — where it involves other women — every damn
where I go. If I start going off on these bitches and fuckin'
their asses up, then I'm going to be wrong. Ya know, dear
Diary? If I fuck them up about fuckin' with me for no other
reason save envy and jealousy, I'm going to be wrong. I
swear, I should just fuck them up. I should just take all of my
anger out on their asses. But then if I do that, I'll go to jail,
won't I?
God, I am just so sick and tired of women fuckin' with me
all the time. I swear, I wish I could just destroy their asses.
Seriously, if I could, I would. I would tear their asses up!
Like pieces of paper!

What is it about me, dear Diary? Why am I always the one
they fear and hate? Nita said it's because God gave me a
unique beauty and height and I stand out. She tells me that
I'm just too much for some people and they can't take the
aura of my existence. And judging by the way so many
women out there are allowing themselves to act towards me,
I'm inclined to believe my Nita.

Sometimes I wish that a lot of these miserable ass women
(such as the ones who are tempted to dislike me without just
cause) had everything they're tempted to covet. Because if
they did, I bet they still wouldn't be happy. They wouldn't
be satisfied at all because peace would still be absent in their
lives.

425

What such women fail to understand is that happiness in life is all about having faith in God and self-love. Those are the most important things to have, but such people want to believe that it's only about material things or physical beauty because they're surface-minded. And that trips them up every time. Any woman can look her best if she feels her best. And anyone can have material things if they work hard enough to obtain them. And that's the truth. But can you tell the truth to any of these people? No, because they don't want to hear the truth, they only want to hear and believe lies. They just need an excuse to hate someone else, because they hate themselves.

I came from extreme obesity and humble beginnings. And what these hateful and envious ass women see on my surface today was not always. In fact, dear Diary, I would bet a pretty penny that were I still big as a fuckin' house these same women (and other self-hating women like them) would be mocking me, ridiculing me, and looking down on me, and doing everything in their power to shame me, just like the ones who came before them did when they knew me as a fat girl. Seriously, if I were still a big fat cow with acne-prone skin and crooked teeth, they wouldn't envy or fear me, they would love it. Because while they are tempted to see themselves as being less than average anyway, at least they would be better off than some fat and sloppy ass slob. And in a spirit of perversity, they would gather themselves around to falsely embrace me because I wouldn't be a threat to them at all.

But guess what? God had other plans for me. He took me out of the fat suit that had been my shell, cleared my skin up, straightened my teeth, and bestowed honor upon my head on this Earth of His. He did not come slow.

Before, people detested me because I was a despicable fatso; now they detest me because I am the complete opposite of a despicable fatso. The Lord did that. The Lord stopped their heads from wagging at me a long time ago, and He shut up their mouths from laughing at me a long time ago. The Lord shut down their mockeries and their ridicule of me a long time ago, and now they just fear, hate, and envy what truly was all along. Beneath the fat suit of my former body, I was a young woman of promise, I was just hidden. The little fat girl that I used to be always had a sense of style that she was born with, the Lord just didn't allow it to be revealed then. My sunny personality was always the same as it is today, it's just that many people chose not to embrace me for it. The witty sense of humor was always within me, it was just ignored and repelled by the biases of many people. I have always had the "pretty smile" so many people adore today, it was just concealed by my former crooked teeth. I was always who I was, I was just hidden beneath layers and layers of extra weight. And when God saw that I'd had enough, He chose to release me. And out of the shell, I hatched.

While it was not always easy, I had to learn how to love myself one day at a time. I had to learn how to walk down the street without crossing my arms over myself because of lingering self-consciousness about my former weight. I had to learn how to look in the mirror and see the new me, and not the little fat girl that I had once been. And while it took some time to get used to the new me, I eventually started to become more and more comfortable in my new body with each passing day, week, month, and year. And I told the little fat girl — who will always be a part of me, no doubt — that I would NEVER again allow anyone to hurt her, emotionally or otherwise. I promised her that I would ALWAYS fight for her and take good care of her. And I meant every word that I spoke because she will always be within me. She will always be a part of my genetic fabric and that will never change. She can never be allowed to leave me because she is forever a part of me. And to this day, I still fight for her. To this day, I still hold her near and dear. And I will cherish her until my dying day because had she not been allowed to exist, I wouldn't be who I am now.

This is what so many people don't understand about me, dear Diary. They want to believe a lie that they know me, but they don't know me at all. They are only allowed to see whatever face I choose to show them. But they don't know my history, else they would understand me better.

Their ignorance and egos are what will destroy them every time and cause them to miss their blessings in life. The Lord had placed a sparkling diamond right in front of them. And rather than picking it up, they were tempted to treat it as though it were a mere rock and overlook it. And that's shameful.
I could've been used by the Lord to be a great blessing to them, but they're so full of fear — combined with self-hatred and hatred — that they can't even receive it. They're so full of low self-esteem, that they can't even take helpful advice and constructive criticism from me. And that's a shame.

Dear Diary, these days will too perish into eternity. But I will keep moving forward in life living and enjoying what time I have left. I'm just passing through, I have no intention of setting up shop here long term. I'm just passing through.
And once it's over, I will never have to see these miserable people again. Because I don't know them. I never have and I never will. I didn't know them yesterday, I don't know them today, and I won't know them tomorrow.
But while I'm here, they're not gonna be allowed to fuck with me lest I have to do them physical harm in self-defense. And I will do them physical harm quick, fast, and in a hurry if need be.

Anyway, enough about those self-loathing women. Let's get positive!

Milli Vanilli's "Baby Don't Forget My Number" is on KDWB right now, and it sounds so good. God, I love Milli Vanilli. I love Rob and Fab, I swear I do. I love everything about them. They're just so beautiful, both of them.
I should call the station and ask them to play "Girl I'm Gonna Miss You" because I could really go for that one right now. That is such a gorgeous song.

(Gentle sigh)

My four walls are all covered with photographs of print and fashion models who look so lovely. And I'm now looking at a photo of Iman in a Virginia Slims ad, which I can see needs a new strip of scotch tape. Ohhh-kay gotta fix that because I can't have my girl falling off any wall of mine.

Paula's "Straight Up" is coming on the radio now, and it's lively. Every time I hear it, I think about that sexy ass video with Arsenio doing his cameo.

(Smiles)

That's my girl, Paula Abdul! She can dance her ass off, and that black and white video is just too fuckin' gorgeous. Nessa and I were just talkin' about it the other day, how perfect Janet and Paula are. Love those women!

You do know what I'm doing, don't you, dear Diary? Yeah, I'm contemplating whether or not I should return Hawk's call. He's got a game coming up, but I'm not going because I don't feel up to it. I'll watch it on TV, though.

Should I or should I not call him?

Oh shit, dear Diary, am I boring you now?

(Laughs)

I'm sure that if you could talk, you would say, "No! Don't be silly, Cat! Keep writing to me, girl!"

(Giggling)

The Pinot Gris that I'm drinking right now is making me feel silly. And someone is knocking at my door. Hold on, my dear Diary.

(Pausing to answer the door)

(10 minutes later)

I'm back, dear Diary. Guess what? Nessa just walked in, and she's loaded with bags of Leeann Chin!!! Hey, that rhymed! Hehe. Anyway, I've got a hearty appetite and I'm gonna have to chat with you later, alright? Hey, that rhymed, too!

Hey, woohoo!

Love,

Cat

"The Attorney"

THE POEM:

A man of beauty,
Tall in darkness,
Invited me
To dine out in elegance.
I'll honor him.

THE ENTRY:

6th April 1991, SATURDAY

Dear Diary,

I had been strolling through the frozen foods aisle at
Rainbow in the Midway center singing along — although
off-key — to Taylor Dayne's "Love Will Lead You Back" as
he approached my cart. And as I was so preoccupied with
how much Walleye I wanted to buy — not to mention
Taylor Dayne, whose distinctive vocals were ringing out
loud and clear from the store's sound system — I didn't see
the man pulling up alongside me. I just looked up and there
he was, tall and draped in a rich shade of ebony flesh. While
his left hand held a plastic produce bag full of Bosc pears,
his right hand was outstretched to shake mine in a friendly
gesture of greeting. He smiled at me politely and I smiled
back at him in return. And when he spoke to say hello, I
instantly detected an accent. I said hello and accepted his
handshake, then I asked him about his unique accent,
curious as to where he was from. He told me that he's from
Nigeria, and I replied, "Oh, that's so lovely. Nigeria is such a
beautiful country." He agreed that it most certainly is and we
soon embarked on a brief conversation.

I probed further inquiring about his tribe, and he told me that
he's from the Yoruba tribe. He also told me his name,
Kemba Lawson. I told him my name is Kimberly but he
could call me Cat.
"Cat?" He asked, amused. And I answered him that Cat is
my nickname by which I prefer to be addressed. Then he
proceeded to compliment it, saying that it fits me and asking

me how I came to acquire it. "It's a long story," I answered dismissively. He chuckled, quipping that maybe I could explain it to him over dinner.

I was thinking: *A date? Is he really asking me out on a dinner date? Right here in the frozen food aisle in front of the Stouffer's entrées?*

(Inwardly amused)

I knew it was coming, but even still, it caught me off guard. As I searched for words with which to answer him, my ears were attentive to the sound system: the ladies of Wilson Phillips singing "Release Me." I asked, "How do you know I'm not already seeing someone?" And he replied, "I don't know, but I can only hope you're not. You're so beautiful I had to come over and introduce myself. You're turning so many heads here today." His accent was heavy and the moment was awkward, but he hung in there, asking, "If I give you my phone number, will you call me?" I smiled and asked, "How old are you?" He told me that he's 44 and works as a corporate attorney for a downtown law firm. He then queried me as to my age and what I do for a living. And I told him that I'm 20 and work as a junior buyer for a major department store. He responded with an "Oh wow."
To move things along, I agreed to take his number as a kind gesture. It wasn't a guarantee that I would call him, it was simply a kind gesture. But before he handed me his number, he said, "Will you please call me, Cat? Please? Please call me?" And I told him that I would.

While I wanted to continue with my shopping, he wanted to keep talking to me. And I told him that there would be plenty of time for us to talk when I phoned him. He took the hint and said, "It was very nice meeting you, Cat." I told him that it had been nice meeting him, too. And with that, we exchanged smiles and parted ways. Well, at least I did. He never moved an inch, he just stood there in the same spot staring at my back.

As Alannah Myles sang the first verse of "Black Velvet" from the sound system, I made my way to the Kemps frozen yogurt and Mrs. Smith's pies.

In my peripheral vision, I could see him watching me. And I thought to myself, *Lord, I hope this man ain't a wacko.* As an afterthought, he called out to me, saying, "Cat? That is a very beautiful wrap you're wearing. And you smell good." I smiled, said "Thank you," and wished him a gorgeous weekend ahead.

The wrap he likes so much is a gift from the House of Yves Saint-Laurent; and the fragrance? Elizabeth Taylor's Passion.

I'm home now and settled, but I'm undecided on what to eat tonight. Hey, wait a minute. I have a ton of La Choy downstairs in the cabinets. I'll open a can of Stir-Fry Vegetables, steam a pot of rice, uncork a bottle of White, do it all just right, and call it a groovy ol' night. Until next time, dear Diary.

(Wink)

Love,

Cat

26th April 1991, FRIDAY
(Three Weeks Later)
3:07 p.m.

Dear Diary,

After I left my cousin Jackie's house today, I decided to stop
by Mr. Tillman's store on the way home to pick up a few
things: Certs, Caress soap, a big bag of Munchos for my
dear mother, and three big bags of Earl's Cheese Curls for
moi. And it was while I was leaving the store that I
remembered Kemba, the Nigerian attorney whom I'd met at
Rainbow in Midway weeks ago. He had come over to
introduce himself to me while I was selecting Walleye and
started up a conversation, eventually asking me to have
dinner with him and giving me his phone number. I agreed
to call him, but I never got around to doing so until today.
We just finished our call a little over twenty minutes ago, and
here I am sharing the details of it with you.

Excited to finally hear from me, he gushed into my ear, "Oh
my God, I don't believe you called me! Oh my God, it's so
good to hear from you! How are you doing?" I told him that
I was doing good and then I asked him how he was. He said
that he had been doing great but that he was even better now

that he had me on the phone. And I chuckled in response. We caught up on the goings-on over the past three weeks: work, play, more work, more play, etc. And after that, we made a date for dinner. He told me that he would make reservations at L'Exquisite for next Friday, and I told him that that sounded great. As we chatted about the best cuisine the city had to offer, I asked him if he's ever been to Kincaid's, to which he replied "Yes." Like me, he loves its menu and suggested that maybe we could have lunch there sometime. Of course, I accepted his offer as I love Kincaid's. It's one of my favorite restaurants in the city and I told him as much. Kemba then shared with me that he lives right down the street from Kincaid's, and how unbelievable it is that I'm so fond of the dining establishment.

Me: "Really?"

Him: "Yes, Cat, yes. We could walk to Kincaid's from my place."

Me: "Oh, how groovy."

Him: (Laughs)

He wanted to know the name of the perfume I had been wearing the first day we met at Rainbow, and I told him that it was Liz Taylor's Passion. I also told him that the wrap he liked had been a gift to our store from Yves Saint-Laurent, and that my supervisor was kind enough to let me keep it, seeing as I love the French designer so much.

He then said to me, "Cat, you must love your job." And I replied, "I do, I do! We're like kids in a candy store, Kemba!"

(Laughs)

We chatted about a few more things before we prepared to end the conversation with him asking if he could call me later on tonight. I told him, yes, that would be fine, and then we said good-bye. Now I'm sitting here looking at Naomi, one of my dress forms named for Naomi Campbell, of course, and wondering what I should wear to L'Exquisite next week.

Think: *The silk Dior blouse! Yeah, I can wear that. It'll match my Raspberry Sizzle lipstick to perfection! Yeah, that'll work. I'll wear it with a black pencil skirt, my felt cloché with the plum-colored pattern, and some black suede boots! Yessssss. That'll work. And I can carry a black suede Gucci bag to knock it all out! Yessssss. That's how ya do it, girl! Work it! Now for the jewelry...*

(Emerging from the thought process)

I think I've got it all figured out, dear Diary. Talk to ya soon.

Love,

Cat

"Deflated Balloons"

THE POEM:

They'll all blow you up.
Then you'll float
On gaseous winds -
Until you are no longer.
Pop! Gone like that!

THE ENTRY:

20th May 2019, MONDAY
4:54 p.m.

Dear Diary,

I had a few minutes to kill and figured that I would use the
time to do what I do best: write.
I need to vent on your pages again, dear Diary. I need to
purge out my aggravation in this entry. I need to unleash my
feelings. I need to tell it like it is, and I need to tell it like it is
right now. May I?

It's this present generation, ya know? I cannot *stand* it. I
don't hate the people who constitute for it, I just can't stand a
lot of them because many of them, *not all of them*, but many
of them, are so full of pride, laziness, covetousness, anger,
bitterness, neediness, perversity, and greediness. They seem
to want nearly *everything* handed to them, but they don't
want to work for too much of anything. And I just hate that
about so many of these people out there in the world today.

My guess is that many of these so-called Millennials have
always been lazy as the word itself, but their shortcomings
were hidden by the obscurity they dwelled in before the
creation of social media.

Social media pulled the rug back to reveal a whole lotta shit.
And while many people choose to turn their heads the other
way and pretend not to see the blatant desperation festering
in so many people out there in the world, it's safe to say that
we're in a really bad place in these current times.

Fear and madness — mingled with desperation — has come
for the throats of many of those who call this present

440

generation their own. And the aura of their ways has spread like an invisible plague. It's sad, but many of these people today, especially those of the Millennial generation, need social media to validate their lazy asses. Case in point: recognition.

It makes me sick to my stomach to see certain people being referred to as "Web stars" or "Internet famous," because such people are nearly always without merit.
What the hell are these people famous for? What contributions to the arts, or sports, or fashion, or journalism, or broadcast media, or politics, or religion, have they made?
What legitimacy do they have? What credibility do they have? Why do the people who run these social networks and Internet websites feel the need to feed the people out there in the general public a bunch of friggin' lies? Why do so many (visual and print) media outlets and corporations join forces to help feed the system of lies? I'm sure they have many self-seeking reasons, one of which is *survival*.
In my personal opinion, the whole sham is pathetic, and it says a lot about everyone involved. I'm not judging any of them, I'm just stating facts.

Having a ton of followers on a social media platform is not an equation of legitimate notoriety by any standard. True fame is gained by way of public work, not fleeting popularity on a bunch of social media platforms. And because such outlets can be manipulated in a variety of ways, the same should not be deemed credible to make such declarations.

Whether people can handle the truth or not, there is nothing legitimate about a so-called "Web star" or a so-called "Internet famous" person. Both expressions are fabrications created by the human operatives of Internet companies (and corporations) to make certain members of the general public feel good about themselves, even if for only fifteen minutes. But there is no truth to any of it whatsoever.

Because many people in the general public are being tempted to hate themselves and envy those who are truly renowned for their works — creative or otherwise — in the public sector, the human operatives within many of the corporations that fuel the machines of the social media systems feel as though they have an obligation to at least try to fill up a bottomless well of low self-esteem. But they will fail every time because that empty well will never be filled, it's bottomless. It always has been and it always will be. Those who prefer to believe such lies "believe" for a little while, and then they lose interest because they *know* it's a lie. But because it makes them feel good to "go viral" for only a moment, the companies and the masses follow suit and applaud them so that they do not lose hope in society. Because "a lot of likes" and "a lot of views or followers" makes them feel good about themselves for only a moment, the companies and the masses follow suit and applaud them so that they do not lose hope in society and give up on life. That's how bottomless self-esteem is in countless numbers of people out there in the world. That's just how weak they are in spirit.

Truly, they'll snap like twigs should the wind gust too strongly upon them. And that's a damn shame.

In short, "Internet fame" is bogus, unreal, and unmemorable. And while corporations and media outlets work hand in hand to feed starving egos and cater to many people who have low self-esteem, they also go from bad to worse, deceiving and being deceived. Because the people they're constantly trying to inflate don't truly believe it; therefore, the wind goes out of them quick, fast, and in a hurry.

Another thing that I detest about this generation is the power-hungry spirit of its women. Too many women have forgotten themselves, striving to take the place of men in every aspect of society. And they too will fail because God made the woman from the rib of the man, not the man from the rib of the woman; therefore, the woman is the weaker vessel. And while there is absolutely nothing wrong with that, many women in today's society are being tempted to both hate themselves as women and covet having power over men. And that's just not a good look.
As women, we don't have dicks, we have vaginal cavities, and ovaries, and uteri. Well, *I* don't have a uterus anymore because mine was spayed in 2008, but you know what I mean. I still have my ovaries, though, thank God almighty for that. I love my womanhood, and other women should love theirs also.

Women don't need to impose themselves on men, but many are being tempted to do just that. There are too many women in today's society moving as one body to infiltrate themselves into the orbit of men, whether it pertains to business, sports, certain areas of politics, etc. And seeing it daily irks me.

Women are not designed to play contact sports like NFL football, NBA basketball, NHL hockey, or MLB baseball because their bodies were not produced to handle that type of physicality. But will they listen to the words of truth? No, of course not, it only makes them hate the bearers of it more so. Such women are defiant in their ignorance and prefer to go on coveting the power of men. But they are destined to fail because of their self-hatred, low self-esteem, covetousness, malice, and vindictiveness.

The malice that many of those women out there in the world foster towards men is ungodly and stems from a wicked source, period. And there is no going around that truth.

It just looks to me like women (and girls) are trying to replace boys and men on every level of society. One can see the evidence of it in real life, commercials, movies, and even in many works of literary fiction. And it's ungodly. Something is driving such people and it's not the Spirit of Truth.

A woman cannot do everything a man does, it just doesn't work that way. And those women out there in the world, the same women who are being tempted to covet power and have power over men, will not only destroy themselves but also their daughters.

Women have been given a place and they ought to stay in it. Because no matter what they do, they will NEVER be men, nor will they ever take the place of men. Men are the strength, and women, the weaker vessels. And these women out here in the world should humble themselves that they should come to an understanding and learn the true power of self-love.

The following is my understanding:

"Men are physically stronger than women, who have, on average, less total muscle mass, both in absolute terms and relative to total body mass. The greater muscle mass in men is the result of testosterone-induced muscular hypertrophy. Men also have denser, stronger bones, tendons, and ligaments."
—*Psychology Today, 02 July 2012*

An eloquently-spoken truth, indeed.

Oh shoot, I forgot about the time. Sorry, dear Diary, but I have to cut this conversation short because dinner is served. Hehe, chef Patrice has hooked up a meal to salivate for: Lobster mac & cheese, Caesar salads, and cupcakes. Hot damn. Gotta go. MWAH!

Love,

Cat

"Serenaded by Kenny G"

THE POEM

His magnificence,
It enveloped us
On the Island:
The smooth horns of Kenny G,
They enraptured me.

THE ENTRY
26th May 1989, FRIDAY
11:22 p.m.

Dear Diary,

*T*his has been the most beautiful day! I had a ball tonight, and I will love Otis forever for treating me out to such a wonderful evening!

From the moment I woke up this morning, even till now, I've been a solid body of energy and excitement! I know I need to bring it down a bit, but I can't! At least not right now because I'm still too jacked up! Whewwwww! Whew!

Okay, okay, hold on. Hold on.

(Breathe slowly, Cat, breathe slowly, Cat, breathe slowly, Cat, breathe slowly, Cat…)

Okay, dear Diary, I'm calm now. Ready for the details? Okay, here goes.

After I woke up this morning, I showered, had breakfast, got myself dressed, and went to beauty school. I was only in for four hours today, but it was a fun four hours that I used to color a client's hair and do a manicure. I also received a lovely gift today in the form of three tubes of lipstick, all violets made by Ultra Sheen cosmetics: Sultry Violet, Vivacious Violet, and Midnight Violet. And I love all three of them because they look great on my complexion!

Anyway, after I left school, I went to Walgreens in the Midway Shopping Center to buy a new bottle of Chloé and a jar of La Toya Jackson's Mahogany Image cream foundation. The weather was on the cool side today, so I decided that a light application of cream makeup would do just fine under the circumstances.

After I left Walgreens, I went next door to Rainbow for smoked Gouda, blue cheese, cantaloupe, and apple juice, then I came home to pick out something to wear on my platonic date. And it had to be something jazzy because Otie (you know that's Otis) would be picking me up around 4:30 for the show. He was taking me to an outdoor concert (The World Series of Ribs Festival) starring Kenny G on Harriet Island. And I was on a natural high all day, dear Diary. Because you know I love, love, love Kenny G! And I couldn't wait to get downtown on the Island for the concert.

I powered on my Pioneer stereo system component, put *Silhouette* on the turntable, and proceeded to let it spin all the way through on both sides while I picked out an outfit to wear. And it was during the middle of "Summer Song" that I finally decided on what to sport: white button-down Donna Karan blouse, burgundy necktie (to match my Posner Blast-Off Burgundy lipstick and High Kickin' Wine nail color), black Donna Karan tights, pleated black and white plaid flare-legged pants, gold thigh-length trench coat (for the cooler temps along the river), black patent leather wingtip shoes, and my black patent leather Chanel mini bag.

After my outfit was selected, I brought my jewelry box to the bed to sit and pick out some earrings (the brass ones), a bracelet (the chunky brass and Topaz one), and a ring (the large brass and Topaz ring to match the bracelet). Done! I had my outfit and jewelry ready, dear Diary! And I was ready to go when it came time to.

After I put the needle on "Against Doctor's Orders," I took another shower and layered it on, the Chloé: scented body crème, scented dusting powder, and a couple of spritzes of Eau de Toilette spray — in that order, dear Diary. I then took a seat at my vanity and went to work on my hair and makeup. For the outfit I picked out, I decided that wearing my hair in an upsweep would do the ensemble supreme justice, so I piled my tresses up allowing a few wispy hairs to hang freely. I then lined my lips and filled them in with Blast-Off Burgundy. After that, I lined my eyes, blended my eyeshadow, contoured my nose and brows, and applied another coat of Great Lash. Voilà! I am now ready!

Allowing everything to set, I was sitting on my bed in my kimono and reading the album's liner notes for the umpteenth time when my phone rang. Otie called to inform me that he was on his way. And I was giddy, dear Diary! I was so giddy, I couldn't wait.

(Laughs)

I couldn't help it, dear Diary, I just love Kenny G! Love his music, love his spirit, love his finesse, love everything about his creativity. And I couldn't wait to finally see him. Hey, I'm a Jazz girl, no shame.

(Smiles)

Six Hours Later
(After The Concert)

Otie bought me a pink rose wrapped in gorgeous pink paper for our concert date, and I carried it with me downtown. The weather was perfect. We arrived on Harriet Island early enough to get the perfect spot on the lawn: 5:45 p.m. or so. We spread out our blankets and took in the view as KQ92, the station hosting the show, blasted classic rock from the huge sound system. More people were arriving and setting up their pallets on the lawn as "So Into You" by the Atlanta Rhythm Section played loud and clear. We had a few minutes to relax before showtime, and all I could think about was the glass of chilled Pinot that I planned to have afterward.

Before Kenny Came out on stage to greet his adoring fans — including me — KQ paved his way by playing Steely Dan's "Deacon Blues," which I thought was very creative, considering that the G-man is a saxophonist. By the time our guy got ready to go on, the sun had still not set but it was getting there. When he (Kenny) stood on stage and spoke to those of us in the audience about how ironic it was for him to be a vegetarian playing a ribs festival, we all chuckled in response. I felt like blurting out, "I'm a vegetarian, too, Kenny!" But I refrained myself.

Clad in jeans, a black T-shirt, a white blazer, and black shoe boots, Mr. G's set got underway. And he came out of the gate smokin' it! I could not believe that I was looking at one of my biggest crushes live and in the flesh! Oh my God, it was a dream come true! And the evening was beautiful.

The sun had now set and it was time for Kenny to wrap up his show. And as is his tradition, he left the stage to come out and engage (personally) with the audience. He performed on his alto sax as he worked his way through the crowd, stopping briefly along the way to shake hands with a few of his fans before moving on. As he approached our section, my heart was racing from an overdrive of excitement. And when he crossed my path (pun intended), he looked directly at me, did a double-take, and then backed up to stand right in front of me while playing his famous horn in flawless harmony. Our eyes became locked. All I could do was look at both him and that horn. Honest to God, I cannot remember the song he was playing, but it may have been a track from *G Force*. A beautiful man to behold, Kenny G was still looking directly into my eyes (I know this because I was looking directly into his) when I heard a member of his security detail say something like, "Kenny, come on man, you gotta go!"

Otie's voice brought me back to Earth. I can remember him telling me that Kenny didn't want to move and that his people had to nudge him along through the crowd. I can remember Otie chuckling and saying that it was as if Kenny had been playing that song "especially for you, Cat!" I came out of my trance and saw many of the people who had been surrounding us looking at me. I couldn't talk because my mouth felt dry, and I could barely walk because my legs felt weak. All I could feel was the breeze. Otie had to guide me away from the island.

I didn't return to normal until Otie and I got to Kincaid's, where we had a reservation for dinner. I sipped my chilled Pinot and Otie sipped his beer while we awaited our meals: Calamari and Oysters on the Half Shell for me; and a Porterhouse steak, baked potato, and a side salad for Otie. I looked up to see my favorite Marine (Otie) waving his hand in front of my face and asking me if I was alert. I told him that I was, and then we both shared a good laugh.

Otie: "Kenny G serenaded you tonight! Damn!"

Me: "Oh my God, did that really just happen?"

Otie: "Yep. It was as if y'all were the only two people out there on that lawn tonight."

Me: (Laughs) That is my guy! You know how I am about Kenny G, Otie."

Otie: "I know, I know, he's my guy, too. (Laughs)"

We ate our meals in quiet serenity. And then Otie brought me home.

I was still jacked up when I came in, dear Diary. And while I peeled off my clothes and hopped into my comfy camisole and teddy shorts, I told mama all about everything that happened at the show. She burst out laughing and then asked me if Otie had to pick me up and carry me out. I chuckled and told her, no, he didn't, but that the butterflies were still fluttering around in my belly. It was exhilarating. I opened a can of apricots in light syrup and ate them while mama humored me: "See, it's because you're such a beauty, baby…"
I heard my mother's words, but they trailed off because my mind focused on something else not about the evening's events. I was thinking about the weekend ahead and how I

planned to spend it: staying inside, drinking coffee, eating frozen yogurt, listening to music, writing, etc.

My mind returned to the present as mama was still talking, by now telling me that she was so glad that I'd had a good time at the show. And she was right, ya know? I had a good time. I had more than a good time. And I needed a change of pace.

Sitting here in my bedroom now, I'm looking at the pink rose that Otie gave me tonight. I put it into a slender vase with some warm water and a little bit of sugar to help keep it beautiful. I love its life. And I love what it represents. Life is to be lived and enjoyed while we have it. Because like a flower, it soon withers away.

Thank you, God, for a wonderful evening. I finally got the chance to see someone that I truly admire up close and personal, and it was way too cool.

It happened to me. I was serenaded by Kenny G.

Love,

Cat

"Memory… is the diary that we all carry about with us."
—Oscar Wilde

I couldn't have said it better.

Coming July 2020

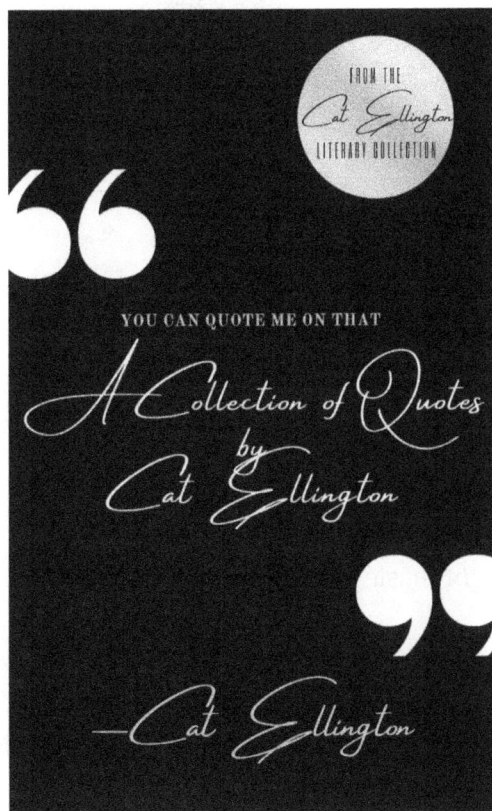

You Can Quote Me On That: A Collection of Quotes by Cat
Ellington
Imprint: Quill Pen Ink Publishing
Cover Tint: Bumblebee

About the Author

Cat Ellington is an American songwriter, casting director, poet, and author from Chicago, IL. She is best known for her creative contributions to the diverse industries and fields of music, movies, art, and literature.

Outside of her professional element, the award-winning lyricist enjoys reading, listening to music, cooking, collecting vintage and modern charm bracelets, watching LMN, film noir movies, and classic TV shows, sailing, jet skiing, playing tennis, and eating lots of frozen yogurt.

Cat Ellington lives in Chicago with her husband Joseph Strickland, their three children Nathaniel, Nairobi, and Naras, and the family's pet Pomeranian, Aspen.

Cat Ellington on Amazon: Books, Biography, Blog, Audiobooks, Kindle

Cat Ellington at the Award-Winning
Boutique Domain

Cat Ellington: The Review Period with
Cat Ellington

Cat Ellington at IMDb

Bonus Material

Previously Unpublished Works

"Tulips in Poetry"

A Poem About Flowers

Watercolors by Ateli

Decorative tulips,
So dainty in two;
Painted in shades of red, orange, and blue—

Their stems are of green,
Curvaceous and lean—
They sway on their bodies,
In breezes unseen—

Their splendor and graces
Invites and embraces the glorious sun
That shines on their faces—

Decorative tulips, so dainty in two;
Painted in shades of red, orange, and blue.

The Commentary

I wrote *Tulips in Poetry* on a whim after Quill Pen Ink Publishing acquired the beautiful watercolor painting of the tulips pictured above. Although the piece was featured - but only briefly - at The Boutique Domain (my official website) to lead my Poetry Page, it has never appeared in my books.

However, I decided to include the flower poem in this compilation, well, just for the hell of it. I have never believed myself to be that great at poetry, especially where the subject matter involved flowers, which I love, but I thought I would give it a shot anyway. The tulips are gorgeous, wouldn't you agree?

I know you would. :)

"The Abusive Marriage"

A Poem About Racial Oppression

Watercolors by Ateli

Why do you mistreat me?
Your hands, like hands of lead,
Show off their rage:
They take it out on me—

Your face, a resemblance of cracked paste,
Resorts to falsehood:
For it has two sides:
One of kindness for the foreigner,
And the other of meanness for me:

Yet, with you, I am yoked.

Like a rusty sword is your tongue:
For whatever it may speak ill of me,
It speaks—
Your eyes, milky from being soulless,
Look upon me with a ravaged disgust;
Scorn unwarranted:

Yet, with you, I am yoked.

Power has teamed with you,
To skin my existence alive;
To scalp any honor I may have—
Society has teamed with you,
To slash the wrist of my dwelling;
To bleed out my dignity:

Yet, with you, I am yoked.

You have a heart of cement;
And a conscience that drips dry—
Your integrity is a hypocrite,
And your making is a lie—

For our guests,
You assume the role of the perfect host;
But when their backs turn,
It is my neck -
By which the sole of your foot becomes provoked—

You are my abuser,
My hater,
And my oppressor:

Yet, with you, I am yoked.

This thing between us is like being in an abusive marriage:
for we two are of a separate culture; we are of a different
heritage. But our history together is like that of an abusive
marriage.

The Commentary

Not every white person is a ravenous wolf, just like every
black person isn't an innocent lamb. The flesh is sinful by
nature. And many humans defile themselves daily.
Concerning the production, appropriately titled *The Abusive
Marriage*, I was motivated by the Spirit of Truth to speak
about the nature of racism that plagues this current society in
which we live: the lying and denying and the hypocrisy of it
all: even to this day, those White Americans who perpetrate
evil in America refuse to acknowledge their actions, their
rebelliousness to God, their perversities. They refuse to
admit to any wrongdoing, and they despise anyone who
dares to call them out. They (constantly) kick and spit on the
Black American and then expect the same to smile and say
it's okay. They mistreat African Americans on every level of
society and walk around pretending that it's okay. They
expect to eat only the best but feed others slop. They don't
mind seeing others at the bottom suffering in the worst

463

conditions so long as they're okay. And that's not right; it's downright evil.

Over four hundred years is a long time to be subjected to oppression, especially when the oppressors refuse to admit, much less deal with, their heinous actions. Yes, the European establishment in America has done tremendous evil. And yes, it will pay the price for its sins, even to the fourth generation, as is written in the Holy Scriptures.

The people of this nation claim that it is in God whom they trust. They even have the declaration printed on the currency of the country. But one should ask the question: How can you say you love God whom you have not seen while you hate your brother (otherwise known as your fellow man) at whom you look every day? It is a lie on which the foundation of America stands. And its people have yet to rebuke it.

Life in America, particularly for African Americans, can most times be likened to residing in an asylum. Madness abounds when many White people want to treat African Americans as if they just got here, when in fact, the people have been here for over four hundred years. The same people who helped to build the country into what it is today. African Americans, contrary to popular, delusional beliefs, are NOT second-class to anyone.

To the foreign eye, the falsity gets shown: the oppressors profess to admire an oppressed culture but hate its people. They claim to love the attributes of African culture, but they mistreat the very people to whom those qualities are natural.

464

For example, such people cannot profess to love Michael Jordan while they hate his people, Black people. Such people cannot claim to love Jazz music or Blues music, while they hate African Americans from whom those two genres originated. For such people are liars—and the truth is not in them.

The devil has worked, on every level of American society, through many wicked people. And they have worked hard to carry out his wicked-and-depraved wishes: an evil spirit whom they cannot see but who lies to them and tells them that they are the master race, superior to others, especially the native of Africa. But there is a price to pay, not with people, but with the Lord. And when he rewards the sins of a generation, He destroys both body and soul—for eternity. He made humans, and he can, and will, destroy humans. And we, as human beings, should not forget that.

There are many people, not only in the United States but also in other parts of the world, who would compare the treatment of African Americans at the hands of an untold number of White Americans to an abusive marriage: an abusive marriage that we, the descendants of Africa, were forced into when we entered this country, against our will, over four hundred years ago.
We had no rights; we had no money; we had no power; we had no say, and we were without dignity. Compassion shunned us, empathy scoffed at us, love detested us, and our coal-hued flesh betrayed us. The stench of our poverty clung like the stench of dung to our existence, and we were laid waste. As black people, we did not ask to come to America. We were sold as property by those of our kind and trafficked

here. On the ocean—during our voyage over—we were wretched: those who bought us and brought us saw to that. They were raping our human pride, sodomizing our dignity, and spoiling the richness of our culture—like thieves in the vault of our consciousness.

Like night and day, where their contrary flesh was concerned, the black and the white merged. And together, they formed an ugly shade of gray: a dreary-and-gloomy history where the white would dominate—and hate.

Now one might be compelled to ask, Hey, if it was so bad, why didn't Black people leave America and go back to their native continent or the Islands? And the answer would be simple. The Lord didn't allow it. It had all been preordained for us, as a people, to be transported to these shores. Why? One might ask. Well, because God didn't forget. Once upon a time, Black people were the oppressors. Tens of thousands of years ago, during the Old, Middle, and New Kingdoms, BC, the native of Africa, particularly ancient Black Egyptians, ruled with iron fists and subjected the ancient Jewish people, or the Hebrews, if you will, to four hundred and thirty years of brutality and inhumane treatment. Four hundred and thirty years. That is a long time. We had enslaved the Jewish people. And the Lord had hardened our hearts against them. We had done evil in His Holy sight, and He never forgot us. But because the Lord had a divine plan for the descendants of Africa, whom He would thousands of years later call into a new faith of Pentecostal Christianity, He caused us to be enslaved and mistreated in a new land called America for four hundred years. Beneath the feet of a foreign people whom we knew not, we fell prey to the cruelest of treatment. And in the eyes of the Lord, who called us, it was allowed—for an allotted time—because we, as Black people, had done the same to the Hebrew people thousands of years before. In this way, the Lord humbled us because we had been a (very) proud people from Africa.

In this way, we had to reap what we sowed. And that is not to say that it was okay what the European establishment in America subjected us to as a people: for they, too, will pay the price for their evils—many as they are.

For then, we shall see the wrath of God when He commands death and destruction to gorge themselves on the flesh and souls of the wicked and the rebellious—just as He had done in times past.

"The Spirit of Obsession"

A Poem About Envy, Jealousy, and Covetousness

Watercolors by Ateli

Ob·ses·sion
/əbˈseSHən/

My every thought rotates around your reality:
I eat, breathe, and sleep you;
You are my sustenance, my daily multivitamin;
You are the reason that I can face each day...

I feel coerced to hate you,
But I need to focus on you:
I hate myself more because of you—
You are like a brightly-lit galaxy in my inky-black universe:

Your happiness taunts my misery;
Your achievements insult my failures:

I need to blame you for everything that I lack in my own
life...

You are my sole absorption, my ultimate preoccupation—
I wish to be you because I loathe being me:
Your happiness only intensifies my sadness;
Your vivacious confidence arrogantly thumbs its nose at my
contemptible low self-esteem...

I believe you to be my better,
But I will never give you your deserved props;
I will never give you the satisfaction of knowing that you are
indeed greater than I.

You—and only you—have the alpha power to command my
every other thought:
I cannot exist without your validation—

I regard your every move, and about you, I am inclined to
know every detail—
Everything you have I want;
Everything you are I wish to be:

Your very existence only reminds me that I am nothing.

The Commentary

Once again, the spirit of wisdom speaks:

Spiritual warfare. Spiritual warfare does not suffer the faint-hearted lightly. For once it takes possession of a human mind, it will by no means release its hold on the host until not one scintilla of logical sanity remains in him (or her). Obsession stems from unrebuked spiritual warfare in the human mind.

—Cat Ellington

Self-hatred is a breeding ground for envy to sprout the seeds of jealousy and its closest kin, after envy, covetousness. The preceding poem is one that I wrote to expose this particular spiritual warfare. Envy is an ugly spirit. And once it takes possession of the human mind, the results can be detrimental—for both the person under its assault and those targeted by it. There is no such thing as healthy envy because envy stems from a spiritual place of darkness. And the same goes for jealousy and covetousness: they all lead to destruction and self-destruction. There is no going around that truth. It is one thing to admire the advantages that someone else appears to have, but it is something else to become envious of that person's accomplishments. Because like all spiritual warfare (in the human mind), negative thoughts always present themselves to be harmless, but they grow and lead on to sinful actions—if they don't get checked and replaced with faith, hope, and a positive outlook. Some factors contribute to a person being susceptible to this type of demonic warfare in their mind. And a few of these include low self-esteem, self-hatred, and self-pity.

According to Merriam-Webster, the difference between envy and jealousy is this: Envy means **discontented longing for someone else's advantages**. Jealousy means **unpleasant**

suspicion, or apprehension of rivalship. Envy is most often used to refer to a covetous feeling toward another person's attributes, possessions, or stature in life.

Excellently defined.

"Words of Encouragement"

A Poem About Faith

Watercolors by Ateli

Be of courageousness,
And not of cowardice.
Be of strength,
And not of weakness.
Be of joy,
And not of sorrow.
Be of joy,
Because there is a better tomorrow.

Be of love,
And not of hate.
Be of an emboldened spirit,
And stand in your faith.

Whatever offenses you may encounter in the world,
Even if they be doubled,
Remember that it is written:
Let not your heart be troubled.

The Commentary

Through the trials and tribulations of life, strength builds a
foundation of resilience, and character takes form. Faith
meets challenge; however, her hope remains undefeated.
Tears flow down their streams, but they soon dry up in the
parch of drought. Joy constructs her house, and patience
makes itself at home in her perfection.
—Cat Ellington

Words of Encouragement serves as my (personal) witness.
—Cat Ellington
American author and poet

Do you feel like you are all alone? Do you feel alienated and
overlooked? Do you sometimes feel hopeless? Do you feel
fearful? Tearful? Do you feel confused? Do you sometimes
wonder why you and not someone else whenever the bottom
appears to be falling out? Do you feel victimized by society?
I have felt all of those things. And to be honest, I sometimes
still do. When I wrote *Words of Encouragement*, I was
feeling many of those things. And when the words started

flowing, I could not seem to write them fast enough. But I got them all, thank God. And by the time I completed the faithful work, my tears had dried up. My joy returned, and I felt a renewal in my spirit. As long as we are alive (in this physical world), the enemy will be *allowed* to attack our faith. But we have to be strong and hold on because nothing will last forever - not even our so-called troubles.

That's the thing about the flesh: it is deceptive. And to defeat the deception of it, we have to stay focused on the spiritual things. Because unlike the physical - which is temporary - the spiritual is permanent, eternal. Always remember: it is an honor for people to know *you*, not the other way around. And whenever you sense those negative thoughts trying to penetrate your mind, you remember these words. Remember *Words of Encouragement.*

"The Spirit is Willing, But the Flesh is Weak"

A Poem About Enemies and Persecutors

Watercolors by Ateli

The soul and the flesh,
They are engaged in a tug of war:
The soul prefers to love,
But the flesh desires to hate.

And in this life, the flesh tends to win.

The soul and the flesh,
They are engaged in a tug of war:

The soul prefers to forgive,
But the flesh desires to castigate;
The soul seeks to encourage,
But the flesh desires to denigrate.

And in this life, the flesh tends to win.

The soul and the flesh,
They are engaged in a tug of war:
On the shoulders of life,
The soul on the right is the angel,
And the carnal on the left is the Devil,
The mind is the battlefield;
And it wills to do evil.

And in this life, the flesh tends to win.

For the flesh seeks instant gratification. It is sweet and
succulent.

The Commentary

Cat Ellington:

I am writing the following words in freestyle. I speak to
encourage those, who like me, have endured hostility
without cause, and bore the brunt of the bully.

They say revenge is sweet. And for that split second, it
seems true. But the price for revenge is eternal.
Here is what I have free will to do:
At liberty, I can destroy you;

But my anger, I reel it in,
Lest I give in to sin.

Spiritually speaking, I must control the body I'm in.
The Devil on the left,
The angel on the right—
The mind is a battlefield,
And faith wins the fight.

I have free will to adulterate,
And I desire to hate;
But my mind must be in control;
The weakness of my flesh,
It cannot tolerate.

Sometimes, I want to kill:
For I have free will— to do it.
I could maim—
But I don't,
Lest I become like Cain.

I could fuck you up,
And make you drink from the wrath of my cup—
But what good would that do me?

You rebellious goat,
I could cut your throat—
But what good would that do me?

My soul has a will to love,
To mimic the ways of my Heavenly Father above—
But my flesh disdains,

My mind is insane— with this vengeance.

I could knock your fucking brains out,
And at the top of my lungs,
I could scream and shout—
But I don't;
Rather I encage my rage.

Your lies are visible in my eyes,
And your actions, hardly a fraction,
My flesh wills to despise:
But with you, my soul holds its peace.

I cough you up and spit you out like phlegm,
Lest like yours, my soul is condemned.

Wisdom:

Beloved, do not avenge yourselves, but *rather* give place to
wrath; for it is written, "Vengeance is Mine, I will repay,"
says the Lord.
Therefore "If your enemy hungers, feed him; if he thirsts,
give him a drink; for in so doing you will heap coals of fire
on his head."
Do not be overcome by evil, but overcome evil with good.
—Romans 12:19-21

The soul and the flesh,
They are engaged in a tug of war:
The soul prefers to honor and live by these words,
But the flesh desires to be willful and rebel against them.

And in spiritual life, the soul reigns as the victor.

Live by these blessed words, and you will have peace.

Love,

Cat

Coming Soon

REVIEWS BY CAT ELLINGTON

A TRILOGY

OF

UNIQUE CRITIQUES

#2 IN

Caribbean Fuchsia

BY

CAT ELLINGTON

FEATURING BOOKS 4-6 FROM THE REVIEWS BY CAT ELLINGTON SERIES
WITH BONUS MATERIAL BY NARAS KIMONO AND JOSEPH STRICKLAND

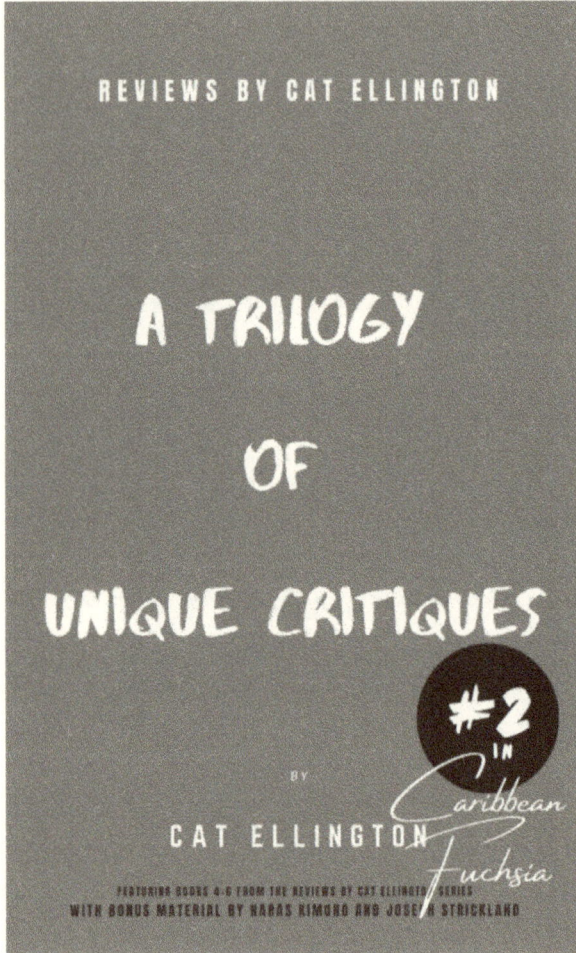

Reviews by Cat Ellington: A Trilogy of Unique Critiques #2
Imprint: Quill Pen Ink Publishing
Cover Hue: Caribbean Fuchsia

I Do: Sheet Music
(Cat Ellington, Princeton Brown)
Publication date: December 3, 2021
Publisher: Vital Vision Publications

The Book of Us: Sheet Music
(Cat Ellington, Princeton Brown)
Publication date: December 3, 2021
Publisher: Vital Vision Publications

I'm Still in Love: Sheet Music
(Cat Ellington, Princeton Brown)
Publication date: December 3, 2021
Publisher: Vital Vision Publications

Something in Your Eyes: Sheet Music
(Cat Ellington, Princeton Brown)
Publication date: December 3, 2021
Publisher: Vital Vision Publications

Gett Out: Sheet Music
(Cat Ellington, Joseph Strickland,
Greg Schutte, Princeton Brown)
Publication date: December 3, 2021
Publisher: Vital Vision Publications

About the Author

Cat Ellington is an American songwriter, casting director, poet, author, and entrepreneur from Chicago, IL. She is best known for her creative contributions to the diverse industries and fields of music, movies, art, and literature.

Cat Ellington's professional credits list a collection of nonfiction books, including the Reviews by Cat Ellington series, The Making of Dual Mania, More Imaginative Than Ordinary Speech, Memoirs in Gogyohka, You Can Quote Me On That, and The Cat Ellington Sheet Music Collection. In film and music, Ellington's credentials include her work on the psychological thriller, "Dual Mania," and its soundtrack--on which she wrote five original songs: "The Book of Us," "I'm Still in Love," "Something in Your Eyes," "Gett Out," and "I Do."

Outside of her professional element, the award-winning creative enjoys reading, listening to music, cooking, collecting vintage and modern charm bracelets, watching movies and classic TV shows, sailing, jet-skiing, playing tennis, and eating frozen yogurt -- lots of it.

Cat Ellington on Amazon: Books, Biography, Blog, Audiobooks, Kindle

Cat Ellington at the Award-Winning Boutique Domain

Cat Ellington at the Review Period with Cat Ellington

Cat Ellington at IMDb